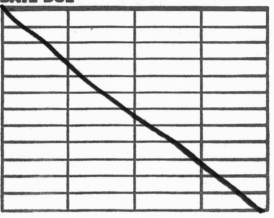

THE POLITICS OF NATIONAL PARTY CONVENTIONS,

Revised Edition

Paul T. David
Ralph M. Goldman
Richard C. Bain

A condensation of the 1960 Brookings Institution
Study edited by Kathleen Sproul and Paul T. David

With a new Epilogue by Austin Ranney
on Recent Changes in the Presidential Nominating Process

**UNIVERSITY
PRESS OF
AMERICA**

LANHAM • NEW YORK • LONDON

Foreword to 1984 Edition

Renewed interest in all phases of the presidential nominating process makes it timely to republish this condensation of the massive Brookings Institution study of 1960. That study was a breakthrough in research on presidential nominating politics. Nothing like it had ever been published before. It represented the culmination of eight years of intensive research in which more than 300 political scientists and their associates had been involved.

The work began when the American Political Science Association commissioned a cooperative study of national convention delegations in the spring of 1952. That activity let to the publication in 1954 of the five volume report, *Presidential Nominating Politics in 1952*, edited by Paul T. David, Malcolm Moos, and Ralph M. Goldman. The research continued at The Brookings Institution, delving into the historical materials beginning in 1789, with many analyses of the convention system of nominations from the election of 1832 onward. This led to the unabridged edition of *The Politics of National Party Conventions*, by Paul T. David, Ralph M. Goldman, and Richard C. Bain, published by Brookings in 1960. A paperback condensation by Kathleen Sproul followed later that year, and was updated by the undersigned for republication in 1964 by Random House in its Vintage Books series.

In the present edition, the text and tables of the 1964 edition have been reproduced without change, except that the two tables of presidential nominations at the end of the book have been updated. An important addition is the Epilogue by Austin Ranney on "Recent Changes in the Presidential Nominating Process." This is reprinted, with permission, from *The Key Reporter* of Summer 1983. We are much indebted to Professor Ranney for this brief but comprehensive survey of the changes of the last twenty years.

My own most recent work in this field is the book entitled *The Presidential Election and Transition 1980-81*, edited with David H. Everson and published by the Southern Illinois University Press in 1983. In working on that book, similar in format to the one that I had edited on the election of 1960, I too was impressed by the sweeping changes that have occurred in recent years. Nevertheless, a thorough knowledge of the historical roots of the nominating process is basic to understanding why this essential process of

1984 Foreword
leadership selection in the United States is so different from that of any other country. With my co-authors, I believe that the evolution of the convention system of nominations continues to deserve study. The materials of the present book offer a concise and convenient way of getting at that evolution.

> Paul T. David
> Professor Emeritus
> University of Virginia

February 1984

Foreword to 1964 Edition

In January 1960 the Brookings Institution published *The Politics of National Party Conventions,* which was addressed mainly to scholars and specialists. In the spring of 1960, Brookings issued a condensed paperback edition intended for the general reader. The present book is an updated version of that edition.

The senior author, Professor Paul T. David of the University of Virginia, has rewritten substantial portions of the text to reflect the events of the 1960 conventions and to utilize further research, including that for the Brookings book he edited, *The Presidential Election and Transition, 1960-1961.* The new data developed in 1960 have also been included in the tables when relevant. Certain parts of the book's analyses, however, have remained unchanged, for reasons indicated in the respective chapters. One alteration has been made in the chapter order: the present Chapters 1 and 2 were Chapters 10 and 11 in the 1960 condensation. They have here been moved to the beginning of the book because of their contemporary importance; following them, the other chapters continue in the original sequence.

The 1960 edition of the condensation was prepared by Kathleen Sproul, who had skillfully assisted the authors in editing the original manuscript. The Institution is grateful to Mrs. Sproul and to the three authors for their cooperation and suggestions in the preparation of both condensed editions.

The original study was made possible by the generous grants of the John Randolph Haynes and Dora Haynes Foundation of Los Angeles. The Foundation should not be understood as approving or disapproving the conclusions or recommendations in the original unabridged volume or in this edition. The views expressed are the authors', and do not purport to represent those of the trustees, officers, or other staff members of The Brookings Institution.

ROBERT D. CALKINS
President

August 1963

Contents

Foreword to 1984 Edition   vii

Foreword to 1964 Edition   ix

Introduction   xv

1. The Changing Character of Nominating Campaigns   1
   Styles of Campaigning   2
   Campaign Finance   11
   The Content of Nominating Campaigns   17
   The New Picture   20

2. Mass Media, Public Opinion Polls, and Voter Preference   24
   The Role of Mass Media   24
   The Record of Voter Opinion   30
   Delegate Polls   33
   Voter Influence   36

3. Origins of the National Convention System   39
   The Constitution and Executive Leadership   41
   Leadership Recruitment from Washington to Jackson   43
   Early Party Conventions   53
   The Legacy of the Formative Years   56

4. Changes in the Party System   65
   The Ante-Bellum Years, 1832-1860   66
   The Post-Civil War Period, 1864-1892   69
   Republican Dominance, 1896-1924   71
   Recent Times, 1928-1956   74
   Party Competition and the Nominating Process   79

5. *Leadership Centers of the Party in Power* 82
The President as Party Leader 83
The Vice Presidency: Dead End or Stepping Stone? 90
The Cabinet 93
National Committee and Convention Officers 94
The Congressional Leaders 96
Factional Centers 98
Leadership Integration 99

6. *Leadership Centers of the Party Out of Power* 103
Titular Leaders 104
National Committee and Convention Officers 110
The Congressional Leaders 112
Other Members of Congress 115
The Governors 116
Interest Groups and Their Leaders 119
Bosses and Kingmakers 121
Leadership Integration 122

7. *Patterns in the Nominating Process* 126
Patterns in Confirmation of Leadership 127
Patterns in Leadership Succession 131
Continuity and Change in the Patterns of Nomination 138

8. *The Candidates* 143
The Geography of Ticket Selection 144
The Age Factor 147
Backgrounds in Private Life 150
Governmental Experience 151
Electoral Success 157
Is There a Type That Emerges? 158

9. *Apportionment and Voting Structure* 166
Evolution of Apportionment Rules 166
Apportionment in 1960 170
Voting Power Under the Apportionment 171
Apportionment Issues 176

Apportionment Within States 180
The Unit Rule 183
The Two Thirds Rule 186
Massive Size and Its Consequences 189

10. *Presidential Primary Systems* 193
Delegate Election Systems 195
Presidential Preference Polls 202
Open vs. Closed Primaries 204
Effects on Participants 205
Which Primaries are Effective? 209

11. *Other Systems for Mandating Delegates* 213
Party Processes for Mandating 215
Seating Contents 219
The Mandates Compared 224

12. *The Delegates* 229
Age 230
Women Delegates 231
Negro Delegates 232
Religious and Ethnic Group Representation 233
Education 234
Income Levels 235
Occupations and Connections with Interest Groups 238
Public and Party Officials as Delegates 240
Experience and Leadership 243
The Evolution and Recent Status of Delegate Characteristics 244

13. *The Delegations* 248
Delegation Leadership 250
Decision-Making and Candidate Support 253
Voting Behavior as End Product 258
Voting as the Final Test of Representativeness 261

14. *Voting Power and Strategy: The Road to Consensus* 265
Voting Procedures 265

Nominating Votes as Measures of Effective
    Power   269
Regional Patterns of Effectiveness   270
Big States vs. Small in Winner Support   273
The Idiosyncrasies of the States   275
Voting Strategies   279
The Strategy of Non-Nominating Roll Call Votes   280
Reaching Consensus   284
Split Conventions   287
The Processes of Alliance   289
The Limits of Convention Action   290

15. *Convention Action and Election Results*   292
Fluctuations in Growth in the Party Vote   293
Convention Action and State Voter Turnout   295
Nominating Conflict and Election Victories   309
Mechanisms of Long-Term Change   316

16. *The Nominating Process and the Future of the*
    Party System   320
The Central Position of the Nominating Process   321
Problems of Preparation   327
Problems of Popular Control   332
Problems of Bringing the Conventions Up to Their
    Potentialities   338
Dilemmas in Out-Party Leadership   347
Goals for the Party System   353

Epilogue, "Recent Changes in the Presidential
Nominating Process," by Austin Ranney   357

National Party Nominees, 1832-1980   366

Index   369

Introduction

The two major American political parties and their quadrennial conventions to nominate candidates for the Presidency and Vice Presidency represent a paradox in a nation created by and devoted to a written Constitution. They are wholly the products of custom and usage—developed to fill a gap when the constitutional provisions for selecting the Chief Executive proved unworkable in the manner originally intended. Put to public test every fourth year for more than a century, the interrelated institutions have been amazingly durable. Today they are without doubt central to the American political system.

Yet the conventions have been almost continuously subject to attack. They have been described as "unwieldy, unrepresentative, and less than responsible." They have been called a serious obstacle to responsible party government because of the reputed undue control of party bosses. And many a party voter has doubted their effectiveness and sometimes their honesty. The argument has always been complicated by a basic uncertainty: is nomination by a party organization proper at all?

In recent years a national primary for nominating presidential candidates, in which all voters could take part, has been repeatedly suggested as a substitute for the conventions. Such a procedure in its timing as a one-day, one-ballot choice would basically resemble an election. The point most often overlooked by those who advocate the change is that a nomination is *not* an election. The function of the nominating process in a two-party system is to reduce the number of available candidates in successive stages to the two who will be the final alternatives for electoral choice. The conventions can and do perform an essential service that is practicable only in a general parley, and they cannot be judged by standards appropriate to an election. The reasons why this is so are given attention throughout the book, with a final discussion in the concluding chapter.

The book begins with a review of the striking changes that have occurred in nominating campaigns since the Willkie campaign of 1940, which was in some respects the forerunner of the new type of campaign that was consolidated in the Kennedy victory of 1960. The increasing influence of the mass media of communication and of the public opinion polls is a part of this development; this is discussed in Chapter 2. These two opening chapters raise most of the contemporary problems regarding candidate strategy, voter influence, and public policy. The book then turns to examine the background against which these problems must be assessed: the historical setting in which the national conventions were created and the long-term evolution of the party leadership structures and of the competitive relationships between the major parties.

The role of the conventions must be judged not only in regard to the idiosyncrasies of the nominating process but also in relation to the survival, stability, and effective operation of the party system and the structure of government as a whole. This book seeks, therefore, to present a comprehensive view of how the candidates emerge and are nominated in the national conventions; its primary objective in so doing is an improved perception and understanding of the process in all its major phases.

1

The Changing Character of Nominating Campaigns

■

Since the early 1940's presidential nominating campaigns have been subject to real and significant changes, for which the combined impacts of the primaries, the public opinion polls, and the mass media of communication seem to be mainly responsible. The effect can be seen in many elements of the campaigns—in the augmented efforts of candidates (and their managers) to prove that they have popular support; in the marked rise of voter participation; and in the number of candidates already billed as popular national favorites that the conventions increasingly find at their doors on opening day.

Many factors have of course been at work, directly and indirectly, including the growing power of the Presidency and a greater concern about the kind of leadership the United States must have to carry out its role in the world at large. But the strategists who plan campaigns show themselves very aware that the primaries, the polls, and the mass media must be taken into account as parts of the nominating process.

Styles of Campaigning

Before presidential primaries were invented, the ancient doctrine that the office should seek the man, not the man the office, still had a marked restraining effect upon the public behavior of potential candidates. To announce a candidacy or stump the country before the convention met was not customary. Any man mentioned as a possible nominee prior to the convention was expected to respond with modest deprecation and continue his previous pursuits with a minimum of ostentation. Flat disavowals of candidacy were common. The nominee finally chosen was expected to affect ignorance of the event until officially advised, some weeks after the convention, by a committee dispatched for the purpose.

Quiet anticipation is still the rule for potential candidates who await a draft or hope for possible nomination as a compromise choice. But nearly all active candidates of recent years have eventually rejected the old doctrine—and those who enter the primaries are required by law to do so. By coming into the open, each one has encountered many difficult decisions.

Should a candidate with substantial support announce early or late? Should he enter all of the primaries, some, or none? How should he behave toward the party organization's in strongly organized states, or the factions where organization is weak or divided? Under what conditions if any should he enter an open contest with a favorite son? If he stays out of the primaries, what other means are available for attracting national attention and approval? How much help can he anticipate from the mass media? Is popular support more important than good relations with party leaders and strong state organizations—or vice versa? Is it possible to have both? What kind of headquarters should he set up at the convention city? What campaign should he plan for the final days? What fund-raising commitments will be involved in these decisions? Where will the money come from?

Every one of these questions has undoubtedly been argued over by the inner circles of friends and supporters of major candidates in recent years. The decisions made have produced a wide variety of styles, which in turn affect the extent to which popular mandates come into existence in support of the candidacies.

AVOWALS OF CANDIDACY

Formal avowals of candidacy now occur frequently in the fall and winter preceding the presidential year, but the manner of avowal differs according to the status of the candidate. Incumbent Presidents in modern times have rarely considered it necessary to announce candidacy for a second term on their own initiative, but will usually admit or deny their availability at some point in a press conference. When an incumbent President is available, others of his party who announce their candidacies assume the role of challenger automatically.

Titular leaders have been treated with considerably less deference than Presidents.* Thomas E. Dewey's prospective availability for 1948, for instance, did not deter other candidates, some of whom announced unusually early: Harold E. Stassen in January 1947, a year and a half before the convention, Robert A. Taft in October 1947, and Earl Warren in November. Dewey himself did not announce until January 1948.

---

* Although an incumbent President is often referred to as "titular leader," this book applies the designation only to the defeated candidate of the out-party, both for clarity and because in modern times the two leadership roles differ greatly.

The only nominating campaigns from 1940 to 1960 that involved neither an incumbent President nor an openly available titular leader were those of 1952 on the Republican side and 1960 on the Democratic. In the first case, Taft announced in October 1951 as part of his decision to enter the Wisconsin and Ohio primaries, where formal consent was required. Warren announced in November and Stassen in December. In January 1952, Eisenhower stated from Paris that under no circumstances would he seek relief from his NATO assignment in order to run, but he permitted his name to stand in the New Hampshire primary. He later returned from Paris and retired from the army; his opening campaign speech was made in Kansas on June 4.

The 1960 preconvention campaigns began officially with the announcements by Senators Hubert H. Humphrey on December 30, 1959, and John F. Kennedy on January 3, 1960. Each indicated that he would enter a number of primaries. Senator Stuart Symington became a candidate later in 1960, but entered no primaries where his consent was required. Senator Lyndon B. Johnson deferred announcing until July 5, two days after Congress recessed for the conventions.

Reluctant candidates have usually announced late, if at all. Adlai Stevenson repeatedly disclaimed candidacy up to the time of the Democratic convention in 1952 and again in 1960, although never going so far as to say that he would refuse the nomination if offered.

PRECONVENTION CAMPAIGN PATTERNS

The first impact of the primaries on campaign practices was felt mainly in the Republican party, and in 1920 conspicuously so, when three leading candidates were involved: Governor Frank O. Lowden, General Leonard Wood, and Senator Hiram Johnson. In the end, large expenditures and hectic campaigning, which tried to make the most of both the primaries and the party organizations, led to stalemate. Since none of the three was willing to compromise or to support one of the others as a second choice, the convention in effect was returned to organization control, and Warren G. Harding was chosen as a dark horse.

In the Democratic party, most of the leading candidates for the nominations from 1912 to 1932 avoided the primaries when they could. In 1932, Franklin D. Roosevelt conducted a long-prepared and most active preconvention campaign, mainly through the more traditional channels. He was entered in several primaries, however, and suffered defeats in Massachusetts and California, which he had probably been drawn into by erroneous information and might have declined had he anticipated contests. Roosevelt never let himself get into the position of seeming to stump the country before the convention.

The long period of the Roosevelt and Truman incumbencies led to a profound lack of interest in open preconvention campaigning on the part of opposing Democratic candidates. Meanwhile, insurgency and open campaigning were also largely out of fashion in the Republican party—until 1940 when Wendell Willkie mounted his remarkable campaign directed partly to the voters through the mass media and partly to influential local citizens through advertising, commercial, and banking channels. The combination brought him the Republican nomination in a new type of convention stampede, which had the appearance in its final stages of being generated by gallery enthusiasm, but was probably influenced considerably by a flood of telegrams and long-distance telephone messages to delegates from leading citizens at home.

Republican attitudes on preconvention campaigning changed substantially as the result of the 1940 experience. The mass media and the new public relations techniques were seen as methods for arousing the voters and so bringing pressure on the delegates. The primaries, however, were still looked at askance as an effective means of winning a nomination, and after Willkie's defeat in 1944 were feared as potentially fatal. In 1948, Dewey attempted at first to campaign mainly through organization contacts and traditional channels, but he finally entered a number of primaries by request and with assurances of strong support. Taft entered fewer primaries, worked through his associates in appealing to the state party organizations, and relied for popular support upon his work in the Senate.

Stassen, running mainly as an independent but with relatively ample campaign funds, entered as many primaries as possible, and attempted to mount the broadest appeal to the voters. His tactics had some early success, with the result that Dewey found himself compelled to campaign actively in Oregon. There he not only accepted Stassen's challenge to a nationally broadcast radio debate but also campaigned throughout the state for several days by bus, making six to ten speeches a day—a performance the like of which no previous candidate of major stature had ever felt called upon to endure.

The 1952 Republican campaigns made the fullest use of every available technique, but with noteworthy differences in the style of the leading contestants. In some respects the primaries may be said to have come into their own for the first time. The basic strength of the campaign for Eisenhower lay in his evident ability to get votes; the record of the primaries was only one facet in demonstrating that ability, but clearly an important one.

The problems of preconvention campaigning were rediscovered in the Democratic party in 1952. President

Truman showed vast confidence in his ability to name his successor, but he evidently underestimated the danger in letting Kefauver pile up a lead in the primaries. Kefauver's showing in the primaries was clearly a surprise; he never came close to winning the nomination, but the brutal manner in which he was rejected left scars on the party and weakened its position in the general election.

In 1956, Stevenson occupied a position as titular leader analogous to Dewey's in 1948; equally reluctant to take on a heavy schedule of primaries, he found himself not only facing Kefauver, whose campaign style was similar to Stassen's, but also under heavy pressure from state organizations and local factions to enter the primaries against him. The result was four months of grueling primary campaigning for both candidates.

In 1960, Kennedy's virtuoso record in the primaries was an essential feature of a campaign that was also an expert performance on other fronts. Contests in the primaries are evidently here to stay, and in all probability will be increasingly influential in out-party nominating situations.

ACTIVITY AT THE CONVENTION CITY

Before 1896 candidates seldom came to the conventions. From 1896 to 1936 the practice was mixed; the eventual nominee was rarely present at the convention city, but leading contenders were frequently there. Incumbent Presidents were never present for any purpose.

In 1932, when Governor Franklin D. Roosevelt flew from Albany to Chicago to accept the nomination in person, the old tradition of candidate aloofness was publicly disavowed, but the Republicans still maintained it in 1936 by sending a committee to Topeka in late July to notify Alfred M. Landon of his nomination in early June. In 1940, Wendell Willkie ambled around the hotel lobbies of the convention city, asking delegates to vote for him. After his nomination he appeared briefly at the convention—with Mrs. Willkie—and promised to make the campaign a crusade. Nevertheless, the notification ceremony was again performed— but turned to modern public relations uses by elaborate arrangements for an acceptance speech at Willkie's childhood home, Elwood, Indiana.

In 1944, at the height of the war, Roosevelt's acceptance speech was broadcast to the Democratic convention from a naval base on the Pacific coast. The Republican convention, on nominating Thomas E. Dewey, named a committee to notify him at once, to invite him to address the convention, and to escort him if he came—and Dewey promptly did come. This completed the transition; since 1948 each party's nominee has appeared before the convention in its closing hours, and the principal candidates (other than incumbent Presidents) have been present throughout.

What are the consequences of having the candidates at the convention city? First of all, more responsible attitudes in the private discussions that occur at the final time and place of decision, and a considerable curtailment of the wide latitude previously allowed to the candidate's managers: no longer can a candidate pretend that he did not know what his managers said on his behalf. The way has also been opened for personal contacts between the candidate and the delegates whose support he is seeking; the delegate may thereby feel his duty and responsibility more acutely.

Perhaps the most important consequence is the impact on popular mandates in the final days of choice. Through the intensive radio and television coverage of activities at the convention, the voters of each party can reassess their previous positions if they see fit to do so. Their information is nearly as extensive as that available to the delegates, and if they choose they can then communicate with their delegates by mail, telegram, and telephone. The results are not necessarily the same as those of a national referendum or plebiscite, but undoubtedly make themselves felt.

CAMPAIGN STYLES AS A PRODUCT
OF PRESSURES

The specific effects of the public opinion polls and of the greater activity of press, radio, and television will be discussed more fully in the chapter that follows, but enough has been said here to show that, combined with the primaries, they have created opportunities of competitive self-display for the candidates. No candidate is as helpless under these pressures as it might seem, but the public nonetheless increasingly expects the candidates to respond.

It can be argued that the whole history of nominating campaigns in recent years would have been different but for the presence of two individuals, Harold E. Stassen and Estes Kefauver. Both had reason to think that they would never be seriously considered for a presidential nomination unless they could make a spectacular success in the primaries. Both were accustomed to slugging it out in state campaigns, and could hope to make a showing in the presidential primaries by using the same style. Both were successful in finding groups of backers who would put up the necessary campaign funds.

In the absence of primaries, these men might never have started or might have followed an entirely different style. The primaries thus may have made possible the appearance of candidates of this type—but did not make it inevitable that they would appear. Both Stassen and Kefauver seem to be genuine examples of personalities who created the role they played in making use of the available instrument.

Without these men, therefore, the nominating campaigns of 1948, 1952, and 1956 might have been different. But the assumption, for example, that Dewey and Stevenson would otherwise have been allowed to coast into their second nominations seems a little too simple. Other opposition probably would have made less noise in the primaries, but opposition there surely would have been.

In their respective ways, Dewey and Stevenson did as much to demonstrate the possibilities of active campaigning in the primaries as Stassen and Kefauver. Yet some observers have suggested that both Dewey and Stevenson were foolish to meet the challengers with their own weapons. The question presumes that both were wrong in their early decisions to enter selected primaries, and wrong again in deciding to campaign actively in the later primaries after being beaten in the earlier ones.

Any such conclusion would require guessing at many factors on which no adequate information is available; but some aspects of the situation are certainly obvious. Dewey faced his party's record of nearly a century in never renominating a defeated candidate; Stevenson needed new evidence of popular appeal after his crushing 1952 defeat. Neither man had much reason to think that he would be the convention choice if he let all primaries go by default. All available evidence indicates that each went into his first primaries cautiously, reluctantly, and under some pressure from friendly state party organizations. Once entangled, there was no retreat. Neither man desired to assume the campaign style he eventually accepted, but both demonstrated that spectacular victories in the primaries late in the season could rejuvenate a candidacy that might otherwise be eliminated—as Willkie's had been in 1944.

Eisenhower and Kennedy were the candidates who brought this sequence of development to consummation. Each won not only nomination but also election; in each case the preconvention campaigning in the primaries was an essential ingredient and the style of campaigning a response to the inherent pressures.

Eisenhower probably would not have accepted candidacy in 1952 but for his remarkable showing in the early New Hampshire and Minnesota primaries. In midseason, while he was still in Paris and his intentions were still ambiguous, he lost ground. After he had become committed, although not yet actively campaigning, his victory in Oregon and near-win in South Dakota were final demonstrations of vote-getting ability as the convention approached.

Kennedy's effective use of the primaries in 1960 seems to have ended the argument over their importance even among the professionals in the Democratic party, who held out longer than anyone else. His victories in Wisconsin and West Virginia were seen in retrospect as decisive. He was undefeated in any open contest. His strategy was the result of careful calculation; by mid-1959 he had concluded that, in his case, victory in the primaries was essential to win the nomination.

Campaign Finance

To active candidates and their supporters the problem of money has always been important, but with the advent of primaries, and still more the new campaigning styles since 1940, the availability of campaign funds has become an enormous factor in running for the presidential nomination. This raises questions of public policy. The available information on the problem is scanty.

State laws on election finance rarely include information on expenditures in nominating campaigns, and federal law has required no routine reporting of contributions or expenditures in such campaigns. Special investigations to uncover such information have been infrequent, the Kenyon Committee investigation of 1920 being the most noteworthy.

FINANCING PRE-ANNOUNCEMENT ACTIVITIES

Building up a potential candidacy before any overt announcement is made can cost a good deal of money, although the activity seldom attracts much attention, involving mainly the potential candidate, his principal backers and managers, and sometimes a formally organized committee.

When the objective is to persuade a reluctant candidate, voluntary committee operations take on a special importance. The Citizens for Eisenhower Committee reportedly spent $1,200,000 in its campaign to secure the 1952 nomination for Eisenhower. A considerable part of this sum was collected and spent before Eisenhower had returned from Paris and accepted his candidacy. Additional sums were undoubtedly collected and spent by state and local groups. The Stevenson for President Committee is reported to have collected only $20,300.91 during its entire existence in 1952, of which a balance of $507.13 was eventually contributed to the general election campaign. The greater part of its work was made possible by the services contributed by many talented volunteers. The Eisenhower committee also made use of large amounts of unpaid, contributed services of all kinds. The activities concentrated on these two candidacies before the principals consented to run were unique in extent. Something of the kind, however, happens in connection with many candidacies, and even a willing potential candidate hesitates to announce until he has had substantial assurances of support.

A potential candidate who seriously expects to run is usually involved in a series of complex, delicate, and time-consuming activities. If he is a governor or senator, the activities blend into phases of his official activity, but to the skilled observer there are many telltale clues: statesmanlike utterances that have no apparent connection with an immediate contingency or official duties; a willingness to devote time and travel to speaking engagements from one end of the country to the other; most of all, the recruitment of a task force of associates, whose subsequent extensive travel and intensive busyness have no visible explanation.

This kind of activity was being demonstrated to some degree as early as 1957 and through 1958 by at least three potential candidates for the 1960 Democratic nomination: Senator John Kennedy, Governor G. Mennen Williams, and Governor Robert R. Meyner. By mid 1959, the two governors were less conspicuous and three more senators had made moves into the limelight —Hubert Humphrey, Lyndon Johnson, and Stuart Symington. Humphrey was preparing actively for an open campaign in which he seemed likely to be Kennedy's main opponent in several contested primaries. Johnson and Symington seemed less likely to mount open campaigns before the primaries were over, but were preparing for the possibility of aggressive campaigning through organization channels. Governor Edmund (Pat) Brown of California was also attracting attention as something more than a favorite son possibility.

On the Republican side, the widely ranging and well-organized activities of New York's Governor Nelson Rockefeller in late 1959 proclaimed him a presidential candidate in all but name for many weeks. Then on

December 26, 1959, his announcement of a definite decision not to run took even some members of his own staff by surprise. His withdrawal—at least for the time being—left the field to Richard Nixon; his large and expensive stable of task force associates, however, did not disband.

The financial requirements for the usual activities of this kind (Rockefeller's task force was unusual) are not large compared to what it costs to mount a campaign after announcement. But they can easily become large enough to outgrow the personal and official resources of a man who has no private fortune, especially when a task force including several full-time professional staff members is put to work.

FINANCING OPEN NOMINATING CAMPAIGNS

The public act of announcement or acceptance of candidacy provides a legitimate basis for a broad fund-raising operation by a committee of supporters. Home-state financial support is essential for most candidates in the early stages of their campaigns. Early support from other quarters depends on how successful promoters of the candidacy have been in locating potential contributors before the announcement. If the campaign develops well, further financing becomes relatively much easier; if it drags, the sources of money dry up. Failing campaigns usually end with deficits—which in some cases may remain as a personal obligation for the unsuccessful candidate to work off over a period of years.

The 1952 expenditures on preconvention campaigning undoubtedly reached levels higher than had been known before. Alexander Heard, in his study *The Costs of Democracy* (1960), estimated the total outlays as at least $7,000,000, with contributed goods and services also being counted in millions. Most of the expenditure was the product of the Taft-Eisenhower struggle. Cash outlays for the Eisenhower nominating campaign were estimated at $2,500,000 (on the basis of incomplete but substantial evidence and including the previously noted $1,200,000, of which there is public record). No authoritative information is available for the Taft campaign expenditures but, in view of its scale of activity and duration, they were probably at least as great as those for Eisenhower.

In 1956 the active contest for the Democratic nomination may have involved a total outlay exceeding $2,500,000. The cost at all levels of the Stevenson campaign was probably at least $1,500,000; the Kefauver campaign, widely reported as ending in a deficit of more than $40,000, probably cost in total at least $350,000, and substantial expenses were doubtless incurred in the Harriman campaign.

In 1960, at least $2,100,000 was spent in the campaigns for the Democratic nomination. Kennedy campaign expenditures, controlled and documented more carefully than most, were a reported $912,500. Expenditures for others were reported or estimated as follows: Humphrey, $266,500; Symington, $350,000; Johnson, $250,000; Stevenson, $250,000; others, $100,000.*

Political money in general, according to one political writer, has five principal sources: (1) wealthy "fat cats," (2) organized labor, (3) government employees, (4) the underworld, and (5) unorganized voluntary contributors. In range and relative importance of the sources, however, nominating campaigns probably differ substantially from election campaigns.

The contributors of great wealth—those affected by

---

* For details, see the chapter by Herbert E. Alexander in Paul T. David, ed., *The Presidential Election and Transition 1960-1961* (1961), esp. pp. 119-122.

the legal limitation on contributions to a single political fund in the general election—undoubtedly have had a special role in nominating campaigns, where there is no such limitation. Organized labor's contribution at the national level has not so far been a substantial factor in the nominating campaigns of either party. Federal government employees probably contribute even less to nominating campaigns than to general election campaigns, although some state employees may be obliged to contribute for a favorite son candidate.

Since contributions from the underworld are never publicly welcomed by a candidate, one can only suppose that such contributions are more important in sustaining certain county rings and city machines than in state politics generally, and more important in the politics of some states than in federal politics. But county rings and city machines do play a part in presidential nominations. A candidate may wish to avoid tainted money and yet find it impossible to maintain the rigid discipline in his campaign organization that such avoidance would require.

Unorganized voluntary contributors, especially those who will contribute in amounts of $5 to $500 if invited to do so, may be the hope of the future in political finance. The national parties have been directing special fund-raising efforts toward this group. Such appeals to civic duty are still a long way from general success, but they may well be making it easier to raise money for nominating campaigns—provided the campaign managers can manage to locate and appeal to potential contributors.

THE INFLUENCE OF MONEY ON MANDATES

Money may not be able to buy a nomination, but it can buy prominence for a candidate if he is otherwise eligible. Wealthy candidates start with a substantial advantage, yet in the end their wealth may be held against them unless they can project a particularly clear image of public-service motivation. On the other hand, a "popular" candidate who is not wealthy may make his need for funds an advantage, with contributors from one end of the country to the other becoming increasingly involved in a self-financing and self-inspiring type of campaign.

The uses of money in nominating campaigns have been so unregulated that many opportunities for questionable practices or for actual corruption exist; whether such opportunities have been used to an extent that impaired the quality of the choice is a question not easily answered. Some built-in safeguards are provided by the competition itself: under the acute pressures of competition there is always the risk that questionable practices will be discovered and will boomerang. Congressional investigations are also an ever-present threat to potential malpractice.

The need for corrective legislation may be less than the need for avoiding unwise meddling. Recently, for instance, several bills have been proposed in Congress, which, if enacted and proved constitutional, would prohibit voluntary committees similar to those for Eisenhower and Stevenson in 1952 from operating until the men supported announced as candidates. It is, of course, possible to argue that no one should be permitted to raise money for a candidate who has not given his formal consent. But the tradition of the office seeking the man is still strong enough in American politics to merit recognition in any legislation, and especially in the case of the highest office in the land.

The Content of Nominating Campaigns

. . . There's a lot more to winning an election than spending money, as all politicians know though sometimes they won't admit it.

The reason is that money may affect the *volume* of campaign communications and activities, but that has nothing to do with the more crucial matter, their *content*. (Alexander Heard, *Money and Politics*, Public Affairs Pamphlet 242, 1956.)

A nominating campaign involves a great deal of talk, but it is made up of much more than talk. Like a military campaign, it must include movement, supply, attack, defense, and the support requisite to these maneuvers. The candidates and their managers and supporters are continuously concerned with decisions and expressive acts. The voters, on their part, are given an exposure to persons and events as well as to the words the candidates say.

Active candidates for the nominations are involved almost continuously in public display of personality, whether they wish to be or not and whether they can or cannot control the circumstances of the display. Those already holding high office have an obvious advantage: Vice President Nixon during his various official visits abroad and Senator Humphrey in his 1958 conference with Soviet Premier Khrushchev not only were able to create a public image of competence to deal with high matters of policy but automatically acquired page-one newspaper coverage. Comparable opportunities are not often available, but in the strategy and even the routine of the prenominating campaigns any candidate has abundant means of demonstrating his qualifications, if they exist, for the office he seeks.

The kind of campaign strategy chosen and the candidate's manner of carrying it out are highly revealing of whether he is reckless, cautious, bold, or timid; willingly candid or skillfully devious; democratic or authoritarian. He must exhibit the approved virtues of statesmanship, at the same time showing individuality as a person. If he campaigns in the primaries, in each state entered he must adjust to the political situation—including its personalities, its memories of other campaigns, and its specific slant on the issues currently of national importance; throughout he must maintain a position that will do the least harm when reported in other states whose political situation may differ.

In discussing issues, a candidate must express views on a wide range of subjects if he wishes to look like a statesman. But the more definite his position and the more numerous the subjects he talks about, the more are voters likely to disagree with him one way or another. Moreover, a position that may help to win the nomination may turn into a handicap when it comes to winning the election.

The direction and intent of his discussions also create dilemmas. Should he attack the views of a competing candidate of his own party, or only the positions of the opposite party? Should he direct his proposals to the entire electorate or only to his own party?

*   *   *

In sum, a candidate's public display must make a variety of appeals. In the first place, he needs to identify himself as a loyal party member. Second, if the party is deeply split, he must define his own relationship to the conflict—by showing either that he belongs with what he hopes will turn out to be the winning faction or that he is the unifier who can bridge the split. Third, he must discuss the issues, choosing and treating them in a way that will define his individual approach yet not alienate party and voter groups who may disagree in part.

Fourth, he must provide an attractive personal image that includes human warmth and cordiality, a prior record of accomplishment, apparent qualifications for

high office, and recognition by his associates as a leader. This image is sometimes the most important of all the appeals, for when the factional and issue positions of several candidates are all relatively acceptable, choice will then be based principally on personal qualities.

The New Picture

Candidates and party voters, interacting in the nominating contests of recent years, have established a series of precedents that add up to a new picture of what a nominating contest can mean. In years of contest, the standard nominating campaign of the future may prove to be a composite of those that won their first nominations for Willkie, Eisenhower, and Kennedy, and their second nominations for Dewey and Stevenson.

All five campaigns were notable for demonstrating the great extent to which the mass media would report and seemingly seek to influence contests that involved dramatic events and impressive personalities. They were remarkable also for the amount of activity they developed among those persons who do not ordinarily serve in party organizations but who do provide the sinews of war and are in a position to exercise influence when they choose. Action in the primaries was an important part of four of the campaigns (not of Willkie's in 1940), with each candidate proving that a challenge could be repelled where the issues were clear. In all five cases, when the primaries were over, a final push was mounted that reached its climax under the candidate's personal leadership at the convention, with a heavy mobilization of popular sentiment as the delegates reached the point of voting.

When campaign participants discuss these new patterns, the primaries are often a chief focus. In the course of a television interview on June 1, 1958, for example, Adlai Stevenson commented that the presidential primary "is almost a useless institution." He noted the burdens imposed on governors and other busy state executives when required to campaign in the primaries, the usually small turnout of voters, and the confusion and lack of uniformity in the rules.

> Finally, it is terribly expensive; it's exhausting physically; you burn up yourself, you burn up your ammunition, you burn up your means. I think that it's a very, very questionable method of selecting Presidential candidates and actually it never does. All it does is destroy some candidates.

Stevenson's comment was at best incomplete in its implied assessment of how Eisenhower had been nominated in 1952, and was somewhat unfair to Dewey's record in 1948 and his own in 1956. Yet he was merely giving an unusually articulate expression to sentiments that were widely held in 1958. That was the summer in which a Humphrey emissary unfolded a plan under which all of the candidates for the Democratic nomination of 1960 would have avoided contests in the primaries by mutual agreement.* A year later, Humphrey and Kennedy were both convinced that neither could win without a showing in contested primaries; and each obviously needed the other in order to create the contests that were necessary.

Even Stevenson, however, in criticizing the primaries did not seem to question the desirability of campaigning for popular support. It seems to be taken for granted that a direct appeal to the voters is required to assure the legitimacy of the nominations, and that popular mandates, when they exist, must be given weight in the

* See the unabridged 1960 edition of this book, p. 296, footnote 33.

nominating choice to secure popular favor in the election campaign to follow.

It is in the nature of presidential nominating contests that new men are always under consideration and must sometimes be nominated. The Republican choice in 1940, for example, lay mainly between three men whose fame had not yet matured: Dewey, a defeated first-time candidate for governor; Taft, a junior senator of two years' standing; and Willkie, a public utility magnate who had never held public office. The limitations of well-known candidates are likely to be about as well understood as their potentialities. But both limitations and potentialities of lesser-known men can only be guessed at—unless the testing process before the convention is sufficient to bring out evidence.

Without the kind of nominating campaigns that have recently occurred, popular judgment would probably be wholly inadequate for rational choice when new men must be considered. If the nomination were left entirely to the party organizations and the assembled delegates, a much more informed choice (though subject to the obvious limitations of the organization point of view) might be possible with a minimum of campaigning. But even the most knowledgeable party leaders cannot predict how a potential new candidate will act under pressure. The Stevenson nomination of 1952 was at best a calculated risk for those who were active in bringing it about. Stevenson was completely untried in presidential campaigning or in meeting the voters for any purpose in any state other than his own.

The recent pattern of nominating campaigns has undoubtedly increased the possibilities for rational choice. The process extends over enough time to give candidates, voters, party organizations, and delegates an opportunity to reconsider and correct their first impressions. The candidates are required to make a complex series of decisions, each of which is vital enough to test courage and intelligence, but not likely to be fatal. The voters have ample chance to exert substantial influence, without being given full control over decisions that can best be made by the parties in their corporate capacities. The final decision is reserved to a meeting at which there is opportunity for negotiation, exchange of information, and the application of informed judgment.

By comparison, the possibility of rational choice would be greatly lessened if, on the one hand, there were a national primary in which the whole issue would be settled directly by the electorate on a single day, or if, on the other, the national conventions made their nominating decisions on the basis of a campaign in which there had been no direct appeal to the voters and no testing of the candidates in elections outside their own states—as was largely the case from 1832 to 1912.

2

Mass Media,
Public Opinion Polls,
and Voter Preference

■

The evolution of voter attitudes and preferences in the
selection of a first-time presidential nominee has been
singularly neglected in general studies on voter psychology. There can be little doubt, however, that in
recent years the mass media of communication and the
public opinion polls have played compelling roles in this
evolution.

The Role of Mass Media

The competitive two-party system originated some
years before the telegraph came into use (the first line
was authorized by Congress in 1843) and long before
the first commercial telephone exchange was established
(1878). Political communication was for many years
mainly by word of mouth, discussion in meetings, correspondence by mail, printed flyers and leaflets, and the

press as it then existed—limited in circulation and highly sectional and partisan in opinion and behavior. That a truly national means of communication was lacking to the parties until the latter part of the nineteenth century had a great deal to do with their own long lack of a truly national character. When the remarkable acceleration of all of the then available means of communication in the country began in the twentieth century, the effect on political affairs was immediate. But not until the newsreel began spreading visual images of election candidates and events throughout the nation were the possibilities of mass media, as now known, recognized.

Commercial radio broadcasting, which came along in 1920, leapt into political importance in the presidential campaign of 1924. Television broadcasting, which began modestly just before World War II, made its first impact on presidential politics in 1948; by 1952 television receivers were available in 37 per cent of all homes and the average set was used about 26 hours for watching the political conventions. By 1956 sets were available to at least three quarters of the population; an estimated average of 16 hours was spent in viewing convention events. By 1960, television was available in some 45,000,000 homes, but not more than half of the sets were turned on for the conventions at any one time.

The coverage of political events by newspapers, magazines, motion pictures, radio, and television is more ubiquitous in the United States than in any other country. Adverse criticism of this has been often voiced, especially when certain aspects of political life that are still considered privileged and private in other democracies are regularly treated here as in the public domain. But there can be no denying the importance of the mass media to the nominating process.

FUNCTIONS

In making decisions, recognition of the alternatives of choice is a first and vital step. The nominating process has to start at this beginning, although there is actually no single starting point where the potential candidates begin to become visible. It is in the nature of things that, when the identification becomes authoritative, the candidacy ceases to be potential and becomes actual.

The mass media have almost the entire responsibility, so far as the public is concerned, for pointing out the likely candidates during the early period when none of them has as yet formally announced and when party leaders are not yet willing to comment publicly. The early movements of opinion are intangible and ambiguous; their adequate collection and interpretation require constant access to insiders who are willing to talk to their confidants in the press corps, but not for attribution. The result is a highly complex function in which a few top-flight political analysts excel, while other elements in the mass media provide supporting services and the apparatus of dissemination.

The next phase—the clarification of the relative standing of candidates—is of the utmost importance during the period when a field of twenty or thirty potentials is being reduced to six or eight who will actually announce and three or four who will have some substantial chance of nomination. The interpretative reporting of such early evidences of public judgment as the presidential primaries and state party conventions offers useful guidance in the often foggy state of public opinion at this stage. The public opinion polls sponsored and published by newspapers and certain magazines are a special and major part of such guidance.

The candidates that the media refuse to take seriously as news—as indicated by the relative allocations of time and space—are likely to find their difficulties redoubled; those who are given top news treatment take on the appearance of leaders. The cumulative effect of these judgments may well be the point of greatest impact the media themselves make on the nominating process; certainly it is the point at which they are most directly assuming responsibility for decisions of important political consequence.

The function most open to question is the transmission to the conventions of what purports to be the final popular mandate on the nominations. The evidence for any assessment of popular consensus is always incomplete and difficult to view with objectivity. Nevertheless, there is no other route by which most of the voters can send a last message to the convention, and only the media are in a position to make the widest collection of what facts are available. When the media speak with something approaching a united voice in reporting the consensus, as they did in the Taft-Eisenhower struggle of 1952, the impact on the convention delegates can be substantial.

In covering political news, and particularly as complex a sector as the nominating process, the media are especially beset by their traditional problem: where does objective reporting end and partisan commentary begin —and at what point does editorial opinion cease to be admonition and advice and become undue influence? There is no easy answer, because an overlap in performance is part of the problem, and even if bias does in fact exist, the motivations may never emerge from the subconscious. Accusations of media bias in the nominating process have been relatively rare, although motives are often questioned. Its presence as a major factor in a campaign has never been proved or disproved.

Naturally enough, when the media do present something approaching a united front in behalf of one candidate and against others in a nominating campaign, those adversely affected tend to see intentional bias. Senator Taft, for example, after his defeat at the Republican convention in 1952 made no secret of his feeling that the press had been largely responsible and later spelled it out in the memorandum prepared for some of his campaign lieutenants. Specifying the underlying causes of his defeat, he pointed first to "the power of the New York financial interests" and then to the press:

> Second, four-fifths of the influential newspapers in the country were opposed to me continuously and vociferously and many turned themselves into propaganda sheets for my opponent. Of course, this was not true of the McCormick papers, the *Wall Street Journal,* the *Omaha World Herald,* and the *Los Angeles Times.* The *Philadelphia Inquirer,* the Hearst papers, and the Knight papers remained neutral. But most other Republican papers were almost campaign sheets for Eisenhower and were supplemented by the violent support of every New Deal and so-called independent paper.

The problem of the news purveyor's proper role in political matters has been less acute for radio and television than for the press, largely because the legal restrictions under which the broadcasting industry is licensed rule out, in effect, overtly partisan activity as between one candidate and another. But the legal controls aside, the pressures of the market place push the broadcasters toward a general policy of neutrality and avoidance of extreme opinions—the safest way to secure and retain important sponsors and the vast audiences the sponsors want.

EFFECTS

Without the mass media, the vast increase of popular influence on the nominating process in recent years would have been impossible; this can be said notwithstanding the public opinion polls and the presidential primaries that were also closely associated with the increase, for their impact would have been much less without the mass media to support and extend it.

The great number of changes, pressures, and tendencies that have contributed to the increase in popular control are largely the result of the more informed public opinion made possible by the mass media. When, for example, the media made the front-runner position more conspicuous than it used to be, the also-runners were put under strong compulsion to develop counter-strategies that would have popular appeal. When radio and TV opened the conventions to nationwide popular inspection, the way was also opened for changes in convention behavior that might guarantee greater fairness to all candidates.

To the extent that the people take a more informed interest in the nominating process, the popular mandate increases in value and importance. But what can be said about *how* the party voters reach their decisions? What are the effects of mass communication on this complex tangle of individual and group psychology? Answers to such questions will inevitably remain elusive for a long time to come. But some light is shed at least on the existence and timing of voter preferences by the modern-day polls that register public opinion as it changes throughout the successive phases of a presidential election year.

The Record of Voter Opinion

Public opinion polls based on scientific sampling methods have been a feature of presidential nominating and election campaigns since 1936, the year the most grandiose of the earlier type of straw votes, the *Literary Digest's* postcard survey of several million telephone subscribers and automobile owners, was dismally wrong in its prediction of a sweeping victory for Alfred M. Landon over President Roosevelt. The actual outcome of the election was forecast with considerable accuracy through the new sampling techniques used by several other polls, among them the Gallup Poll, conducted by the American Institute of Public Opinion.

In recent years the polls have probably had much more effect on nominating campaigns than on election campaigns, since they provide the only nationwide measurement of voter preference that is available before the conventions. Widely circulated in newspapers of mass distribution, they act as a check on the mandates provided through the primaries and the party processes, and no doubt at times are themselves the source of mandates.

Originally concentrating on the election year, they soon were operating through the whole four-year cycle from one election to the next. As soon as an election is over, a poll is taken among the voters of the losing party on whether the defeated candidate should run again, and, if not, which of the other figures notable in the campaign should run. The query is repeated at intervals; up to the time of the mid-term elections the preferences tend to shift slowly—new names are added to the list, some names disappear, and the ranking order sometimes changes strikingly. During the year following, there is relative stability in the voter judgments, but in the fall and winter preceding the convention, as potential candidates begin their campaigns, preference shifting is again the rule.

In the earliest phases of the cycle, the polls are not very useful to the new men on their way up, but as soon as any previous unknown is mentioned in the listings and begins to move above the 2 to 3 per cent level, politicians and political reporters take notice. For the titular leader of the defeated party and the other well-known figures, the preferences publicized at any period are always of some importance—for good or ill.

From March to June of the presidential year, preferences for various candidates are being registered in both the public opinion polls and the primaries. The primaries undoubtedly affect the polls more directly than the polls affect them. As voters throughout the country read the news of the first-held primary, for instance, their sentiments about candidates may change or may strengthen. The developments are then reflected in the polls, which thus in effect repeat the impact of the primary and clarify its importance for the candidates, party leaders, and delegates, as well as for the voters. The revisions in candidate strategy and behavior that may result affect each later primary, which in turn affects general voter sentiment, which in turn is reflected in further opinion polls. When the later primary results differ markedly from the earlier ones, the polls may also show oscillation, with rapid swings of sentiment in March and April but tending toward equilibrium in May and June as the primary campaigns come to a close.

THE POLLS AND FINAL DECISION

The "trial heat" type of poll is in some respects more relevant than other types to the final decision in the convention, since it tries to discover how a specific candidate of one party would run against a specific candidate of the other if the general election were held at the time of the poll. The candidate leading the preference list within his own party is usually the one who runs best in trial heats against opposing party candidates, but the two choices are not always the same, since the trial heats include voters of both parties and of none. Eisenhower was pre-eminent in the trial heats of 1952 because of his great appeal to independents and to many Democrats, whereas Taft, though at one time reported momentarily as the leading preference of Republican voters, always polled low against a potential Democratic candidate.

The trial heats frequently provide a picture of the total situation quite different from that of the preference polls taken within each party, even when the ranking of the candidates remains in the same order. As of March and April 1940, for example, with the "phony war" dragging along in Europe and before the impact of the French collapse, several Republicans ran strongly against President Roosevelt in the trial heats: Dewey was polling 48 per cent of the total vote, Vandenberg 47, and Taft 42. But among the Republican voters who had a preference, Dewey was preferred by 43 per cent, Vandenberg by 22, and Taft by 17.

The trial heat and preference polls in conjunction sometimes throw light on the distribution and strength of second-choice support. In the example just cited, the figures suggest that Dewey and Vandenberg each had strong second-choice support from voters who preferred the other as their first choice; Taft's second-choice support was relatively much weaker. The distribution of second-choice support is of great importance in nominating contests when all the first-choice candidates fall short of a majority. If any of the polls were to obtain and publish complete tabulations of second-choice data, for instance, this would assist in a clearer understanding of the relationships among the respective candidates and the factions providing their

TABLE 1. PRECONVENTION TRIAL HEATS
AND ELECTORAL OUTCOMES[a]

Year	Democratic Candidate, Per Cent of Popular Vote		Republican Candidate, Per Cent of Popular Vote	
	June Poll[b]	November Actual	June Poll[b]	November Actual
1936	56%	62%	44%	38%
1940	58[c]	55	42[c]	45
1944	51[d]	53	49[d]	47
1948	50	52	50	48
1952	34	44	66	56
1956	36	42	64	58
1960	52[e]	50.1	48[e]	49.9

[a] All trial heat data from American Institute of Public Opinion; trial heat and voting data adjusted to 100 per cent two-party basis in each case to facilitate comparability.

[b] Preconvention trial heat data for the candidate actually nominated, against the other candidate actually nominated.

[c] No Roosevelt-Willkie trial heat was reported, presumably because of the suddenness of Willkie's rise to prominence as a leading candidate; the figures given here were based on responses to a question as to which party the respondent would vote for.

[d] From a release of April 25, 1944; no report for June.

[e] From a release of July 5, 1960; earlier report for June gave Kennedy 49 per cent, Nixon 51.

first-choice support, and the coalition possibilities would be greatly clarified.

When the preference polls report a majority preference within either party, they come close to providing a national popular mandate. But in a hotly contested nominating campaign that involves three or more candidates, there is seldom a majority to report. If the early balloting. of the convention indicates that there is still no majority preference for any one of the leading candidates, the delegates are entitled to look elsewhere for a mandate and a winner. The second-choice suggestions furnished earlier by the trial heat polls then become especially useful.

Since 1936 the preconvention Gallup Polls have indicated each election winner correctly—except in 1948, and even then the polls taken before the convention were more nearly right than those taken in the later election campaign. Table 1 indicates the extent to which the preconvention polls were in accord with the November outcome in the seven elections from 1936 to 1960. In every instance except 1940 and 1960, however, Republican popular strength as it eventually materialized was overestimated by 2 to 10 percentage points, while Democratic strength was similarly underestimated.

Delegate Polls

Popular mandates always exert some influence, but they are not always obeyed. The final vote on a nominating ballot is the point at which convention delegates must decide conclusively whether to carry out or disregard their mandates, but often the final decision has been foreshadowed by earlier ballots on other issues and by the unofficial polls the national press services take of the delegates before and during the convention.

The delegate polls serve as the best available estimate of delegate sentiment at any one time. Those taken before the convention opens are initially a response to the mandates given at the time of delegate choice. As the tension mounts, however, the later polls revealing that sentiment is turning strongly toward a single outstanding candidate may accelerate a development that would otherwise take place more slowly.

In 1956 both the AP and the UP began rechecking

their polls of the Democratic delegates at intervals of a few hours just before the convention and during the opening days, maintaining a running tally that was continuously available. A week before the convention, Stevenson had a strong lead but much less than a majority. Truman's announcement of support for Harriman complicated the situation as the convention opened, along with argument about Stevenson's position on civil rights. Nevertheless, both press polls showed Stevenson steadily gaining during Monday and Tuesday; the majority point was reached and passed in the early hours of Wednesday morning. A band-wagon shift then occurred, and Stevenson polled 66 per cent on the first nominating ballot on Thursday.

At Los Angeles in 1960, the developments were not as striking but followed some of the same pattern. On Saturday, before the convention opened, the Associated Press credited Kennedy with 546 votes and Johnson with 235, with 761 needed to nominate. After delegation meetings on Sunday, the tally went up to 620½ for Kennedy and 273 for Johnson. Thereafter Kennedy continued gaining slowly in the public count but without reaching a majority in advance of the voting; there was no band-wagon shift until the actual balloting on Wednesday in the convention hall. Even so, the continuing revelations of weakness on the part of the other candidates probably helped to hasten the decision.

This kind of acceleration is clearly another demonstration of the changes in the nominating process. When one candidate is showing strength in the delegate polls, other candidates are under pressure to make a similar showing by urging their supporters to become publicly committed; it becomes difficult for any candidate to keep his reserves of committed strength hidden. For any delegate, reticence is also difficult when other delegates are making candid statements. In open contests, the stage is thus set for band-wagon movements even before the voting in the convention begins. In a sharply fought contest between two strong candidates, the uncommitted delegations that have been clearly identified by the polls are so much under the spotlight of public attention that the contest may be concluded very rapidly when the convention finally meets.

Voter Influence

The recent increase of voter influence on nominating decisions is undeniable. But a fair appraisal of the extent to which the influence is usually effective remains difficult—not only because tools of measurement have seldom been available, but also because simple observation shows that the influence has been far more effective in some nominating decisions than in others.

Voter preferences for one candidate rather than another can be highly unstable. When the opinion polls show rapid changes in the standings of the candidates as the preconvention campaigns unfold, it can be assumed the attitudes of the party voters being consulted are not based on very firm convictions. In such a situation the convention delegates may feel no strong compulsion to give the nomination to what may only purport to be the leading popular preference.

Nevertheless, the regard for voter sentiment can be clearly seen in some convention situations. When a front-running candidate reaches the point where he is clearly the majority preference of the voters in his party, as in the case of Dewey in 1944, majority support for him among the delegates comes rapidly and the contest is likely to be over before the convention meets. It is no longer possible without qualification to identify a candidate as the front-runner unless he is the leading preference both of the voters in his party and of the delegates. A candidate who develops a strong lead in delegate strength without leading in voter preference becomes suspect, and has difficulty in maintaining a legitimate claim to the front-runner position.

Situations in which the convention faces two strong candidates, and only two, are undoubtedly those that put the convention system under its greatest strain. The Taft-Eisenhower struggle may long be the classic case in which it was clear that voter strength had accumulated predominantly behind one candidate and delegate strength behind the other. In the end, the convention was forced to decide whether it would go along with popular sentiment or disregard it. Popular sentiment proved controlling—and if it had not, it now seems entirely possible that the party would have lost the election.

When the preconvention campaigns leave three or more candidates in the running, usually with an evident front-runner but with no demonstration of a first-choice majority mandate for any, the extent to which a convention is or should be limited by the available indications of popular choice is a good question. In such cases, it would help if the public opinion polls would more often provide evidence of the kind the Gallup Poll reported in February 1960. In a series of two-way tests among the candidates for the Democratic nomination, Kennedy was preferred to Stevenson by 50 to 43 per cent of the Democratic voters, with 7 per cent undecided. Against Johnson, Kennedy was preferred 58 to 32 per cent, with 10 per cent undecided; Johnson was preferred to Symington by 47 to 28 per cent, with 25 per cent undecided. No similar figures were reported later in the campaign, but Kennedy continued to gain strength as a first-choice preference among Democrats, rising from 35 per cent in February to 41 in June.

Plurality mandates are always suspect, yet are almost inevitable in contests with three or more active candidates. Assessing such a mandate always involves uncertainties about the nature, strength, and basis of the plurality preference. It may also be questioned to what extent the campaigns have permitted the voters to examine all of the valid alternatives—including potential candidates who refused to campaign actively.

The popular plurality mandate registered for Senator Kefauver in 1952, for example, was weak not only because it was merely a plurality and of very recent formation, but also because many other voters were known to be looking for guidance from leaders whose views they wished to hear or were simply waiting for events to develop. The situation was unusual, but not so unique that it may not happen again.

The nominating process is indeed one where there is need for the services of a representative institution— one that can take the situation as it finds it, weigh up all the possibilities, and arrive at a decision in the name of the whole party, as the conventions when at their best can do. If the institution is truly representative, there is little reason to think the party voters will be disregarded when they can speak with a clear voice. When they cannot, there still remains a need for a decision that will rally the party rather than divide it, if the party is to enter the election contest with any hope of success.

The extent to which the conventions have in fact been representative under the rules and practices of recent years receives specific examination in later chapters, especially Chapters 9 to 13. Before moving to these details, however, it seems appropriate to examine how the convention system happened to exist in the first place, and under what conditions it has evolved since 1832.

3

Origins of the National Convention System

■

National party conventions for the nomination of President and Vice President entered the American scene in 1831-1832, during Andrew Jackson's first presidential term. Uncertain in policy and authority and held irregularly at first, within a few decades they had developed the main features that have characterized them ever since. In a world of constant political change, they are among the oldest important political institutions to be found in any country.

In the forty-three years between the ratification of the Constitution and the first nominating convention, two successive systems of choosing a President had been used. In 1789 and again in 1792, George Washington was chosen by the method contemplated by the Constitution as written, which merged nomination with election:

> Each State shall appoint, in such Manner as the
> Legislature thereof may direct, a Number of Electors,

equal to the whole Number of Senators and Representatives to which the State may be entitled in the
Congress. . . . The Electors shall meet in their respective States, and vote by ballot for two Persons, of
whom one at least shall not be an Inhabitant of the
same State with themselves.

Beginning in 1796, the second system, nomination by
party caucus in Congress and choice of electors by
popular vote in the states, gradually supplemented the
constitutional provisions. "King Caucus" persisted, despite criticism, as an off-and-on instrument through
1824, then disappeared for good. The two major nominations for the election of 1828 were made respectively
in the Tennessee legislature and a state convention in
Maine.

In 1832, when for the first time all candidates were
nominated by public national conventions, the electoral
college members were chosen by popular vote in every
state but one. Thus the succession of systems had
moved increasingly in the direction of popular choice.
Each of the three was the combined product of an
earlier history and the circumstances of its own day,
and each of the first two left an imprint on its successor. The institutional origins of the national political
parties can be traced very largely in this evolution of
the apparatus for dealing with presidential nominations.
And throughout every stage of later development, the
practical requirements of the party system have necessarily determined many aspects of the nominating process, and vice versa. Obviously the nominating process
is not an end unto itself; it is preparatory to an attempt
to win an election, which in turn is preparatory to an
attempt to operate a government.

In the light of this chain of relationship, the nominating process emerges, not as an isolated quadrennial
activity, but as part of the complex process of govern-

ment in its widest sense. This concept was implied in the Constitution, yet even the men who wrote that instrument realized only gradually, during the early years of the new government when principles were first undergoing trial by practice, the more far-reaching implications of the relationship.

The evolution of the American political system is not yet completed; it never will be as long as the country survives. As evolution continues and attendant problems arise, it is well to recall the antecedents and the origins of our political customs. The fact that these customs have existed for so long does not prove them beneficial, but does suggest that they should be understood before changes are contemplated that might produce unanticipated effects.

The Constitution and Executive Leadership

One of the most remarkable features of the American Constitution is the fact that is provides for a strong executive. This was not an accident but a firmly guided intention that emerged from controversy dating back to the earliest days of colonial history and still erupting while the Constitution was being written.

The colonial bitterness toward arbitrary governors had been reflected in the structure of government under the Articles of Confederation as drawn in 1777; the only semblance of executive leadership for which they provided was vested in the presiding officer of the Continental Congress, with rotation from year to year. But the conservatives in the Congress never gave up their struggle for a stronger form of government; in 1786 they were able to secure authorization for what became the Constitutional Convention of 1787.

Most of the thirty-nine members of the Constitutional Convention who remained to the end and signed the final document were leaders of the conservative or nationalist wing of the "party of revolution." Well-read and politically experienced, they knew fully, from history and at recent first hand, the record of conflict between executives and protesting assemblies. Yet being also intent on the necessity for national integration and the creation of a government able to govern, they decided that the Executive Branch of the new government must be personified, not by a committee, but by a single head of state.

How, then, would this chief executive be chosen? The basic premise widely held among the Founding Fathers, themselves mostly bred in an aristocratic tradition, was that there exists a "natural aristocracy" of men imbued with such qualities as virtue, talent, wealth, distinguished descent, learning, and even physical strength. The problem was to devise a method for selecting "the best" from among this natural aristocracy to serve as President of the United States.

The Virginia delegates, having high regard for the parliamentary model evolving in the mother country, where the prime minister was chosen by the legislative majority, proposed that Congress should choose the President. This, however, would violate the principle of separation of powers, to which the Founders were dedicated. Nor could the President be chosen by the governors of the states, as proposed by a Massachusetts delegate, since this would undermine the establishment of a national authority independent of the states. Direct election by the people was also considered impossible, for it was believed that the electorate, even limited as it was then, would be incapable of employing the "proper" standards for soundly judging which one of the natural aristocracy was "the best."

The Convention finally settled on the method of an *ad hoc* electoral college. Each state would convene separately its most capable individuals to serve briefly as presidential electors, who in their wisdom would choose "the best" American for the office of President; the runner-up would become Vice President. Each state legislature was left to work out its own method for choosing the electors.

The Founders were soon engaged in a hot national campaign to secure the adoption of the Constitution. Calling themselves Federalists, these members of the "party of the Constitution" met opposition in nearly every state, but showed themselves expert in argument and in the art of circumventing established political institutions. They had wisely provided for ratification by a minimum of nine specially elected state conventions—instead of the sitting state legislatures, most of which were under the control of agrarian, Antifederalist majorities. By June 1788 the ninth state had ratified the document that presented a new structure of national leadership and government, including what was thought to be a strong but nonpartisan Presidency.

Leadership Recruitment
from Washington to Jackson

The sixty-nine presidential electors who cast their ballots in February 1789 had no trouble making their unanimous choice of "the best." George Washington was the acclaimed military genius of a successful revolution, had presided over the Constitutional Convention, was one of the wealthiest men in the country and the leading citizen of Virginia—the state with the largest electoral vote.

EMERGENT PARTISANSHIP

In the brief span of Washington's first administration many political leaders realized that elections are critical

occasions for change, even revolution, by constitutional
means. They saw that when officeholders were chosen
and legislative policies adopted on the basis of numeri-
cal majorities, organized efforts to win those majorities
were automatically invited. The recurring elections provided by the Constitution had set forces in motion that
rapidly produced groups of opposed partisans in Congress and among the electorates in the states. Any incumbent of the Presidency, intended by the Founding
Fathers to be a nonpartisan office, soon owed his position to the efforts of a political party.

The four principal figures in the opening years of the
new government were President George Washington,
Secretary of State Thomas Jefferson, Secretary of the
Treasury Alexander Hamilton, and Representative
James Madison. Washington, although basically a Federalist, endeavored to remain neutral in the Hamilton-
Jefferson feud, in which Jefferson and Madison were
allies, and also kept himself clearly above the party
battle that took place in Congress and the electorate.
As President, he made all major, and many minor, decisions in matters of administration, and here did tend
to give some preferment to the Hamiltonian program.
Fundamentally, his nonpartisanship rested on the assumption of continued Federalist dominance in public
policy.

In the opening session of the First Congress, Madison
held the initiative in legislative business, pushing through
the Bill of Rights amendments and working hard to
carry out the provisions of the new constitutional system as he understood them. Hamilton, acting through
his congressional friends, seized the initiative in the
second session on behalf of the Federalist program.
Party identifications were vague, but the Hamiltonians
appeared to have a majority in each House. In the elections of 1790 for the Second Congress, they won small

but definite majorities: 37 to 33 in the House of Representatives, 16 to 13 in the Senate.

Jefferson, pondering the lessons of these elections, began looking toward the general electorate for ultimate support of his philosophy of government. He promoted organizing work in many states through personal correspondence, but New York State, as Hamilton's main political base, required special attention. In May and June of 1791, Jefferson and Madison took their famous "botanizing expedition" up the Hudson Valley. The result was a political alliance between forces in New York and Pennsylvania that shortly produced further results in Congress and in the electoral college.

By 1792 the "Hamiltonians" and the "Madisonians" were rapidly becoming identifiable political parties. Jefferson, eager to come out openly against the Hamiltonian program, several times offered his resignation as Secretary of State, but was also among those urging Washington to serve a second term. When Washington agreed to do so, the party struggle focused on the Vice Presidency and the congressional seats. Local campaigning was intense. An increasing number of Antifederalists, finally obliged to admit the success of the Constitution, dropped the old designation and called themselves "Republicans"—signifying that they were opposed to monarchy, which they accused the Federalists of trying to establish.

Washington received the unanimous vote of the electoral college—now 132 members. Of the second votes, the Republicans mustered 50 for George Clinton, not enough to beat the Federalist 77 for John Adams, who was thus re-elected Vice President; 4 Republican votes went to Jefferson and 1 to Aaron Burr. The Federalists retained their majority in the Senate, but the opposition took control of the House of Representatives.

Jefferson left the Cabinet late in 1793, after which

the Republican opposition increasingly made itself heard in the press, in Congress, and occasionally from Monticello. In 1794 Hamilton also left the Cabinet and devoted himself with increasing vigor to party politics. With the approach of the third presidential election year, 1796, it was clear that the electoral college provisions of the Constitution were to receive their first real test.

Article II, in requiring each elector to vote for "two Persons" without indicating preference between them, contained the seeds of trouble. In 1789 and 1792 when each elector gave one of his votes to Washington, the problem was simple, but the emphatic division of the vote for Vice President in 1792 indicated the effect of the growing party activity. In 1796 there would be 138 electors, and with each of them having two officially nonpreferential votes it was possible that many different presidential candidates might win only a few votes each. It was also possible that if enough electors shared the same clear preference for a single candidate for Vice President, they could actually give him the Presidency when none of the intended first choices had mustered a majority.

NOMINATION BY CAUCUS

If electors of like mind were to be mobilized in full strength, some kind of influential leadership was clearly needed to unite them on a slate of first and second choices. Throughout 1795 and early 1796 the problem engrossed Madison and his Republican colleagues; they finally settled on the plan of open nominations made by a congressional group. During the summer the Republicans in Congress held a caucus and agreed to support Thomas Jefferson for President and Senator Aaron Burr for Vice President.

When the electors met in December 1796, the cross-currents of constitutional design and party competition produced thorough confusion. Ballots were cast for thirteen candidates. The majority winner was Adams, with 71 votes; the runner-up was Jefferson, with 68. Thomas Pinckney, Adams' running mate, received 59 votes, and Burr 30. Twelve of the Adams' electors had dissipated their second-choice votes, and at least one elector had voted for both Adams and Jefferson, since between them they received 139 votes.

Thus a Federalist became President, with a Republican as Vice President. The experience emphasized the importance of pledging the electors to vote for *both* the presidential and vice-presidential nominations of their party. This step in planning, however, was subject to still another possible dilemma—a tie vote between the two candidates of the same party if all electors cast their ballots as instructed by the popular vote.

Between 1796 and 1800 increasing reliance was placed upon the congressional caucus to organize national and local party effort. The Republican caucus united again upon a Jefferson-Burr ticket for 1800, but unity was not so readily achieved among the Federalists. Adams' administration had alienated many of his own party, particularly Hamilton, who considered the prospect of his re-election intolerable. Nevertheless most Federalists were constrained to support their incumbent President for re-election; for second place they chose Charles C. Pinckney of South Carolina.

THE TWELFTH AMENDMENT

Preparing for the presidential contest, Aaron Burr led Tammany Hall in an unprecedented "get-out-the-vote" drive during the elections for the New York state legislature.* Among other innovations, he introduced the use of a card index file, thereby enabling party workers to ferret out every possible supporter on election day. The Republicans carried a majority into the legislature, which then selected Jefferson-Burr partisans for New York's full quota of presidential electors.

So perfect was Republican organization that every one of the party's electors voted for Jefferson as his first choice and Burr as his second. The outcome was the ultimate arithmetical absurdity of the system: Jefferson and Burr were tied for first place with 73 votes each. Adams received 65 votes, Pinckney 64, and John Jay 1 vote.

Burr, certain of at least the Vice Presidency yet eligible for the Presidency, did nothing to clarify the position as the election went into the House of Representatives for decision. Ironically, the lame duck Federalist majority had the power to frustrate the election of Jefferson merely by voting for Burr. But Hamilton, now that the hated Adams was safely out of the running, convinced his Federalist colleagues that Jefferson, although "a contemptible hypocrite," was incorruptible, and therefore better than Burr.

Jefferson's personal popularity made his re-election in 1804 a matter of course, but he was uneasy about Burr's ambitions. In 1802 he began to encourage the influential New Yorkers De Witt and George Clinton to undermine Burr's political base in their state. He next moved for a constitutional amendment that would separate vice-presidential and presidential voting in the electoral college. On October 17, 1803, the opening day

---

* Named for an Indian chief, the Tammany society of New York City was organized in 1789 as one of a number of patriotic societies using the name; surviving all the others, it early became a center for political activity among the Republicans, later to be known as Democrats.

of the session, the proposed Twelfth Amendment was introduced into Congress, specifying that the electors should "name in their ballots the person voted for as President, and in distinct ballots the person voted for as Vice President." The debate was intense; within eight weeks, however, the proposal was sent to the states. Ratification was completed on September 25, 1804, just in time to free Jefferson, who had earlier been renominated unanimously by the Republican caucus, from a possible repetition of the risk encountered in 1800.

The election was a triumph for Jefferson and the Twelfth Amendment. The revised electoral college system produced 162 votes each for Jefferson and George Clinton, and 14 each for Federalists Charles C. Pinckney and Rufus King. Republican majorities in both houses of Congress had been steadily growing since 1800; their further enlargement in 1804 initiated two decades of one-party government at the national level.

THE DECLINE AND FALL OF "KING CAUCUS"

In the Federalist party, "King Caucus" had never been fully enthroned. When Pinckney and King were nominated in 1804 by caucus, strong objection followed from the state Federalist leaders in New York and Massachusetts, who were more powerful on their home grounds than the party minority was in Congress. In 1808, therefore, at the instance of a committee of Massachusetts legislators, a Federalist delegate convention was held in New York. The delegates, representing eight of the seventeen states, endorsed Pinckney and King.*

The Republicans in Congress caucused again in 1808, despite the growing objections to the system. With the

---

* Although this was in essence the first national nominating convention, it is usually not awarded that distinction because it was held without public notice and with its sessions closed to the public.

support of Jefferson, who refused to consider a third term, they nominated James Madison for President and George Clinton again for Vice President. Madison won the election by 122 electoral votes to Pinckney's 47.

Nominating procedures in 1812 were carried on in the shadow of war with Great Britain. Madison received unanimous renomination in the Republican congressional caucus, but a group of bolters in New York backed De Witt Clinton as the Republican choice. A secret Federalist convention again meeting in New York also chose Clinton as a fusion candidate. Madison won his second term with 128 votes, but Clinton's 89 votes showed the renewed strength of the Federalists, who also gained in Congress.

By 1816 the war was over, and the Federalists had been considerably discredited in the process. Madison's heir apparent was Secretary of State James Monroe, but Secretary of the Treasury William H. Crawford was popular—despite his disavowals of candidacy. Monroe was nominated by the most sharply divided Republican caucus vote so far to occur, 65 to Crawford's 54.

The Federalists held no organized caucus or convention; by common consent Rufus King, their twice-defeated candidate for the Vice Presidency, was given the empty honor of a hopeless race for the Presidency. The party had a small representation in Congress until 1824 and then disappeared—mainly the victim of its incapacity to adapt to the requirements of an expanding electorate.

The election of Monroe in 1816 inaugurated a period in which there was neither an important opposition party nor a clearly defined set of divisions within the majority party. Several strong congressional leaders were competing with each other, and turbulence was growing among the various factions and cliques in the country, but in 1820 all welcomed a postponement of any showing of electoral force. Monroe was renominated by common consent without formal action. With an opposition party virtually lacking, his candidacy went unchallenged, and his electoral college vote was almost unanimous. Not surprisingly, popular interest in the election was at low ebb.

Monroe had the makings of a strong executive, but he had inherited a position that was in the process of being stripped of its real power. He owed his nomination to the members of his party in Congress—who had no need to depend on him for their own electoral success since there was no effective opposition party. As President, he could preside but not rule, the end result of trends that had required two decades to unfold.

In the country at large the political environment was changing rapidly. State constitutions were being overhauled and popular suffrage extended. Population changes had shifted Virginia from first to third place and put New York first and Pennsylvania second. The urban centers were becoming pivots of power, not only because of their wealth, but also because of their voting strength as more and more wage-earners gained the franchise. The frontier areas were also growing—and insisting on a greater voice in political affairs.

As 1824 approached, five major candidates emerged for the presidential nomination of what was now called the Democratic-Republican party: John Quincy Adams of Massachusetts, Secretary of State; William H. Crawford of Georgia, Secretary of the Treasury; John C. Calhoun of South Carolina, Secretary of War; Henry Clay of Kentucky, Speaker of the House; General Andrew Jackson of Tennessee, the national hero now back again in the Senate.

The congressional caucus had not functioned at all as a nominating instrument in 1820, and there was opposition to its revival in 1824. Several proposals for a national Democratic-Republican nominating convention came to nothing. The Tennessee legislature nominated Jackson, then issued a formal resolve that caucus procedure in Congress was unconstitutional. The Georgia legislature favored Crawford, but declared that only a congressional caucus could legitimately make the nomination. In Congress, a committee ascertained that most members deemed the method "inexpedient"; nevertheless, Crawford was nominated by a caucus—sparsely attended and the last ever held for the purpose.

Presidential electors in 1824 were chosen by legislatures in only six of the twenty-four states; the total popular vote in the other eighteen states was slightly over 350,000. Jackson won 99 of the 261 electoral college votes for President, not enough to elect; Adams won 84, Crawford 41, and Clay 37. For the Vice Presidency, Calhoun's 182 votes led a field of six and provided a majority.

The presidential choice was thus thrown into the House. Clay, as the low man and as Speaker of the House, was put in the role of kingmaker and swung his influence to Adams. The vote taken on February 9, 1825, showed 13 states for Adams (a majority), 7 for Jackson, and 4 for Crawford. When Clay subsequently became Secretary of State, the Jacksonians immediately sent up the cry "corrupt bargain" and, declaring that the people had been cheated by "the dynasty of the Secretaries," vowed revenge in 1828. An estimated breakdown of the popular vote, the first such in American history to be widely publicized, indicated that Jackson had led with about 42 per cent, lending substance to the popular outcry when he was denied the office.

END OF AN ERA

Thus the stage was set for the new alignments: the Adams men—now being called "National Republicans"

—versus the Jackson men. President Adams, professing opposition to parties, made little use of his office and its prerogatives to organize for his own re-election. The Jacksonians turned their very willing and expert hands to the creation of what was to become a new party— legislative and electoral, state and national.

As early as October 1825 the Tennessee legislature again nominated Jackson, who resigned from the Senate to begin his campaign. In January 1827, Senator Martin Van Buren of New York, who had placed himself at the head of the anti-administration forces in Congress, proposed that a national convention be called to nominate candidates for President. No action followed the suggestion, but it prompted Adams to call Van Buren "the great electioneering manager of General Jackson."

In 1828 the popular vote for presidential electors rose to 1,155,000; in only two states were they still chosen by legislature. The electoral college outcome was 178 for Jackson, 83 for Adams. Calhoun, with 171 votes, was re-elected Vice President.

Jackson came to power as a result of a highly organized popular movement in which he owed nothing to those members of Congress who had refrained from becoming his announced supporters. The election of 1828 brought with it a revolution in party politics, and began a new era in the development of the Presidency both as an office and as related to Congress.

Early Party Conventions

The first national party convention in the modern sense was held in Philadelphia on September 11, 1830, as a public organization meeting for the new Antimason party, which had evolved from strong anti-Jackson groups in western New York and Massachusetts. Since only a few men among the groups held public office, the leaders were well aware that the party's chances for nationwide growth and success depended mainly on appealing to voters in the areas where it had not yet won any elections. A congressional caucus was obviously useless as a nominating device; some structure had to be built from the ground up, with recognition for adherents who had no representation whatever in public office. The organization meeting therefore called a national nominating convention for September of the next year, which would be open to the public. Delegations were to be chosen in a manner determined by each state attending, and each delegation would have as many votes as its state had representatives in Congress. A majority of three fourths was set as the requirement for presidential nomination.

On September 26, 1831, 116 Antimason delegates assembled at Baltimore and nominated former United States Attorney General William Wirt for the Presidency. Other business included the appointment of a national committee to carry on until the next convention—but the party did not survive to hold another of national scope. Several of its convention rules, however, were to have lasting effects on both the convention system and the party system, and one of its principal leaders, Thurlow Weed of New York, was soon playing a key role in the new Whig party.

By 1831 the National Republicans had so few members in Congress that they too needed some device to give them a semblance of nationwide representation for the coming election. Accordingly, delegates were called to a public convention in Baltimore on December 12, and nominated Henry Clay for President and John Sergeant of Pennsylvania for Vice President. In May 1832 a group of so-called "younger" National Republicans met in Washington to draw up a set of resolutions that purported to define the party's stand. But Clay's overwhelming defeat in the subsequent election effectively disposed of any further attempts to maintain an organized conservative party under the National Republican banner.

On May 21 and 22, 1832, the Jacksonians held a convention, also in Baltimore, of what was still called the Democratic-Republican party. The bitter split in the administration between the supporters of Vice President Calhoun and those of Secretary of State Van Buren had made it necessary to find some new means of pulling the party together. Since Calhoun had a strong following in Congress, Major William B. Lewis, of Jackson's "Kitchen Cabinet," suggested the convention as an instrument that would draw on Jackson's vast strength among the people. He also suggested the timing: the convention should be held after Congress had adjourned and gone home, thus preventing "an improper interference by members of Congress."

The convention used the Antimason model in three procedures: each state could use its own judgment in choosing delegates; delegation votes were allotted on the electoral college basis; and a special majority—two thirds—was required for nomination. To minimize public signs of disunity, each delegation was required to elect a spokesman to cast its vote. Jackson's renomination was unanimously endorsed; Van Buren was named for Vice President, 208 to 75, the Calhoun men failing to muster a third of the votes in opposition.

Only one ballot was necessary on this occasion, but the rules of the convention had provided for other contingencies: ". . . if a choice is not had upon the first ballotting, the respective delegations shall retire and prepare for a second ballotting, and continue this mode of voting, until a selection is made." There was no provision for compulsory elimination in run-off balloting. The convention retained maximum freedom in its search for a choice—a feature of great importance in the later development of the system.

Thus the national convention system was inaugurated as an agency for party representation independent of Congress. With the party system itself in flux, some years were required to establish the authority of the conventions to determine the presidential nominations, but the Democratic-Republicans did not hesitate to hold a second convention in 1835. The upcoming Whigs held their first in 1839, the Democratic-Republicans their third in 1840. Thereafter, nominating conventions of the major parties were uniformly held in the presidential election years.

The Legacy of the Formative Years

The years between 1832 and 1860 saw the establishment of most of the institutional forms of the party system and the nominating conventions that were to survive. When the second Democratic-Republican convention met at Baltimore in May 1835 (purposely early, to head off moves against Van Buren for the Presidency), its permanent chairman justified it as follows:

> . . . the democracy of the Union have been forced to look to a national convention, as the best means of concentrating the popular will, and giving it effect in the approaching election. It is in fact, the only defense against a minority president.

The convention of 1840 was a brief one, quickly confirming Van Buren's renomination, but its historical distinction was assured by two other actions: the party was officially designated the "Democratic party," and a statement of principles was issued as a "party platform."

The opposition vacuum left by the demise of the National Republican party began to be filled in 1834, when the Whig party, spreading out of the South, became the principal vehicle for the anti-Jackson forces. Thurlow Weed, who had promptly assumed the role of Whig organizer in New York State, was instrumental in the strategy whereby several Whig candidates with strong local followings ran regionally in 1836. The party's first national convention was held on December 4, 1839, at Harrisburg; after a heated contest it nominated William Henry Harrison, hero of the battle of Tippecanoe in the War of 1812, for President and John Tyler, a former Democrat new to Whiggery, for Vice President.

The lively "Tippecanoe and Tyler, too" campaign proved too much for the divided Van Buren forces. The total popular vote jumped to nearly 2½ million (a gain of about 60 per cent over 1836), of which the Whigs polled 53 per cent.

Thus the two-party system once more received strength by the creation of a new second party with wide popular support. In the four successive elections from 1840 through 1852, the party in office was defeated in each election, the two parties alternating at four-year intervals. This display of mutual strength coupled with instability was accentuated by two presidential deaths. Not only did five different Presidents hold office during the twelve years, but two of them— Whigs Tyler and Fillmore, who succeeded deceased Presidents in 1841 and 1850 respectively—were to a large extent opposed by the central councils of their own party.

In 1845 a federal statute established a nationally uniform election date—the Tuesday following the first Monday in November. Previously the presidential electors had been chosen on dates variously appointed by the states, with campaign managers concentrating their efforts first on one state and then another. The statute reflected the growing intensity of the interparty struggle.

In view of the changes in campaign tactics made necessary by the uniform election day, the Democratic convention of 1848 established a continuing committee to serve until the following convention, for which it would send out the call and at which its membership would be renewed. It was made up of "one from each state, to be named by the respective delegations, . . . to promote the democratic cause, with power to fill vacancies, . . . and designated 'The Democratic National Committee.' " Benjamin Hallett, former Antimason, was elected chairman of the first committee. The Whig convention of 1852 took similar action.

Both party conventions in 1852 were held amid increasing strain over the slavery issue. The Whigs denied renomination to President Fillmore, although his administration had a good record, and chose—on the 53rd ballot—General Winfield Scott. Thereafter, the party rushed rapidly into limbo. The Democratic nominee, Franklin Pierce, defeated Scott sweepingly, mainly on the basis of hope that he would maintain the Compromise of 1850 and keep the slavery issue out of politics for a few more years.

The hope, of course, was not fulfilled. By the next convention year, bitter struggle had brought about defections from the Democratic party in the North, the final breakup of the Whig party everywhere, and the rise of two new parties. The first of these, the American or "Know-Nothing" party, took over various Whig elements and briefly developed considerable strength; by 1856 it too had begun to split on the slavery issue. Many of its antislavery adherents then went over to the other Whig successor, the Republican party, organized in 1854 and greatly strengthened when Weed brought his antislavery "Woolly Heads" into its camp in 1855.*

The Republicans held their first nominating convention in June 1856 at Philadelphia. John C. Frémont, California's maverick hero, was chosen as the presidential candidate; in the election his 1,341,264 popular votes, to Democrat James Buchanan's 1,838,169, testified to the rapidly accumulating strength of the new party.

The widening national schism was dramatically symbolized in the conventions of 1860, which resulted in the only four-cornered election so far held in American history in which each party candidate had to be taken seriously and actually did win votes in the electoral college. The drastic Democratic split produced two conventions and two candidates: Stephen A. Douglas of Illinois for the northern Democrats, John C. Breckinridge of Kentucky for the southern. Remnants of the Know-Nothings and of southern elements of the erstwhile Whigs met as the Constitutional Union party and nominated John Bell of Tennessee. The Republicans discarded Weed's candidate, William H. Seward, in favor of Abraham Lincoln of Illinois, and evolved a platform

* The shifting of parties and the irregularity of convention dates in the earlier years presented certain minor problems for the analyses in this book. To what extent, for instance, should the National Republican convention of 1831 and the Whig conventions of 1839-1852 be treated as predecessors to the conventions of the Republican party? The National Republicans of 1831 were not identical with the Whigs of 1839, and the Whigs of 1852 were certainly not identical with the Republicans of 1856. But since each of the two earlier parties formed the principal current opposition to the Democrats and elements of each did participate in the formation of the Republican party, the predecessor relationship seems sufficiently valid when discussing the major party experience from 1832 onward. To simplify further, from here on in the book all conventions have in general been dated in terms of the election years; that the National Republican nominations for the election of 1832, for instance, were actually made in 1831 is therefore usually disregarded.

skillfully designed to attract all northern elements. In November, Lincoln received only 40 per cent of the total popular vote, but won the election because he held popular majorities in the states with a majority of the electoral vote. By Inauguration Day in 1861, seven southern states had seceded. In a little over a month the Civil War began.

* * *

The Civil War was as decisive as the War of the Revolution and the Constitutional Convention of 1787 in the formation and development of American institutions. On the field of battle it was demonstrated that the United States was to be, not a mere confederation of independent sovereign nations, each of which might withdraw at will from the Union, but in fact "one nation, indivisible. . . ."

In 1860 the political system had seemed in the greatest confusion imaginable. Yet when the war was over, it was apparent that there would be a reversion to a two-party system not differing greatly, except probably in being stronger, from the one in existence from 1840 to 1852. It was also clear that the national convention had decisively replaced the congressional caucus for negotiating and deciding on each party's most important recurring concern, the nomination of its presidential candidate. This was probably the most limited activity through which a political party could achieve identity as a national institution, but it was sufficient; since 1832 the presidential nominating process has been central to the party system.

Before 1832 it had been repeatedly demonstrated that no caucus of a party's members in Congress could adequately represent all party elements, especially in the case of the minority party. Each party's first convention was an attempt to meet its need, in a specific situation of strain, for a wider representation in the rapidly expanding electorate. By 1852 the conventions were able to provide representation for the internal party constituencies, such as they were, in all of the states and in most of the congressional districts, without depending on party fortunes in Congress.

Each of the four major functions of the conventions had been substantially developed by 1860. The nominating function had been stabilized for both the Presidency and the Vice Presidency by 1840, after the lesson had been learned that failure to unite on a complete ticket at the convention would merely invite party defeat.

The platform-drafting function, evolving out of the occasional efforts to prepare "an address to the people," had become a normal part of convention routine. In the early conventions, platform-drafting, if any, was usually deferred until after the nominations had been made. In 1852 both the Democrats and Whigs adopted platforms before acting on nominations, a specific reflection of the deep fissures in each party over the Compromise of 1850; the action set a precedent that has, with few exceptions, prevailed ever since.

The campaign-rally function was recognized implicitly in the initial decisions of 1831-1832 to hold the conventions as public meetings. From then onward it grew in importance, although seldom openly remarked.

The governing-body function was first exemplified specifically in the election of a continuing national committee. After 1848 for the Democrats and 1852 for the Whigs the national committee issued the convention calls. The Republican party was called to its first convention by a previous organizing meeting; thereafter its national committee issued the calls. Thus for over a century the presidential element in each national party has been in a position to assert its independence of congressional control, even in such matters as choosing the convention site.

The voting methods by which candidates were nominated reached early stability, but with unsolved problems that still harass the parties. From the first the electoral college model was used for the apportionment of voting strength among the states, but it obviously gave over-representation to the states where a party was weak, and still does. Another early rule simplified the taking of record votes; the convention roll was called by state delegations—a procedure that thenceforward gave the conventions a much more federal aspect than Congress has ever had. The unit rule, by which all votes in a delegation are cast as determined by its own majority, became an early fixture in Democratic conventions, and some remnants of it were still in use in the 1960's.

One fundamental decision on voting procedure may have been taken by default of any consideration of alternatives. This was the practice (first established by the Democratic-Republicans in 1832) of continuing to vote as long as necessary in search of a choice, without any forced elimination of low men or any bar to the introduction of new contenders. One can wonder what would have happened to American history if the first conventions had adopted the rule that only the two highest on the first ballot could be considered on any later ballot. Under conditions of sharp factional division within a party, such as prevailed especially in the early years, any elimination rule might have made it impossible to nominate the party's most preferred candidate.*

* With a field of three candidates, it can be shown mathematically that the one running third on a first-choice basis may be in fact the most generally preferred choice. This occurs especially when the two leaders are strongly opposed by each

The two thirds rule adopted by the Jacksonians in 1832—taken over without much thought from the Antimason convention procedures—probably had the most important unanticipated consequences of all. Adopted anew by each subsequent Democratic convention until 1936, it specified that a vote aggregating two thirds of the convention was required to nominate for President or Vice President. The convention of 1844 retained the rule even at the expense of its majority preference, former President Martin Van Buren, whose position against the annexation of Texas had set the southern slavery states against him. The result was the dark horse Polk, whose candidacy was a synthesis wrought in a convention deadlocked by hostile factions. The choice

---

other's supporters, with the man in the middle as the second choice. See Duncan Black, *The Theory of Committees and Elections* (1958), Chaps. 9 and 10.

The British experience of 1963 illustrates the point. In the Labour Party, two ballots were taken when the leadership fell vacant. On the first, the vote was Harold Wilson, 115; George Brown, 88; and James Callaghan, 41. Callaghan was then eliminated under the Labour Party's rules, and Wilson defeated Brown on the second ballot, 144 to 103. There was no proof at any point in the procedure that Wilson could have defeated Callaghan in a straight two-man test.

Some months later, the Conservative Party faced the same problem. This party has no formal procedure for choosing its leader, believing that the choice should emerge from the general will. In the divided opinion of 1963, however, the Conservative members of Parliament were privately polled and were asked to give their first choice, second choice, and last choice. This had the effect of eliminating the three front-runners: R. A. Butler, Viscount Hailsham, and Reginald Maudling. Lord Home then emerged as "the choice"; apparently he was a reasonable second choice in a situation where there was no first choice majority for anyone, although there was no public record of the balloting to prove it.

Devotees of the British party system may well contemplate the muddled way in which the British are still handling a problem that in the United States required early solution if the American political parties were to be able to function at all on a continental scale.

seemed to justify itself in the electoral results: Polk was accepted by the party, won the election, and proved to be one of the abler Presidents in an era of congressional ascendancy.

But what might have happened if the two thirds rule had never been adopted in the Democratic party? It seems probable that Van Buren would have been nominated for President in 1844, and that the power of the slavery states in Democratic party affairs would have been markedly reduced as a consequence. Had Van Buren won election, he would have anticipated by nearly fifty years Grover Cleveland's demonstration that a former President could make a comeback after a term out of office. Had he lost, Henry Clay, the Whig candidate, would have become President. In either event the structure of national leadership and the form of the party system would have been different, perhaps in many notable respects.

This is only one striking example of the many occasions when the choice of a presidential nominee has hung on a party rule or its application in a convention —and when the result possibly altered history. No occasion of this sort can be unimportant in a political system that is so largely dependent on the personality of its President. And by the same token, all of the institutional features of the American party system take on a heightened importance as the country becomes larger, more powerful, and more involved in the problems of world order. This was spelled out in the comment of a leading British newspaper, looking toward the 1960 contest in the United States: "No political contest in the world casts longer shadows than the American presidential election."

4

Changes in the Party System

■

To provide a basis for gauging the amount and kind of change in both the party system and the nominating process—since neither can be studied in isolation—the authors of this book made a search for the time divisions that might be used most effectively in considering the facts and patterns of convention and party history in relation to other concurrent national events. The four periods 1832-1860, 1864-1892, 1896-1924, and 1928-1956 finally emerged. Each contains eight presidential elections, and each also includes years in which White House incumbency changed from one party to the other. As a unit in party history, each period has enough identity to lend considerable support to the thesis that major political change tends to occur at intervals of about a generation.

For some purposes, 1960 can now be added to the fourth of these periods. For others, it can better be considered separately, since it may be the beginning of a comparable new period that is still in progress.

The Ante-Bellum Years, 1832-1860

There is a frequent assumption that the two-party system did not really begin on a national scale until the founding of the Republican party in 1854. Yet the Whigs and the Democrats had alternated in power during most of the generation before the Civil War, and a Whig was occupying the White House when the election of 1852—which in effect destroyed the Whig party—was held.

The relatively equal division of the major-party popular vote in the earliest years, a remarkable feature of the period, and the increasing unbalance and tendency toward third-party voting that followed are demonstrated in Table 2.

In geographic distribution the Whig and Democratic electorates were truly national in the years from 1840 to 1852, the cleavage line in the two-party pattern being drawn mainly in terms of the economic conditions in local areas. Each party could count on majorities in 400 to 500 agricultural counties throughout the nation. Those that regularly went Democratic included predominantly the low-income districts in mountain, upland, and frontier regions; Whig counties were likely to include the high-income, well-settled lowlands. Among the cities of the time, all still relatively small, New York, Baltimore, and Chicago were usually carried by the Democrats, and Boston, Philadelphia, St. Louis, and New Orleans by the Whigs. Although the total size of the electorate was not large by present standards—the popular vote in 1840 was about 2.4 million in a population of 17 million—the era was the first to provide experience with mass electorates in the modern sense.

At the same time, party organization in the nation at

TABLE 2. THE POPULAR VOTE FOR PRESIDENT,
BY PARTIES, 1832-1860
(in thousands)

Year	Democratic	National Republican, Whig, and Republican	Other
1832	707	329	255
1836	765	740	—
1840	1,128	1,275	6
1844	1,338	1,300	62
1848	1,222	1,361	295
1852	1,601	1,385	171
1856	1,833	1,340	872
1860	1,383	1,866	1,441

large was still extremely loose, even though hierarchies of committees and chairmanships had been created at county, state, and national levels by 1852. The tradition of party loyalty had yet to achieve real emotional strength; voters and officeholders alike could march out of one party and into another without much regret for the past or concern for the future.

Basically, the legitimacy of a system of party politics was not yet clearly understood or fully accepted. The wide extension of the franchise had arrived as a fact, and massive electorates were the product, but there was little public acknowledgment that a mass electorate could become effective *only* through party organization. The practical necessities of political action were recognized early in the organization of the Democratic party, but only tardily by the Whigs, who at first expressed abhorrence—at least in public—of all partisan organization. Among the Whig leaders, Thurlow Weed was a notable exception in this respect. Boss of a powerful machine in New York State for decades, and a principal architect of the party's national apparatus, he was an unabashed believer in organization, later carrying the tradition into the Republican party.

Though national in name and in membership, both parties were essentially a collection of localisms. Nominating conventions were nationalizing institutions of a kind, but hampered in becoming more so by the lack of a national system of communication. Political opinion was developed mainly in local discussion and with little reference to any truly national leadership. The party turnover in the White House every four years from 1840 to 1852 was a sign, not of the strength of the parties when in opposition, but of the inadequacy of either party as a national instrument when given executive power.

The congressional leaders were almost all highly sectional in their followings and outlooks. Friction between the Executive Branch and Congress was on the rise. The conventions, not yet having found a means to discover or develop strong national leaders, were being used mainly to select weakness for the presidential office.

Third-party movements were conspicuous in every presidential year from 1844 to 1860, as the slavery issue generated increasing bitterness. Most of them were essentially northern protest movements, asking for stronger resistance to southern demands than either major party was prepared to countenance. In 1844 the third-party vote evidently cost New York State for the Whigs, in 1848 for the Democrats, and in each case probably affected the national outcome on the Presidency.

In 1860 party bolting and the third- and fourth-party vote were at their maximum, yet they did not decide the outcome. Instead, a partisan plurality of the electorate within a sectional majority of the states was able to demonstrate a new phenomenon: that a substantial majority could be polled in the electoral college with less than 40 per cent of the popular vote. The immediate result was the Civil War; a longer-term result, central to the history of the Republican party, was the discovery that a winning party did not have to be truly national in scope in order to win.

The Post-Civil War Period, 1864-1892

During the first twenty years of this period, the Republican party held the White House continuously. Yet the balance of popular votes was nearly always close, and at the end of the period the parties were again alternating in power at four-year intervals, as Table 3 indicates.

TABLE 3. THE POPULAR VOTE FOR PRESIDENT,
BY PARTIES, 1864-1892
(in thousands)

Year	Democratic	Republican	Other
1864	1,804	2,207	1
1868	2,707	3,013	—
1872	2,843	3,597	19
1876	4,284	4,037	85
1880	4,414	4,453	346
1884	4,919	4,850	283
1888[a]	5,538	5,447	388
1892	5,555	5,183	1,323

[a] In 1888 the Democrats polled the larger vote but lost the election.

After the Civil War ended the scene slowly changed from northern politics to national politics as southern states were progressively returned to participation. There was also a march of new states into the Union, with the spread of settlement throughout the West, cul-

minating in 1889-1890 in the admission of North and
South Dakota, Montana, Wyoming, Idaho, and Washington, bringing the total number of states to forty-four
and offsetting southern power in Congress.

A vast extension of the railroad network brought
many changes in population movement, travel, and
communication. Agricultural production was expanding
rapidly, but so was industry. Immigration was still on
the rise, cities were growing, and the strains of an industrial civilization were involving a steadily increasing
proportion of the population. National politics, still
dominated by monetary, tariff, and Civil War pension
questions, did little to clarify the new problems of labor
and general social welfare. The economic system frequently appeared to be dangerously unbridled, with recurring hazards for the party in power as a result.

The Democratic party was effective in opposition but
produced no great national leaders in Congress. Still regarded by the northern tier of states as not quite respectable, its increasing monopoly in the South emphasized its appearance of being only sectional. Without the succession of New York governors as its more
effective candidates for the Presidency—Horatio Seymour (1868), Samuel J. Tilden (1876), and Grover
Cleveland (1884, 1888, 1892)—its position would
have been desperate indeed.

Political activity was increasingly more organized but
at the same time devoid of issues by which one party
might be distinguished from the other. Within each
party, issues were often fought over, but the presidential
candidates eventually nominated by either were so conservative as to offer little choice on election day. (In
Democratic platforms from 1844 to 1892, Thomas
Jefferson and his tradition were never mentioned.)

Beginning in 1876 this rigidity was accompanied, not
surprisingly, by a steady rise in third-party movements.

The Greenback party polled over a million votes in the congressional elections of 1878 and was a factor in the presidential election of 1880. Intense agrarian and labor unrest led to the formation of the Populist or People's party, which held its first national nominating convention in 1892. The platform advocated a soft-money policy—free coinage of silver at 16 to 1; government ownership of railroads; direct election of senators; adoption of the secret ballot, the initiative, and the referendum; a shorter work day for labor; restrictions on immigration. The party polled over a million popular votes and 22 electoral votes in the election of 1892. Grover Cleveland's electoral vote of 277 was the Democratic party's greatest in forty years, but the size of the Populist vote made the victory a hollow one.

Misfortune dogged the Democrats during the second Cleveland administration. The financial panic of 1893 led Cleveland to insist on legislation to protect the gold standard; he obtained the legislation, but only by a bitter fight that deeply split the Democrats in Congress. In the mid-term elections of 1894 the Republicans made striking gains in the House of Representatives. The Democratic party showed signs of going the way of the Whigs in 1852, to be replaced by a new party that would give voters a chance for expression on issues vital to them. But in 1896 the Democrats swallowed the Populists, or vice versa. In name, at least, it was the Democratic party that survived.

Republican Dominance, 1896-1924

With Grover Cleveland in the White House, former Congressman William Jennings Bryan, age 36, won the Democratic nomination of 1896; Governor William McKinley of Ohio was the Republican nominee. The Democrats were committed to the unlimited coinage of silver, the Republicans to the gold standard. Factional bolting occurred in both major parties—silver Republicans met and endorsed the Democratic ticket, gold Democrats met and nominated other candidates. McKinley won election by 7,104,779 popular votes to Bryan's 6,502,925, with an electoral college majority of 271 to 176.

This ending of the twenty-year struggle with third-party interests was in striking contrast to what happened in 1860, when neither major party was willing to pay the price demanded by the party bolters. In 1896, the Democrats paid the price of absorbing the Populists and the Republicans that of consolidating party support among the monetary conservatives. (In a balanced voting situation the "price" of tie-breaking pivotal votes goes up, but it must be paid in one way or another. In the closer party balance of recent years, it remains to be seen whether the national conventions can cope with dissident party factions without making excessive concessions for support and without incurring excessive penalties when agreement proves impossible.)

The election of 1896 marked a realignment of party electorates that was to endure for a considerable time—in part ideological, in part sectional, and in part along social and economic class lines, with all the divisions cutting across each other in a pattern of some confusion. Ideologically, the Democrats were again identified with radical soft-money agrarianism, as in the days of Andrew Jackson; the Republicans with sound money, high protective tariffs, and an active concern for the workingman's welfare and prosperity—"the full dinner-pail."

The divisions were expressed in the most sharply sectional vote since 1860. McKinley carried every county in the six New England states and state-wide majorities in New York, New Jersey, Pennsylvania,

Ohio, Indiana, Illinois, Michigan, Wisconsin, and nine other states. Bryan carried the South and most of the Plains, Mountain, and Pacific states, for a total of twenty-two states to McKinley's twenty-three. The Republican party's subsequent long dominance in both the nation and most of the northern states earned it the reputation of being the party with a "natural majority." Meanwhile the Democrats consolidated their control in the South, as the sectional party of white supremacy.

The upset in 1912 was primarily the result of the split in the Republican's own ranks, when former President Theodore Roosevelt, as leader of the party's insurgents, challenged President Taft, who had been his hand-picked successor in 1908, for renomination. After the convention chose Taft, the Progressives bolted and nominated Roosevelt. The Democrats had a long struggle of their own before the convention nominated Woodrow Wilson. In the electoral college Wilson won 435 votes to Roosevelt's 88 and Taft's 8—but he received only 42 per cent of the popular vote. In the close contest of 1916, Wilson was re-elected, but in the postwar election of 1920 the Democrats were decisively swept out of office. Seemingly the minority party could not win except when the majority party was divided and ineptly led, and then could hope at most for eight years in office. Yet the top-heavy Republican majorities of both 1920 and 1924 were accompanied by ominous discontent and another strong third-party movement.

Elements tracing mainly to the Progressives of 1912 coalesced in 1924 to nominate Senator Robert M. La Follette of Wisconsin for President and Senator Burton K. Wheeler of Montana for Vice President. The ticket, endorsed by the Farmer-Labor party, the Socialist party, and officers of the American Federation of Labor, won 13 electoral votes and almost 5 million popular votes. For the Democrats the election was a fiasco. They managed to hold their place as the second major party, but their share of the popular vote was a meager 28.8 per cent; the Republican candidate, President Calvin Coolidge, won with 54.1 per cent.

During the whole period, internal factional opposition to national party leadership was almost constantly present in the states where one party or the other was dominant; from it stemmed the reforming energy that resulted in the first mandatory, state-wide primary election law (adopted in Wisconsin in 1903) and the Seventeenth Amendment, providing for popular election of senators (ratified in 1913). By 1916, gubernatorial and congressional candidates were being nominated in primaries in about two thirds of the states.

A measure of democracy was thus restored, and boss rule sometimes circumvented, in states where one party had become so dominant that the other no longer provided effective opposition. But the longer-term consequences were detrimental to the survival of two-party government in those states. In a two-party system, a monopoly of the opposition is probably the most important asset of the minority party; when ample facilities for opposition are provided within the dominant party in a state, the second party may easily tend to atrophy.

Recent Times, 1928-1956

The accumulative realignment of the electorates during the elections of 1928, 1932, and 1936 reshaped the pattern of the social and economic cleavage lines between the parties. Allowing for always-present overlap, the Republican party was increasingly identified with the white-collar, proprietary, professional, and upper-income classes, the Democratic party with manual workers, organized labor, ethnic and religious minorities, lower-income groups of various kinds, assorted categories of intellectuals, and maverick high-income individuals.

The realignment thawed some of the sectional patterns that had been frozen since 1896. With the Democratic party in power nationally most of the time after 1932, state after state in the erstwhile "solid North" became the scene of active party competition. The South retained the appearance of solidity in local elections, but in the three presidential elections won by the Republicans—1928, 1952, and 1956—its vote was split almost evenly. Several states, including Virginia, Florida, and Texas, went Republican in each case.

The increase of competition is indicated by the two tabulations that follow. The first shows the percentage of electoral college strength possessed by groups of states, classified according to their party alignment in presidential voting in the two most recent periods. States that voted for the same party no more than five times in the eight elections of each period are here classified as competitive, those voting one way six times or more as aligned with the party for which they voted predominantly.

Alignment of States	Percentage of Electoral College Strength	
	1896-1924	1928-1956
Democratic	29.2%	23.9%
Competitive	12.0	67.5
Republican	58.8	8.6

As can be seen, a generation ago one-party states controlled over seven eighths of the electoral college vote; recently less than a third. The increased competition has resulted in a more even distribution of the electoral college votes polled by each party in the various regions, as shown in the second tabulation. Lack of regional balance is still evident, of course, but the shift toward balance *within* each party has been notable.*

Region	Perce..ntage of Party Vote in the Electoral College			
	Democratic		Republican	
	1896-1924	1928-1956	1896-1924	1928-1956
Northeast	8.8%	24.7%	44.4%	36.4%
Midwest	16.1	24.4	43.0	37.3
South	66.5	38.1	2.3	13.2
West	8.6	12.8	10.3	13.1

Sectional patterns and the intensity of interparty competition in state politics are well reflected by the party affiliations of the three principal officials chosen in state-wide elections—the governor and the two senators. When one party is dominant in a state, the three offices are held with considerable continuity by members of that party. Where there is genuine competition, each party usually manages to occupy at least one of the three offices a considerable part of the time. From 1896 to 1956 they were divided between the parties on the average in about sixteen states. During the first half of that period Republicans usually held all three offices in seventeen states, Democrats in thirteen; during the second half, the relationship was reversed, Republicans usually holding the three offices in thirteen states,

* A listing of states by regions is given at the end of this chapter. The classification is the same as that used in Paul T. David, Malcolm Moos, and Ralph M. Goldman, *Presidential Nominating Politics in 1952* (1954), and also used in recent years by Dr. George Gallup and various other political analysts. The regions are not of equal importance in the electoral college, but the three older regions have been nearly so, at around 30 per cent each, with the West formerly around 10 per cent and recently just under 15.

Democrats in nineteen. After the mid-term election of 1962, however, Republicans held all three in three states, Democrats in nineteen, and in twenty-eight states the offices were divided.

The competitive characteristics of the period since 1928, in relation to those of earlier periods, are shown in the chart below, in terms of the popular vote for the

POPULAR VOTE AND PARTY TURNOVER, 1832-1960

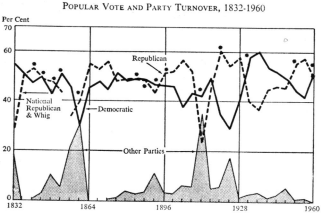

POPULAR VOTE AND PARTY TURNOVER, 1832-1960

The percentage of popular vote polled in presidential elections by Democratic, Republican, and other parties is shown above. The elections that resulted in a change of party administration in the White House are indicated by asterisks. Note the close votes and frequent overturns of 1840-1852 and 1884-1896, followed by the infrequent but wide vote swings and party overturns of 1896-1956, and the close vote and overturn of 1960.

Presidency and of party overturn during the years from 1832 to 1960. In one respect the 1928-1956 period differed from all other periods: third-party movements were relatively unimportant, posing a threat to either major party only in 1948. But the wide swings in party fortunes, first visible in the 1896-1924 period, continued in the more recent period.

The social and economic cleavages that have developed between the major parties during this period are not likely to disappear soon. The great decline in both sectionalism and traditionalism in voting may also be permanent, in view of the continuing importance of economic and political issues that cut across the interests of all parts of the nation. Eventually the nationalizing tendencies that have been at work might even erode the remains of sectional politics in the South.

National politics from 1940 to 1956 were dominated by the events and aftermath of World War II. The new relationship of the United States to the rest of the world has had a heavy impact on the domestic political system. The Democratic party, saddled with the reputation of being the war party, apparently suffered therefrom in the presidential elections of 1952 and 1956, although the Republican revival and the popularity of its candidate played the largest part. The revival was sufficient to win the congressional elections of 1946 and 1952, but in 1954 the previous patterns were notably restored, and in 1956 Eisenhower's victory was largely unshared by his party. In 1958 there was strong Democratic resurgence in the congressional, gubernatorial, and local elections, followed by the presidential victory of 1960.

The recent restless shifting of voting blocs and the increase in split-ticket voting suggest that the current partisan attachments of a considerable part of the electorate are highly unstable. This is a major reason for believing that one of the periodical turning points of political change was in process as the country moved from the conventions and elections of 1956 to those of 1960, and that the present decade may be bringing a further evolution of party institutions.

Party Competition and the Nominating Process

The operation of the nominating process is always affected by the competitive status of the parties and their prospects for victory. A party with no hope of victory approaches the choice of a candidate in a spirit far different from that of a party certain of victory. Still different is the mood of each when either might win but neither is overconfident. The problems of competitive status ramify out into many detailed aspects of the nominating process.

In the current unstable balance, the main point of clarity seems to be that the Democratic party has finally outlived its Civil War legacy of subordination. In none of the several possibilities for the future shape of the party system is it likely to be the permanent inferior. If the vitality it has shown on a broad front in recent years continues—the kind of vitality that has been apparent in the Republican party only in isolated instances—it could be the stronger competitor most of the time; alternatively, the two parties could be so closely matched that either might hope to win the Presidency if it nominates a candidate capable of attracting the independent vote while retaining the party vote.

The tendency toward a polarization of the parties along class and income lines has been welcomed by some as the basis for a more rational politics. Undoubtedly, to many others who prefer the more traditional patterns of American life and politics, the tendency seems sinister. For this group, there may be comfort in the probability that a close competitive balance between the parties would offer many protections to all interests.

No political party is likely to remain for long within striking distance of a national popular majority unless its own moderate elements remain firmly in control of its nominating process. When the parties are competitive because neither can count on a continuing majority, both are forced to put up candidates who will cater for the votes of the neutrals and the independents who have no firm attachment to either. A balanced two-party system is one of the clearest formulas for the organization of countervailing power. Historically it has offered strong protection for most democratic values—including a valid choice for the electorate between candidates who are strong and well-qualified and representative of distinctive points of view.

A Note on Classification of States by Region

The listing order of the states by region, as first developed for use in David, Moos, and Goldman, *Presidential Nominating Politics in 1952,* is based on the following pattern: as far as possible the listing moves from one contiguous state to another, progressing generally from north to south and east to west. Alaska and Hawaii, here listed with the Non-State Areas, would now, of course, in listings dealing with matters from 1959 on be included at the end of the West group.

Northeast	South	Middle West	West
Maine	Virginia	Ohio	Montana
New Hampshire	North Carolina	Michigan	Idaho
Vermont	South Carolina	Indiana	Wyoming
Massachusetts	Georgia	Illinois	Colorado
Rhode Island	Florida	Wisconsin	Utah
Connecticut	Kentucky	Minnesota	Nevada
New York	Tennessee	Iowa	New Mexico
New Jersey	Alabama	Missouri	Arizona
Delaware	Mississippi	North Dakota	Washington
Maryland	Arkansas	South Dakota	Oregon
Pennsylvania	Louisiana	Nebraska	California
West Virginia	Oklahoma	Kansas	
	Texas		

Non-State Areas

Alaska
Canal Zone
District of Columbia
Hawaii
Philippine Islands
Puerto Rico
Virgin Islands

5

Leadership Centers
of the Party in Power

That an in-party wears a face quite distinct from the face it wore as an out-party is especially apparent when a search is made for the sources of leadership and influence most relevant to the nominating process. Most of the rival leadership centers that can be identified are similar in name and primary political function, but the ways of action imposed on them by their party's current power status are widely divergent.

The party in power has the obvious advantage of an incumbent President to act as chief, with all the apparatus of the White House at his command. Even in the days when an incumbent was given little recognition as head of his party, his significance to the nominating procedure could usually not be denied. Today it is taken for granted that the President is the first and most important person to be consulted on the nominating problem.

The President as Party Leader

The first question to be settled is the President's own availability for renomination. Tradition formerly answered the question: a first-term incumbent was usually presumed to be available, a second-termer probably not. But the tradition was not so sacred as to preclude all uncertainty at the end of a second term; Grover Cleveland, for instance, was slow in renouncing third-term ambitions for 1896, thereby further weakening an already weak leadership situation. Franklin D. Roosevelt's third and fourth terms eventually shattered all tradition—and led to the Twenty-second Amendment, proposed in 1947 and ratified in 1951, which prevents any President from being elected more than twice.

For Vice Presidents who succeeded to the Presidency through death of the incumbent, served the remainder of the term, and were thereafter elected President for a full term, tradition offered little guidance concerning a further nomination. Theodore Roosevelt, Calvin Coolidge, and Harry Truman each renounced the possibility in clear and rather dramatic manner.

Traditional or legal availability aside, the decision can be a difficult one, as it certainly was for President Eisenhower in 1956. Although the process of presidential nominations is largely a collective activity, certain questions can be answered only by the individual who might be a candidate. For him every such answer is very personal indeed.

RENOMINATION CAMPAIGNS

Every first-term President, unless he enters office on an announced one-term basis—as no one has done since Rutherford B. Hayes—must give some attention to the problems of renomination from the day of his election onward. This activity usually blends into the other operations of the President and his staff so completely that it goes unnoticed as a separate element. The most effective way to campaign is to do the presidential job well—particularly the many and sometimes dramatic parts of the job that are carried out under the public eye.

Special facets of the presidential routine reflect the necessities of life in elective office. Callers are received whose presence on the official list is inexplicable except in terms of their contribution to the previous campaign and their possible utility in the next one. Much of the massive correspondence pouring through the White House daily is devoted to maintaining friendly relations with political supporters; they may write for a frivolous reason or no reason at all, but a cordial response is essential.

The President is given frequent reminders that his public policy decisions which affect specific groups—whether economic, racial, or religious—may have a critical influence on his political future. The handling of patronage is also of direct political concern. The patterns of the President's distribution of appointments can do much to unify—or dismember—the party he leads.

No other element of party leadership is as vital to a presidential renominating campaign as the President himself. The tradition of renomination for a first-term incumbent is at present so firmly established that only the President, by declination or through his own mistakes, can prevent it from operating.

But every such campaign, easy as it may appear on the surface, involves work and organization looking toward many goals, of which personal renomination is only one. The vice-presidential nomination, for instance, may entail difficulty. And in preparation for the election campaign and for the business of government if the election is won, a platform must be skillfully planned and harmony established within the party on as broad a front as possible. An over-all goal—actually the means by which all the other goals are attained—is solid control of the national party organization. When the renomination itself is subject to challenge, achievement of the other goals becomes doubly difficult.

A modern President's own White House staff normally carries on the most critical parts of the work and organization, maintaining liaison with such important leadership elements in the party as the national committee chairman, the congressional leaders, and the outstanding state governors. In preparation for the 1956 Republican campaign, however, an informal headquarters operated in New York from February 1955 on, with Thomas E. Stephens, President Eisenhower's former appointment secretary, giving virtually full time to the activity.

After the President's heart attack in September 1955, his associates organized to keep his candidacy open and to stall off restless rivals. The strategy line was held until February 29, 1956, when Eisenhower publicly announced his availability. On March 2, Stephens flew to California to deposit the necessary signed statement of the candidacy in the California primary, and plans were then made for choosing the California delegation to be endorsed by the President. Subsequently, similar activities moved rapidly in other states. This is not the only example of a candidacy persistently in pursuit of its occupant, but it may constitute a record in its degree of persistency.

CONTROLLING THE SUCCESSION

The principal business of the Democratic convention of 1835 was to assure the presidential succession from

Jackson to Van Buren. No subsequent President took similar open initiative until the dynamic Theodore Roosevelt, in an excellent position to do so, made William Howard Taft his personal choice to succeed him in 1908.

The next President to face the problem was Woodrow Wilson in 1920. Too ill to perform his duties fully, and with dissension in his Cabinet, he was in a poor position had he desired to control or even much influence the succession. He was apparently opposed on principle to presidential intervention, despite his strong view of a President's importance as party leader. His secretary, Joseph P. Tumulty, reported this statement:

> We must make it clear to everyone who consults us that our attitude is to be impartial in fact as well as in spirit. . . . We must not by any act seek to give the impression that we favor this or that man.

Coolidge seemingly took little interest in the succession after his own withdrawal from candidacy. He showed no enthusiasm for the candidacy of Secretary of Commerce Herbert Hoover, but did nothing to oppose it. Hoover was highly acceptable to the same groups that had supported Coolidge, and in effect inherited the nomination by the absence of overt action on the President's part.

Truman confronted the problem in a characteristically personal way. According to his autobiography, his mind "was made up irrevocably against running in 1952, and I was concerned with the problem of suggesting the right man to the people." He first sought to recruit Chief Justice Vinson, then turned to Governor Adlai E. Stevenson of Illinois. "In Stevenson I felt that I had found the man to whom I could safely turn over the responsibilities of party leadership. Here was the kind of man the Democratic party needed." In January 1952, Truman told Stevenson that "a President in the White House always controlled the National Convention," and urged him to become an announced candidate. Stevenson declined, having already committed himself to run for re-election in Illinois. Truman eventually turned to Vice President Barkley, after considering Averell Harriman along the way. At the convention Barkley encountered opposition and withdrew his candidacy at the end of the first day. Thus, when Stevenson at last became a willing candidate Truman was free to support him.

Truman's personal doctrine on the President's prerogative as party leader to deal with the succession was stated more openly and much more bluntly than that of any of his predecessors. As a statement of prerogative, it is easily open to attack, although Truman probably referred mainly to the simple fact of political power. Implicitly the doctrine concerns the responsibilities of party leadership; certainly, under modern conditions, a retiring President who makes no effort to assure the availability of a worthy successor would be subject to criticism.

Truman also demonstrated that a retiring President can keep a firm hold on the party machinery by the very act of looking about for a successor and using the powers of the Presidency to that end. Whether, with the help of the Twenty-second Amendment, this might become a recurring pattern for future second-term Presidents remains to be seen, but as a substitute for the third-term guessing game formerly employed to maintain end-play presidential authority, an active and responsible interest in the succession could be very effective indeed.

CONTROL OF VICE-PRESIDENTIAL NOMINATIONS

In the present century it has been frequently assumed that the President can control the renomination of the incumbent Vice President, if any, or can arrange a new nomination to suit himself. The historical record suggests, however, that the assumption is only partly justi- fied.

President and Vice President have simultaneously approached renomination in five first-term cases since 1896, including Eisenhower and Nixon in 1956. In 1912, Taft considered finding a new running mate who could balance the ticket in the liberal direction; after the lines were drawn for battle with Roosevelt, he had no choice but to continue with the conservative Sherman. In 1916, Wilson offered no objection to the renomination of Marshall, despite earlier indications of friction. In 1932, neither President Hoover nor Vice President Curtis supported the other for renomination; the party stood on its record and renominated both. In 1936, Roosevelt and Garner were renominated as a team, apparently with little thought of change on the part of either, although some friction had developed between them.

In 1956, Eisenhower refused to give unequivocal endorsement to Nixon, and there was speculation that he might prefer a change. Yet all his public comments highly praised his Vice President. When Harold Stassen launched his move to replace Nixon with Governor Herter of Massachusetts, the only known encouragement he received from the President was permission for a month's leave without pay to advance the cause. The eventual collapse of the move was announced to the press by the President himself, who later told the convention that "it is a great satisfaction to me that the team of individuals you selected in 1952 you decided to keep intact for this campaign."

In all of these cases, the renominations evidently owed more to the passive consent of the incumbent Presidents than to their active support. The record was quite different in the Franklin D. Roosevelt third and fourth nominations.

By 1940, Roosevelt and Garner were so completely at odds that a new combination was necessary. Secretary of Agriculture Henry A. Wallace was an early possibility in a field of more than a dozen availables, but Roosevelt made at least three efforts to persuade his first choice, Secretary of State Cordell Hull, to run— the last on the day before Wallace was nominated. The President finally backed Wallace, only to discover so much Wallace opposition among the delegates as to throw doubt upon the feasibility of the nomination; angered, he wrote out a refusal of his own renomination, which he had just received. Wallace was then nominated.

Early in 1944, Roosevelt considered the desirability of dropping Wallace in the interests of party harmony and improved congressional relations. The name of Senator Harry S Truman emerged as generally preferred at a White House discussion, but no decision was made. In early July, Wallace discovered that the President would probably not back him; at his urging, Roosevelt agreed not to repudiate him and gave him a letter praising his record but stating that the convention must decide. On the same day Roosevelt gave a group of leaders a letter expressing his preference for Truman. On July 20, when a Gallup poll showed Wallace as the vice-presidential first preference of 65 per cent of the Democratic voters, Roosevelt was renominated and the letter expressing preference for Truman was released. Truman himself had been firm in refusing to become a candidate and was managing a vice-presidential campaign for James F. Byrnes. A vote on July 20 might have renominated Wallace; on the next day he led on the first ballot, but Truman was nominated on the second.

Theodore Roosevelt, Coolidge, and Truman each left the Vice Presidency vacant when succeeding to the Presidency; in the choice of the running mate for the following election, each had only limited influence. In 1904, Roosevelt accepted Senator Charles W. Fairbanks, the choice of the erstwhile McKinley supporters, as his running mate, although this was not his own preference.

In 1924, Coolidge's first choice was Senator William E. Borah, presumably in an effort to head off the Progressives; neither Borah, the party leaders, nor the convention were willing. Coolidge then apparently preferred Senator Charles Curtis, but the convention nominated former Governor Frank O. Lowden of Illinois, who declined, and then Charles G. Dawes. (The lack of unity between Dawes and Coolidge was later underlined by Dawes' refusal to sit in the Cabinet.)

In 1948, Truman agreed to the selection of Senator Alben W. Barkley only after Barkley was seen to be the preference of the convention. Truman, in an earlier wide search for an alternative, had vainly tried to persuade Supreme Court Justice William O. Douglas to be his running mate.

The Vice Presidency: Dead End or Stepping Stone?

Benjamin Franklin suggested that the Vice President should be known as "His Superfluous Excellency." Nevertheless, the incumbents in the early days of the Republic were men of stature and the position was a door to the Presidency. After 1840, however, the position and its occupants became the victims of a vicious circle. In each party the vice-presidential nomination was used mainly to secure the votes of an opposing faction for the presidential nomination or to placate them after that nomination had been made. As a result, the running mates were almost invariably incompatible, factionally and personally.

If the ticket won, the new administration was likely to regard the Vice President as an unwelcome outsider, to be isolated as fully as possible in his minor role in the Senate. If the President survived his term and retired, he did not favor the Vice President for the succession. When the Vice President returned to the limbo from which he had come, the post had no value for other purposes of career advancement. If the President died in office, the Presidency was thus entrusted to a secondary leader of a dissident party faction. The unworkable aspects of this formula in its most extreme form were vividly demonstrated during the administration of John Tyler, who took over on his own initiative when Whig President Harrison died and was never considered by Congress and Cabinet as more than an acting and unwelcome incumbent.

Since 1900 the Vice Presidency has been recovering slowly from its previously acquired reputation. Theodore Roosevelt took the nomination in 1900 only under pressure, but he made enough of the job to encourage others. The five Vice Presidents who obtained renomination—Sherman, Marshall, Curtis, Garner, and Nixon —demonstrated that an incumbent can develop his own power base, and one from which he is not easily dislodged.

The tendency to balance party tickets by nominating factional enemies has been less visible in recent years, although such considerations obviously continue to be given weight. The preferable doctrine was pointed up by President Eisenhower in a press conference of May 1955.

> . . . unless the man . . . chosen were acceptable to the Presidential nominee, the Presidential nominee should immediately step aside, because we have a Government in this day and time when teamwork is so important, where abrupt changes could make so much difference. . . .
>
> I personally believe the Vice President of the United States should never be a nonentity. I believe he should be used. I believe he should have a very useful job. And I think that ours has. Ours has worked as hard as any man I know in this whole Executive Department.

Franklin D. Roosevelt was quite obviously applying the principle, then still unstated, when he refused to run in 1940 unless Wallace were also nominated. Wallace was far more active in the administration than any previous Vice President. Under wartime conditions, his activities were accepted without much notice, but they clearly showed that a Vice President could give his main time and attention to duties in the Executive Branch, if the President so desired.

The new conception flowered with the accession of Richard M. Nixon to the office. He attended the President's meetings with the congressional leaders, with the Cabinet, and with the National Security Council, of which he was a statutory member. He was invited to preside over Cabinet meetings in the President's absence, and frequently presided in the National Security Council. He was sent on international missions, some of them apparently more than ceremonial. He carried the major burden of partisan campaigning, particularly for the congressional elections of 1954 and 1958. His political travels were always in the role of a recognized national party spokesman.

In 1960, the position of the Vice Presidency was still further strengthened by Nixon's succession to the Republican presidential nomination and by the close attention each party gave its vice-presidential choice. In office, Kennedy and Johnson proved compatible; the results were apparent when Johnson was called abruptly to duty in the Presidency on November 22, 1963. The Vice Presidency seems to have become firmly re-established as one office that can genuinely prepare a man for the Presidency—something that had been lacking for more than a century in the American system of government.

The Cabinet

In the early decades of the government, Cabinets usually included several members who were powerful political figures in their own right. Often they were active leaders of party factions who held continuing political ambitions of their own. In recent years, Presidents have seldom felt compelled to tolerate openly dissident Cabinet members, and factional leaders have rarely received appointment. For a long time, Cabinet members have been regarded primarily as departmental administrators rather than political leaders, despite their significant role in developing and presenting legislation.

As an agency of inner group political communication, however, the Cabinet has been highly important. Secretaries of the Treasury, Interior, Agriculture, Commerce, and Labor and the Attorney General have long acted as advisers and negotiators, and served as channels between the President and important power-holding groups in the electorate. Each member is also involved in the problem of party patronage—typically, the Postmaster General and the Attorney General especially so.

The Eisenhower and Kennedy Cabinets, as initially appointed, both included a good proportion of men who had been active in the respective campaigns for nomination and election. The Kennedy Cabinet was especially noteworthy for its inclusion of the President's brother Robert, his campaign manager, as Attorney General, but it also included one member of Congress and three erstwhile governors who had been active in the campaign, and who became respectively the Secretaries of Interior, Agriculture, Commerce, and Health, Education, and Welfare. Special counsel Arthur F. Goldberg of the AFL-CIO became Secretary of Labor, and has since been appointed to the Supreme Court.

Since the beginning of the convention system, only two Cabinet members—William Howard Taft and Herbert Hoover—have obtained the nomination of the party in power. This reflects an oddity of the American system of government as compared to various parliamentary democracies: posts that seem to offer exceptional preparation for the highest executive office are largely disregarded in the search for candidates.

The long-term tendency to depoliticize the Cabinet is, however, probably being reversed for at least some of the posts. Members are increasingly available as candidates for the Senate, and service in the Cabinet is perhaps becoming more attractive as a means of advancing a political career. Undoubtedly members will continue to be scrutinized from time to time as potential candidates for President and Vice President, although the road upward may involve a term in the Senate or in a governorship before they can seek one of the higher offices.

National Committee and Convention Officers

In both parties each convention is called to order by the incumbent national committee chairman, who presides until the temporary chairman has been installed. The temporary chairman presides while the convention committees are being organized and the nominations for permanent chairman and other convention officers are being acted on. The permanent chairman serves until the end of the convention.

In legal theory, every convention is an *ad hoc* body, unrestricted by any action of a previous convention and without authority to bind any convention in the future. Actually, precedent acts powerfully to preserve continuity from one convention to another. Those persons who will probably be the officers at the next convention, and those who select them, have a special influence on party affairs that is usually well hidden from view but often of high importance. The influence may be active long in advance of each convention and continue long afterward, in part because the individuals concerned possess strategic information largely unavailable in written form. They are central links in a most extensive and complex network of word-of-mouth communication that normally centers in the national committee chairman.

The convention's temporary chairman does not appear to hold great power, but his post is of some importance, especially when he delivers the "keynote address." From the President's point of view, it is obviously important that the keynote address should present the administration's record in the most favorable terms; therefore the temporary chairman is probably selected by the President or under his close supervision.

The permanent chairman, in presiding over all the major business of the convention, is by far the most important and potentially powerful officer. In 1932 the Republicans began appointing their party leader in the House to the post. In 1948 the Democrats followed suit, with Speaker Sam Rayburn as the permanent chairman, and he served also in 1952 and 1956. In 1960, Rayburn declined the post and was replaced by Governor LeRoy Collins of Florida.

The relative or absolute power of these three convention posts is not easily estimated. For some purposes, they are all obviously much more powerful in the out-party. In the party in power, no President who works at his job as party leader is likely to find his own renomination seriously threatened by opposition from these officials. But if he cannot work well with them as a team, other party business—drafting the platform, planning strategy, and organizing the election campaign —may go very badly indeed.

The Congressional Leaders

The Jacksonian revolt in 1828 put a stop to the "absolutism" of Congress in the nominating process, but of all the inner circles of each party, those that coalesce around the leaders of the Senate and the House are doubtless of the greatest continuous longevity and have had on some occasions the greatest power. The power might be used against an incumbent President seeking renomination as well as for him, but since 1937, when Franklin D. Roosevelt began holding weekly leadership meetings at the White House, an increasingly close relationship between Presidents and the party's leaders in Congress has come about. Presidents Truman, Eisenhower, and Kennedy all continued the pattern of weekly meetings with the congressional leaders of their respective parties, with minor revisions in the ex officio composition of the group attending. The meetings now seem firmly established as an institution.

Do the White House leadership meetings ever discuss nominating politics or national convention arrangements? Perhaps not in any systematic or organized way, since their primary purpose is to review the legislative program, but the whole effect of such a review presumably brings the concerns of the party as a whole into some kind of continuing relationship to the forward planning of legislation, and vice versa. Those attending the meetings are obviously aware that the party's record in Congress will be argued by both sides when the President or his successor run for election—which would seem to have an important disciplinary effect on all concerned.

Powerful members of Congress are no longer often disposed to contest the succession, and so far as is known, no recent President has supported a congressional leader for the nomination to succeed him. During the winter of 1955-1956, Senate Minority Leader William F. Knowland was an announced candidate, should President Eisenhower decide not to run. He was clearly not the President's choice—and he was also clearly ready to enter an open contest if support were given to another candidate. When Eisenhower announced his own availability, the Senator withdrew and promised support.

The more usual pattern in recent years for the in-party's congressional leaders is a position of influence in the prenominating campaigns and the conventions. As noted, Joseph W. Martin, Jr., and Sam Rayburn, the top party leaders in the House, were the permanent chairmen of their respective national conventions for some years. The task of presiding during the critical period of a convention is obviously one requiring parliamentary skills of the highest order. Training in the House of Representatives, with its many members and the close similarity of its basic rules to those of the convention, may well be the best available preparation.

There is an important restriction placed on a permanent chairman: he should not himself be a candidate for either of the nominations. The comparatively recent

custom could therefore be upset if at any future time
one of the House leaders should become a candidate.
However, certain factors traditional to Congress actually limit the availability of these leaders as presidential
material. Members of the House have seldom been
allowed to come within striking distance of leadership
positions until after long service. Martin served fourteen
years, Rayburn twenty-seven, Halleck twenty-four before reaching the top posts; they had thus become
thoroughly tested party "regulars," highly valuable to
the House. But such value is apparently quite different
from the popular appeal that is indispensable for a presidential candidate.

Factional Centers

Factional contests for the nomination of the party in
power may arise under at least three sets of circumstances: (1) when dissatisfaction with an incumbent is
so great that there is overt opposition to his renomination, (2) when there is opposition to an attempt by a
retiring President to control the nomination of a successor, (3) when a retiring President is unwilling or unable
to deal effectively with the succession, so that the convention is more or less open. The existence of an opposing faction does not always produce a contest, for
available candidates to back are often scarce. A faction
with a continuing interest-group basis can suffer defeat
repeatedly and live on to fight another day, but its candidate may depreciate rapidly after only one defeat.

Only a very few potential factional candidates since
1900 were willing to take on an all-out contest for the
party nomination against the entrenched power of an
incumbent President, and the sources of support for dissident candidacies have followed no single pattern. The
Bull Moose revolt of 1912 was an eruption of the

Progressive and Old Guard feuding that had been going
on for more than a decade within the Republican party.
Midwestern agriculture was the source of most of the
overt opposition to Hoover in 1928, and it also produced the Republican vice-presidential nominations of
both 1924 and 1928. The Russell candidacies of 1948
and 1952 were expressions of the sectional dissidence
of the South. So far, neither big business nor big labor
has visibly backed a factional candidate for the presidential nomination in a party in power, although both
have helped in backing majority candidates involved in
factional fights. The support of the business interest
group was important to Hoover in 1928. Organized
labor evidently provided significant support to Henry
Wallace's fight for renomination as Vice President in
1944, but also helped nominate Truman instead.

The relative impotence of dissident factions and their
candidates in the party in power is evident—yet their
impotence is indeed relative, not absolute. Undoubtedly
they retain a kind of veto power, under some circumstances, against other candidates and the policy preferences of other party leaders.

Leadership Integration

American national parties have been almost unique
in their ability to function without any single continuing inner circle of central importance and governing
power. Several inner groups have always existed, but
the fact that they *have* been several rather than one is
a basic characteristic of the system.

The nominating process in the party holding the
White House has been importantly affected by the
rising power of the Presidency and the increased recognition accorded the President as party leader. The
President and his immediate associates now constitute

the innermost inner circle; other circles of influence still exist, but as a loose constellation of groups centering on the power of the White House.

The new status of the Vice Presidency has also altered leadership relationships; the Vice President has clearly been brought within range of a presidential nomination when the succession is open. The office is still uniquely isolated, but it has undoubtedly moved from the outfield to an inner position among the several power centers.

Striking changes have taken place in the role of the national committee chairman in his relationship to the President. During many early decades the national committee chairman was sometimes a factional leader in his own right, sometimes a neutral communication point among factions, sometimes primarily a fund-raiser, but only rarely the accredited agent of a fully accepted party leader. Now he is chosen by the President, occupies a full-time position in command of party headquarters in Washington, and operates essentially as a member of the President's top political staff.

For the convention officers, change is not as easy to document, but it has certainly included a growing recognition of the President's role as party leader. It now seems to be accepted practice that the President has the right to be informed about convention action, to give advice, and, on occasion, to take action himself through his agents or by sending messages. In earlier periods, any presidential interference in the convention was apt to be considered illegitimate.

Four Presidents helped this change to come about: Woodrow Wilson, by his open recognition of the role of party leader as one of honor and legitimacy; Franklin D. Roosevelt, Harry S Truman, and Dwight D. Eisenhower by their successive personal appearances at the conventions, when each chairman found it a distinguished honor to introduce the President of the United States and to appropriate his prestige unto the party.

The new relationships between the President and the congressional leaders of his party, as described earlier, are in some respects the most interesting and significant of all, with the leadership meetings *at the White House* as an important symbol. The practice of using the in-party leader in the House as the permanent chairman at the convention adds the capstone. If the custom continues in future years, an incumbent President seeking renomination or control of the succession cannot select (or at least veto the selection of) the convention's top officer at random; the party caucus in the House of Representatives will have made the choice, perhaps years earlier. At the same time, the House leader, even though almost sure of appointment to the convention chairmanship, is not likely to become so powerful that he can openly defy the President's wishes. The interaction illustrates rather strikingly the forces that appear to be compelling the presidential and congressional wings of each party to work more closely together—even if sometimes reluctantly.

Among the centers of power must be included numerous other party leaders who hold no national public or party office, and who form no single or cohesive group. The list would include a variety of types past and present: such widely different men as Thurlow Weed, Horace Greeley, and Bernard Baruch; the party bosses of major states and of the big-city machines; the former Presidents and former presidential candidates who become elder statesmen within their parties; the governors of major states who were elected on the party ticket.

Interest groups, minority factions, and individual political leaders can of course lobby the President and his close associates to the extent that they can secure access to do so, and in some instances can doubtless threaten sanctions. But the record since 1900 shows few signs of effective interference from such sources; a President seeking renomination or even the nomination of a successor seems to have the situation under his control if he is in health, is prepared to devote himself to the leadership of his party, and is able to hold together the circle of top leaders with whom it has become customary to maintain close working relations.

Apparently either major party, when in power, has acquired the capacity to become a rather tightly-knit organization centering in the President, insofar as questions are at stake that would affect party survival and success in the oncoming presidential elections. From the viewpoint of that central group, every nominating decision is exactly such a question.

6

Leadership Centers of the Party Out of Power

■

The titular leader of the party out of power is the only person whose place in his party even faintly resembles that of the President in his. Yet he occupies no formal position in either the party hierarchy or the government, and thus the post remains a nebulous one.

The national committee chairman might be said to occupy the central out-party post, yet he has no definite responsibility for preparing the next nominations and almost none for leading the party as an opposition force in the government. The party's Senate and House leaders do have the latter responsibility, but in other party matters their roles may be ambiguous, although they must always be considered potentially important as candidates or kingmakers. Other members of Congress, governors, big-city mayors, state party officials, interest-group leaders and a wide scattering of other individuals and groups may all play significant parts of one sort or another.

The result is a bewildering pattern of relationships.

Custom and usage are much more fluid than in the in-party, both for controlling party machinery and for dealing with succession problems. There are certain influence centers that have become relatively institutionalized and stable, yet candidates for the presidential nomination may seemingly emerge from almost any focus of political activity—and any candidate who has strong backing becomes, for a time at least, a center of leadership himself.

Titular Leaders

The titular leader has no clear and defined authority within his party. He has no party office, no staff, no funds, nor is there any system of consultation whereby he may be advised of party policy and through which he may help to shape that policy. There are no devices such as the British have developed through which he can communicate directly and responsibly with the leaders of the party in power. Yet he is generally deemed the leading spokesman of his party.

This was Adlai Stevenson's comment in 1956 on the titular leadership. Nevertheless, the post, perhaps even because of its ambiguity, has become one that offers many opportunities for initiative. Like the present concept of the Presidency, which is far different from that held by Madison and Monroe, Buchanan and Grant, the present meaning of the titular leadership must be assembled from the contributions of the incumbents who have exercised initiative.

In modern times, six defeated major-party candidates for President have made substantial efforts toward renomination at the next convention: Grover Cleveland (D), William Jennings Bryan (D), Alfred E. Smith (D), Wendell L. Willkie (R), Thomas E. Dewey (R), and Adlai E. Stevenson (D). The record of the titular leadership can be read most conveniently in the activities, experience, and status of these men.

THE DEMOCRATIC BREAK WITH TRADITION

Cleveland in 1892 and Bryan in 1900 first gave vitality to the titular leadership by ending the tradition —unbroken in both major parties from the beginning of the convention system—that a defeated presidential candidate is finished as a national party leader. Cleveland's break with tradition was especially resounding in that it included election victory over the man who had ousted him from the White House in 1888. But Bryan's performance was also remarkable, particularly in the length of his availability as a candidate and as a figure of importance in party affairs—demonstrating that the leadership role could be sustained meaningfully both in and out of election years. He was renominated by the conventions of 1900 and 1908, played a power role in those of 1904 and 1912 (in the latter contributing significantly to Woodrow Wilson's victory), and was still a figure to be reckoned with at the convention of 1924, the last before his death.

From 1913 to 1928, the out-party leadership was usually vacant except during election years. The Republican party, when it became the out-party in 1913, had scant regard for the precedents set by Cleveland and Bryan; as part of its sixteen-year attack on "Bryanism," it had been discrediting the notion that an out-party leader should be given any recognition whatsoever. Ex-President Taft was nevertheless influential in party matters, but Charles Evans Hughes, after his narrow election defeat of 1916, not only rejected any suggestion of renomination but also specifically refused to act as party leader, ridiculing the idea that a defeated candidate could do so successfully.

James M. Cox, the defeated Democratic candidate of

1920, made almost no use of his opportunity to be the first in his party to carry on the Bryan tradition, although he took some credit for the compromise decision to nominate John W. Davis in 1924. Davis, crushingly defeated, did little as titular leader.

The role once more came alive when Alfred E. Smith was its incumbent after his defeat by Hoover in 1928, even though his assertion, shortly after the election, that he would never run again for public office was generally accepted as his true intention. In 1929, when his efforts had significantly reduced the Democrats' large campaign deficit, he was widely hailed as party leader. His wealthy friend John J. Raskob continued as national committee chairman until 1932, and Smith himself participated in the arrangements to create a permanent national committee headquarters in Washington. Later, the pressures of his job as head of the company promoting the Empire State Building reduced his party activity, but he always assumed the leadership role when needed—as when in October 1930 he made a radio speech, under the auspices of the national committee, urging the election of a Democratic Congress.

Meanwhile, Franklin D. Roosevelt, whom Smith had sponsored for the New York governorship in 1928 and placed in nomination in 1930 for a second term, was coming into increasing prominence as the most likely Democratic candidate for the 1932 presidential race, especially because Smith gave no indication of changing his 1928 decision. The eventual rivalry between the erstwhile friends when each announced his own candidacy for the presidential nomination put an end to Smith's leadership, but the new vitality he had brought to the post and the ready acceptance accorded him in the role had decidedly advanced the concept.

The Republican candidates of 1932 and 1936, Herbert Hoover and Alfred M. Landon, made no strong effort to challenge the party's tradition against renomination of defeated leaders, but both were more active than either Taft or Hughes had been, Hoover as party spokesman in denouncing the Roosevelt administration, Landon as an energetic leader for party organizational matters.

Wendell Willkie, after his election defeat in 1940, was both leader and instrument for a group of Republicans intent on reorienting and reviving the party. His claim to leadership was strongly opposed by the isolationist wing, prominent in which was Senator Robert A. Taft, who said in his 1941 Lincoln Day speech that Willkie did not and could not "speak for the Republican party," and that there was "no justification in precedent or principle for the view that a defeated candidate for President is the titular leader of the party." Soon after Taft's speech, Willkie, the political amateur, was recognized as party leader at a national committee meeting. On returning from his 1942 "One World" tour—which had been facilitated by President Roosevelt, who continuously accorded him unusual recognition as titular leader of the opposition party—he began active preparation for seeking renomination in 1944. But from here on it was increasingly clear that he was the leader of a faction and not the party as a whole. In April 1944 he was severely defeated in the Wisconsin primary by a slate of Dewey delegates and promptly abandoned his candidacy. He died on October 8, 1944.

THE REPUBLICAN BREAK WITH TRADITION

Thus it was left to Thomas E. Dewey to be the first Republican to break the party's tradition against the renomination of defeated candidates. His first problem, after his defeat by Roosevelt in 1944, was to secure re-election in 1946 to the New York governorship as a base for another try at the Presidency. He also involved himself in national party affairs, and, despite the opposition of the Taft wing, was given considerable recognition as party leader. Meanwhile, there was much jockeying for position by other potential contenders for the 1948 nomination—among them Taft, Bricker, and Stassen.

Dewey continued quietly to build alliances. In January 1948 he announced his candidacy. He entered the convention as the favorite and won nomination on the third ballot. His election defeat by Truman ended his career as a presidential candidate (at least for the time being) but not his status as titular leader. Again elected governor in 1950, he retained great influence in the party, which he used in promoting the presidential candidacy of General Eisenhower. The choice of Eisenhower by the convention in 1952 owed much to the strategic labors of Dewey and his allies.

DEVELOPMENTS SINCE 1952

The Eisenhower victory of 1952 returned the problems of a party out of power to the Democrats. Stevenson, the defeated candidate, and Stephen A. Mitchell, his personal choice as national committee chairman, took on the initial problems of party rebuilding and reduction of the campaign deficit.

In 1953, Stevenson went on a world tour, in the course of which he was acclaimed as a public figure with public responsibilities, in the style of the British concept of opposition leader. Throughout 1954 he continued to devote his time to party matters and the responsibilities of public leadership. His vigorous campaigning in critical states from July to November was recognized as a factor in the remarkable number of Democratic victories.

He then returned to the practice of law and refused to clarify his intentions until November 1955, when he announced as a candidate for the Democratic nomination of 1956. His reluctance to campaign in the primaries was clear, but after his defeat in Minnesota by Senator Estes Kefauver he campaigned vigorously to reverse the score in Oregon, Florida, and California. Kefauver conceded, and Stevenson was renominated, despite Truman's active support for Governor Averell Harriman. The election defeat was more decisive than in 1952, but Stevenson continued to be helpful in party matters. As 1960 approached he disclaimed any intention of running—but remained available until Kennedy was nominated at Los Angeles.

With Kennedy's election in 1960, Vice President Richard Nixon faced the problems of the Republican party as its defeated titular leader. His initial response indicated that he would accept the responsibilities and the somewhat dubious privileges of the role. He received President-Elect Kennedy at Miami on November 14, and expressed the intention of leading a vigorous and constructive opposition. A few weeks later he was toasted at the White House as the incoming leader of the outgoing party. But after the Kennedy inauguration, Nixon retreated from the immediate problems of party reorganization. Resuming the practice of law in California, he performed few duties as the leader of an opposition party.

In 1962 he ran for governor of California, was defeated, and in a bitter press conference announced his retirement from public life. His 1963 move to New York City to continue his law practice provoked a flurry of speculation regarding its portent for his position in the party. Nixon himself gave little indication that he would perform actively as the Republicans' titular leader during the period leading up to the conventions of 1964 but did seem to be anticipating more activity in national politics.

PRESENT STATUS OF THE
TITULAR LEADERSHIP

The net effect of these developments has been to make the position of titular leader even more ambiguous than it was before. Stevenson and his predecessors showed its possibilities, while also suffering its indignities and hazards. Nixon in effect resigned from the position after having received a more complete investiture than had ever been granted any previous Republican— or, for that matter, any Democrat. Partly, one must suppose, Nixon's decision in 1961 was a rational response to the fact that Kennedy looked like a strong first-term incumbent who would be unbeatable in seeking re-election. But Kennedy's death by assassination in November 1963 changed the situation—for Nixon and many others.

The Republican nominee of 1964 will have whatever opportunities the year offers. If he is defeated while running well, it could be expected that he will enter upon the opportunities of the titular leadership with every intention of seeking his party's renomination in 1968. In that case, the role of the titular leadership might again take on new interest as a phenomenon in American politics.

National Committee and Convention Officers

The fortunes of the titular leader and the national committee chairman who goes through a campaign with him to defeat are inevitably linked. Early departure of the man whom the leader chose as chairman is usually interpreted as a sign of weakness in the position of the leader himself, and the change frequently involves a contest in the national committee. The new chairman is not likely to have the old one's relationship of allegiance to the leader. He takes his mandate from the committee, or from the strongest faction within it, but in general he is in a position of considerable freedom.

In one respect, his position differs sharply from that of his in-party counterpart: he is felt to be acting improperly unless he holds himself neutral toward all who might decide to run for the next nomination. In regard to many other matters, however, he has an unrivaled opportunity to exercise initiative. If he feels that the party's leaders in Congress are failing to develop the issues and the party record usefully for the next campaign, he may urge them to take a stronger line in proposing alternatives to the President's program—as Chairman Paul Butler did in March 1956, when he specifically urged action on the Hell's Canyon dam and on the Niagara power project. The unconventionality of this intrusion was commented on with enthusiasm by the official journal of the Republicans; the Democratic congressional leaders made no public response whatever, doubtless concluding that discretion was the better part of valor if they wished to occupy a satisfactory position at the next convention.

Opportunities for exercising initiative are also strikingly available to the permanent chairman of an out-party convention, especially because of its typically high level of factional conflict. As presiding officer, his means of exerting influence include the maintenance of order in the convention hall—or the maintenance instead of levels of "planned confusion" that may permit stratagems otherwise not possible; the power of recognition in debate, which can lend or deny the ears of the convention to delegates equally eligible to be heard; and the rulings on points of order, which can convey or withhold tactical advantages. Collectively, these prerogatives give the permanent chairman great power—to be used entirely as his own ethical standards may dictate.

Now that television has put the activities of all convention officers under public scrutiny, standards of appropriate behavior in these offices are probably rising. Intuitively, the public tends to condemn unfairness on the part of those who administer the machinery of choice in the conventions; pronounced unfairness, therefore, that seems motivated by a factional interest may even boomerang to the detriment of the candidate it was intended to aid.

The Congressional Leaders

Out-party congressional leaders are especially conspicuous as power centers, their positions having been institutionalized through a long evolution. A strong opposition party leader in Congress brings together elements of power that can be used for many purposes; the roles in which he may operate in relation to the presidential nominating process are typically more important in the out-party than in the in-party.

In the candidate role, out-party leaders of the House of Representatives have been little more successful than those of the in-party, but markedly different trends have been operating in the Senate. During the last three decades, the Senate has been developing leaders of a type that can compete with effectiveness for the presidential nominations, particularly in the party out of power. Many of them have the attributes that seem to add up to high availability: the right age, origins in pivotal states, the glamour of a rapid rise in a public service career, and an "executive" personality—one trained by experience to operate across the board in all of the substantive problems of government. Moreover, in an era of national issues cutting across sectional lines, the involvement of Senate leaders in the competitive aspects of national two-party politics brings them to the forefront as potential presidential nominees.

The same factors can also make them powerful as kingmakers. Almost inevitably each one is a center for appraisal and discussion of the possible presidential candidates within his own party. From this, it is only a step to the building of coalitions with his state party affiliates in support of particular candidacies.

SENATORIAL HANDICAPS

Nevertheless, a Senate leader is also under certain handicaps. He has little contact, for instance, with local forces in the states that have sent no senators of his own party; those states nonetheless have voting strength at the party conventions. And senators generally, including the leaders, probably tend to exaggerate their own political power and influence in comparison with governors, whose knowledge of state situations is closer and more realistic. There is a further distorting effect in national political news reporting, which mainly emanates from Washington—where the ablest political reporters in the country rely largely on senators as news sources. Such factors are not measurable, but something of the sort must be at work, in view of the regularity with which senators have been boomed for nominations that they have only rarely received.

THE LEGISLATIVE RECORD

As makers of the legislative record, out-party congressional leaders are directly related to the nominating process. According to what their legislative record shows, a candidate may be able to run with pride—or may have to run somehow in spite of the record. This was illustrated in the Republican party between 1940 and 1952, in the Democratic party between 1952 and 1960, and again in the Republican party after 1960. At the Republican convention of 1948, Senator Taft, in seeking the party nomination, was the champion of the party's congressional record. Dewey, in winning the nomination, took virtually no responsibility for the record, on the development of which he had been little consulted. In his election campaign he said as little as possible about the congressional performance. When Truman won the election, the Republican congressional leaders stubbornly insisted on drawing the moral that their party had failed because of its unwillingness to nominate a candidate who could run on the party's own record. Taft was again their preference in 1952. Eisenhower had been personally associated with many policies long under attack by the congressional leaders. Only the narrowest of congressional majorities accompanied Eisenhower into office, and many of the Republican congressmen refused to support his policies as President. The party lost both houses two years later, and again in 1956 and 1958.

In the Democratic party between 1952 and 1956, the relationship between the congressional record and the choice of a party nominee in 1956 was openly recognized as a problem. Adlai Stevenson, Senate Majority Leader Lyndon Johnson, and House Speaker Sam Rayburn held a meeting in September 1955 at which (according to the press) the two congressmen, with Stevenson nodding approval, "firmly pledged themselves to a congressional program which they hope will put a Democrat in the White House next year."

Johnson later announced his proposals for the final congressional session of the first Eisenhower term, most of which could have been readily endorsed by any Democratic party national convention. But he also saw fit to include the proposed natural gas bill; passed under his leadership, it was the subject of a damaging veto message by President Eisenhower. All three of the leading candidates for the 1956 Democratic nomination—Stevenson, Kefauver, and Harriman—were later reported as saying that if elected they also would veto any such natural gas bill.

Other Members of Congress

Not all of the important candidates from the Senate in recent years have been members of the official leadership groups or even approved by them. Estes Kefauver in 1952 and 1956 was still a relatively junior senator, and apparently campaigned without the approval of the Democratic leadership group and in the face of their tacit opposition.

Kefauver's campaigns were almost unprecedented in the extent to which they attempted to use Senate membership as the basis for developing a massive popular following in presidential politics—with relatively little support from other senators or other political leaders. The total showing was impressive, and raised obvious questions that were answered only in part by the Kennedy and other senatorial candidacies of 1960. With presidential primaries that permit a direct appeal to the party voters, can it be expected that in the future other senators will run without leadership support—as most of them (except Lyndon Johnson) seemed to be doing in 1960? Or will the party leaders be more successful in fencing-in the presidentially ambitious junior senators?

The answer may be determined in part by whether the parties are able to satisfy popular demands for leadership. The Kefauver candidacy had much in common with the important third-party movements of an earlier time; it was a vehicle of dissent, unrest, and the criticism of existing leadership. When the creation of an effective third party no longer seems feasible, the presidential primaries can offer an alternative means of registering dissent; this may be one of their major future functions, with senators as the willing candidates.

The role of candidate manager or principal supporter is one in which members of Congress have appeared with some frequency in recent years. In 1952, Senator Henry Cabot Lodge was Eisenhower's preconvention manager; Congressmen Clarence J. Brown and Carroll Reece were active on behalf of Senator Taft. In 1956, Senator Hubert Humphrey was influential in persuading Stevenson to enter the Minnesota primary and in organizing his campaign in the state; Congressman Robert L. F. Sikes served as Stevenson's manager for the Florida presidential primary campaign.

The role of members of Congress as part of the informal communications network in connection with the presidential nominating process is too intricate for much study here, but the role is too important to overlook. There is no substitute for Congress as a central element in this web at the national party level, especially in its interaction with the press corps in Washington. The effect of this is difficult to assess, but some such network of informal, high-level communication would seem to be essential for the most effective operation of the nominating process. It may be the most important way in which Congress influences the nominations.

The Governors

The history of the national parties has reflected a continuing tension between Presidency, Congress, and state governors as competing centers of influence on the presidential nominations. In recent decades the governors have become increasingly potent in the out-party, but the extent of their influence is dependent on their numbers, their relative cohesion, and the importance of the states they hold.

Shifts in the number of out-party governorships provide important clues to party status and prospects. When the out-party has relatively few governors, it has usually been driven back into the predominantly one-party areas that rarely produce effective presidential candidates, and incumbent governors who look like presidential timber are at a premium if available at all. When governorships in contested territory are increasingly won back, the prospect for presidential victory is also on the increase—and so is the number of governors who can actively contend for the nomination.

Not all governors can be candidates, but all can participate in the nominating process—as convention officers or keynote speakers; as state party leaders and delegation chairman; and as a "third house" for communication and collective influence within each party. At the 1954 governors' conference a story making the rounds recalled a conversation with a youngster at a previous conference: "Do all governors want to be President?" "No, young man, some of them just want to choose him."

In terms of official status, the largest single categories of candidates for the presidential nomination since the beginnings of the convention system have been governors and senators, but neither party nominated an incumbent governor for President until 1876—and then both did so. From 1880 up to 1960, nine governors received nomination, but only one incumbent senator and one former senator. The governors provided a series of noteworthy names among first-time nominees: Cleveland, McKinley, Wilson, Cox, Smith, Franklin D. Roosevelt, Landon, Dewey, and Stevenson, all of them out-party nominees except Cox and Stevenson.

Governors have served repeatedly as temporary convention chairmen and keynote speakers in both parties since 1940. In 1956 the Democratic party had twenty-seven governors in office; nearly every one of them—outside of the deep South—was an active candidate for the convention's keynote role. And in recent conventions, if a governor served as a delegate, he has been chosen delegation chairman in about three cases out of four.

Much of the effectiveness of the governors as secondary power centers at the conventions is due to their established relationships with one another—the result largely of their conferences in which they discuss matters of concern to state governments. In 1956, the *New York Times* estimated the importance of the conferences: "The best political weather station in a Presidential year is the annual Governors' Conference, which comes before the conventions."

The most dramatic exhibit of potent collective action by out-party governors was the manifesto released by the Republicans at Houston in 1952, which led to the first decisive vote at the Republican convention and paved the way for the Eisenhower nomination. Senator Taft, in the memorandum written to some of his campaign lieutenants after his defeat, had this to say about governors:

> The majority of Republican governors were sold on Eisenhower support, although a majority of Senators and Congressmen were in my favor. However, the governors had far more political influence on delegates.

The high level of political power of the governors is undisputable. Yet, according to Louis Harris, on the evidence of public opinion polls he has conducted in many states, more than a few governors elected in recent times are in trouble with their voters. The need for expansion of state programs—in the face of revenue sources that are highly inadequate and difficult to improve or repair—has resulted in "a massive squeeze on the hitherto politically invulnerable position of the governors." The pressures may adjust within ten years or so, but incumbent governors may be compelled to endure much political unpopularity in the meantime.

Interest Groups and Their Leaders

The opportunities for interest groups and minority factions to exert pressure on the nominating behavior of a party are much greater when the party is out of power. Agriculture, business, and labor are the three largest interest groupings that have in modern times been continuously active in national politics. Each operates through a multiplicity of organizations and has its own complex formal and informal structures of leadership.

Organized agriculture speaks with a powerful voice on matters of national legislative policy, and both parties have been intimidated in recent years by the possible drastic effects of a violent swing in the farm vote. Yet the major farm organizations and their leaders have generally continued the traditional policy of nonpartisanship and of nonintervention in the choice of candidates.

Business, industry, commerce, and finance have had no single organization to speak for them, but each of several hundred major corporations is itself a center of economic power and able to exert some political pressure if it pleases. Since 1896 the Democratic party has been viewed with some suspicion by the greater part of the business community, and particularly by northern industries. The business community has thus taken a positive interest mainly in the nominations of the Republican party, while pursuing defensive tactics in regard to Democratic nominations.

The titans of industry, commerce, and finance are not often found in person among the delegates or in other conspicuous positions at either party convention. An exception was the visit in 1952 to the Republican convention by six top officials of the Ford Motor Company and the General Motors Corporation, including Henry Ford II and Charles E. Wilson. According to columnist Marquis Childs, "One of the objects of scorn and anger for loyal Taftites was the box full of General Motors executives. There, muttered one of the Taft managers, are the people who are dictating this convention." Slightly less august business leaders and wealthy industrialists, however, are often delegates—mainly because they enjoy participating.

Organized labor has been involved in politics since the earliest days of unions. But in 1895, after a struggle over socialist control of the labor movement, the American Federation of Labor amended its constitution to provide that "party politics shall have no place in the conventions" of the Federation. Thereafter it was technically neutral between the major parties for many decades, but this did not prevent its leading officers and the leaders of major affiliated unions from taking strongly partisan positions in one major party or the other. With the coming of the Roosevelt New Deal and the formation of the Congress of Industrial Organizations (CIO), the association of labor was increasingly with the Democratic party.

The CIO set up its Political Action Committee (PAC) in 1943 in what has been described as "a hurried effort to save the fourth-term election for President Roosevelt." The AFL created its Labor's League for Political Action in 1947. With the AFL-CIO merger in 1955, the two committees were combined in the Committee on Political Education (COPE).

Bosses and Kingmakers

There has never been a national party boss in the sense in which the term "boss" has often been used in state and local politics. Mark Hanna came the closest to creating the role at the national level, but McKinley, in whose nomination Hanna played a conspicuous part, was his own man in the Presidency. It is one of the glories of the office, in fact, that no President has ever occupied a subordinate position in relation to a recognizable single individual acting as a party boss.

In all periods of convention history, however, state and local bosses have figured prominently in the presidential nominating process. The bosses of major states were at the zenith of power in the period from Grant to McKinley—when, as noted by historians S. E. Morison and H. S. Commager, it could be said that "at the head of the ranks of those who really ran the country were great bosses like Conkling and Platt and Hill of New York, Randall and Cameron and Quay of Pennsylvania, Hanna and Foraker and Brice of Ohio." The type has largely disappeared in recent years, but the leaders of the big-city machines are still visible factors —especially in Democratic conventions.

Party bosses are not the only kingmakers, nor always the most successful. A good many candidates, especially in the out-party, have been tirelessly promoted by men of wealth or strategic position who take a continuing interest in national politics, or by long-time friends and key personal supporters of potential candidates. Harding had his Harry Daugherty, Franklin D. Roosevelt his Louis McHenry Howe. Eisenhower had kingmakers in all parts of the country, including millionaires in Texas and influential newspaper and magazine publishers in New York and other cities.

But party leaders who make politics their business will undoubtedly continue to be important and will receive the name of boss, regardless of the extent to which they may actually resemble the older bosses. Any state party leader may at some time acquire a strategic relationship that will carry through into the final stages of a presidential nomination. This would seem to be the inevitable and continuing consequence of a federal system in which leadership must perennially be renewed from below.

Leadership Integration

In the party out of power, a structure corresponding to the well-knit informal organization of leadership that is possible to the party in power does not yet exist. But a trend toward leadership integration is certainly clearly indicated by some of the developments described earlier in this chapter, and by what appears to be the beginning of a tendency, tenuous and hard to pin down, for the several centers of influence to cooperate more often than formerly in dealing with the over-all party concerns.

During the long period from 1933 to 1953 when the Republicans were out of power, there was generally a fair degree of cooperation between the congressional and national committee leaders and also between the titular leader and the governors. The relationship between titular leader and congressional leaders was usually strained, to say the least. In part this strain reflected the fact that the conservative leaders in Congress lost the contest in the Republican convention on each successive nomination from 1940 to 1952.

THE DEMOCRATIC EXPERIENCE, 1952-1960

In the Democratic party, the level of cooperation among the major centers of leadership between 1952 and 1960 was clearly higher than it had been between 1920 and 1932—and markedly higher than the level in the Republican party at any point during 1933-1953, its twenty years in the wilderness. The Democratic experience was notable for two major precedents. One was Adlai Stevenson's demonstration of the potentialities inherent in the titular leadership. The other was the formation of the Democratic Advisory Council after the defeat in 1956, and its continued operation until the election of 1960 had been won.

Initially, the Council was to include "members of the Congress, Governors, Mayors, and other outstanding Democrats . . . to coordinate and advance efforts on behalf of Democratic programs and principles." But the party's congressional leaders refused to participate and persuaded most other members of Congress not to do so.

Thus, as it shaped up, the Council derived its importance mainly from the active membership of National Committee Chairman Paul Butler, former President Harry S Truman, and the titular leader Adlai Stevenson. Other members included two senators, several governors, a big-city mayor, and all fourteen members of the executive committee of the Democratic National Committee. In 1959 the membership received its most noteworthy additions—the governors of California and Florida and Senators John F. Kennedy and Stuart Symington. (At that point, all of the prospective candidates for the nomination of 1960 except Senator Lyndon Johnson were included as members.)

The Council's principal mode of functioning was to

assemble data and adopt statements on issues of public policy. The statements received extensive attention in the press throughout the country—more, usually, than the congressional leaders could command. In 1958 a "State of the Union" message was issued, containing recommendations for the legislative program of the next two years.

In effect, the Council was recognized as the voice of the presidential wing of the party—the northern and western elements that dominate the conventions, write the platforms, and nominate the candidates—and much of its work was eventually embodied in the 1960 platform. The Council undoubtedly contributed to the party's victory in the close election. Throughout the four years it was disregarded by the congressional leaders, yet it was highly thought of by some congressional segments of the party and not completely lacking in influence even on the legislative record.

THE REPUBLICAN EXPERIENCE, 1960-

Three main alternatives were considered by the Republicans as they faced their out-party leadership problem. One was to provide an institution, similar to the Democratic Advisory Council, for "collective leadership"—a high-level committee that would include the party's two living former Presidents, its defeated candidates on the 1960 ticket, its congressional leaders, the national committee chairman, and others eminent in party affairs. The plan was resisted by the congressional leaders, but was eventually attempted in the form of an "All-Republican Conference," announced June 30, 1962. So far, the Conference seems not to have functioned actively.

A second alternative involved building up the status of the titular leader, perhaps even putting him on salary with staff and offices at the national capital. Various schemes of this sort were debated briefly in 1961, but were not encouraged by Richard Nixon.

A third plan was a form of collective leadership modeled on the in-party's weekly meetings at the White House. This was accepted, in modified form, by the Republican leaders in Congress, who began meeting with each other and the party chairman at weekly intervals. Thus originated the so-called "Ev and Charlie show," in which Senator Everett M. Dirksen and Representative Charles A. Halleck have faced the television newsreel cameras at fairly regular intervals while Congress is in session.

The most significant aspect of the Republican experience since 1960 is the continuing discussion of how best to organize for more effective leadership. The discussion has indicated a discontent that extends to many Republican members of Congress, although not to their highest official leaders. Evidently this discontent has been shared by the Republican governors, who formed a continuing organization in 1963 and began issuing their own public statements as representatives of the opposition party. Whether this ferment will lead to some further and more effective form of leadership consolidation if the party loses the election of 1964 is not yet clear, but the dimensions and importance of the problem seem to be appreciated more fully than ever before.

7

Patterns in the Nominating Process

■

The act of nominating a presidential candidate is primarily a choice of group leadership—the age-old problem of apostolic succession that has had to be solved in one way or another by every human organization that has managed to replace its first leader. The patterns of choice employed by a given organization tend to recur, since their number is obviously limited first of all by the purpose and conditions of the choice, and second by the group characteristics of the choosers. Obviously, too, purpose and characteristics may change if the organization is long-surviving.

In the nominating process, there are two main conditions of choice—the first when an existing party leadership is simply confirmed or rejected, the second when the previous leadership is not available or has been rejected—within each of which various patterns may operate. In each presidential nomination, first-time or otherwise, one of the principal centers of power described in the two preceding chapters has been influential in determining the outcome. Here it is proposed to classify all of the nominations since 1832 in accordance with the type of power center that in each case seemed to be most effective. The comparisons that can then be made between the patterns common since 1896 and those of the earlier period have importance as guide lines to possible future developments in the nominating process.

Patterns in Confirmation of Leadership

In three situations the presidential nomination simply confirms (or rejects) an existing party leadership: the renomination of a President who was elected directly to the office; the nomination for a full term of a President who, originally elected as a Vice President, succeeded to the Presidency through death of the incumbent; the renomination of a titular leader.

Presidents who had been elected directly to the office have generally been far more successful in obtaining renomination than either of the other two classes of party leader, as Tables 4 and 5 indicate. At the beginning of the convention system, Andrew Jackson (1832) and Martin Van Buren (1840) were renominated to succeed themselves; after that no further instance occurred until 1864. This was an era of one-term Presidencies and of frequent rejection of the President as party leader. With Abraham Lincoln and Ulysses S. Grant, the two-term tradition was restored. By 1892, even as weak a President as Benjamin Harrison was able to secure renomination in the face of factional opposition—although perhaps in part because the supporters of William McKinley expected a party defeat and wished to save their man for 1896.

Since then it has been assumed that a regularly elected President is entitled to his party's nomination for a sec-

TABLE 4. SUCCESS AND FAILURE IN
ACHIEVING RENOMINATION[a]

Retired Voluntarily At End of One Term[b]	Sought Renomination Unsuccessfully	Renominated Once or More
PRESIDENTS ELECTED DIRECTLY TO THE OFFICE		
Democratic Party		
Polk, 1848	Pierce, 1856	Jackson, 1832
Buchanan, 1860		Van Buren, 1840
		Cleveland, 1888
		Wilson, 1916
		F. D. Roosevelt, 1936, 1940, 1944
National Republican, Whig, and Republican Parties		
Hayes, 1880	None	Lincoln, 1864
		Grant, 1872
		B. Harrison, 1892
		McKinley, 1900
		Taft, 1912
		Hoover, 1932
		Eisenhower, 1956
PRESIDENTS ELECTED INITIALLY AS VICE PRESIDENTS		
Democratic Party		
None	None	Truman, 1948
National Republican, Whig, and Republican Parties		
None	Tyler, 1844	T. Roosevelt, 1904
	Fillmore, 1852	Coolidge, 1924
	Johnson, 1868	
	Arthur, 1884	

[a] For full names of Presidents and Vice Presidents, see pages 358-359.

[b] The year given in this column is that in which the President would have been required to seek renomination had he not decided to retire.

ond term. Contesting candidacies have rarely been even discussed, unless the President's own availability was for some reason in doubt. The conflict over the renomination of President William Howard Taft in 1912 is the only outstanding exception.

The seven Vice Presidents up to 1960 who became President through death of the previous incumbents sought nominations for the next full term as President. That President Lyndon B. Johnson will also do so is a reasonable assumption.

Of the four nineteenth-century cases shown in Table 4, not one was able to secure the nomination. John Tyler and Andrew Johnson had both been members of the opposite party before their vice-presidential nominations; it was partly for that reason, in a time when party lines were often crossed, that they were selected to balance the ticket. Millard Fillmore and Chester A. Arthur belonged to minority factions in their parties, and they too had been used to balance the ticket; as Presidents, they were in no position to exercise strong party leadership.

The change in practice was striking when it came, and the growing power of the Presidency was probably mainly responsible. Each of the three Vice Presidents succeeding to the Presidency from 1896 to 1960 won nomination for the next full presidential term, and won the election as well. The strength of Theodore Roosevelt as a popular leader was doubtless a factor in the timing of the change, but by 1924 even a Calvin Coolidge could be nominated for the full term without much opposition. In the Democratic party, where the problem had arisen only once, the claim to the nomination was successfully maintained by President Harry S Truman in 1948. There now seems to be general agreement among political leaders, political writers, and the public

TABLE 5. SUCCESS AND FAILURE IN ACHIEVING
RENOMINATION—TITULAR LEADERS WHO
HAD SUFFERED ELECTORAL DEFEAT

Did Not Seek Renomination in Party Convention Next Following Defeat[a]	Sought Renomination Unsuccessfully	Renominated Once or More
DEMOCRATIC PARTY		
McClellan, 1868	Van Buren, 1844[b]	Cleveland, 1892[b]
Seymour, 1872	Cass, 1852	Bryan, 1900, 1908
Tilden, 1880	Smith, 1932	Stevenson, 1956
Hancock, 1884		
Bryan, 1904,[c] 1912		
Cox, 1924		
Davis, 1928		
Stevenson, 1960[c]		
NATIONAL REPUBLICAN, WHIG, AND REPUBLICAN PARTIES		
Clay, 1836[d]	Clay, 1848	Dewey, 1948
Scott, 1856[e]	Willkie, 1944	
Frémont, 1860		
Blaine, 1888		
Harrison, B. 1896[b]		
Taft, 1916[b]		
Hughes, 1920		
Hoover, 1936[b]		
Landon, 1940		
Dewey, 1952[c]		

[a] In this column the year given is the one in which the titular leader would have been required to seek renomination had he not decided to retire. For full names of all candidates, see pages 358-359.

[b] Had served one term as President and had failed of re-election for a second term.

[c] Had previously been nominated and defeated twice when declining to stand for a third consecutive nomination.

[d] The National Republican party disintegrated after holding one convention and made no further nomination.

[e] The Whig party disintegrated after losing with Scott and held no national convention in 1856.

that a Vice President succeeding to the Presidency automatically becomes the leader of his party and will be a strong candidate for the next nomination.

Titular leaders have also gained strength in recent decades, as Table 5 shows, and this also is probably related to the new power status of the Presidency, which confers importance on any candidate for the office. For a long period the possibility of renomination was remote for almost all defeated major-party candidates; in the present century the trend has been the other way.

Martin Van Buren was the first titular leader to seek and fail to achieve renomination. After the unsuccessful tries by Henry Clay (National Republican, 1848) and Lewis Cass (Democrat, 1852), no defeated candidate of either major party sought renomination by his own party's national convention until Grover Cleveland's successful effort in 1892. Many of the candidates dropped out of political life almost completely.

William Jennings Bryan was the first to achieve renomination in either party without benefit of a previous term in the White House. In the Republican party, no defeated presidential candidate tried—at least openly—for a second nomination until the 1940's. Wendell Willkie's attempt came to grief in the primaries of 1944; Dewey's try in 1948 succeeded. Adlai Stevenson won renomination in the Democratic party in 1956 after a period in which no one since Bryan had done so. In both parties the basis has been laid for the claim that a defeated candidate is entitled to another try if he has made a good race.

Patterns in Leadership Succession

When a previous party leader is unavailable, or has been rejected, any one of four major patterns of succession may operate, with variations in each. The instances are brought together in Table 6.

INHERITANCE

Inheritance by an understudy or by an outstanding member of the previous leadership group is a common form of succession in most organizations, but it has not happened often in presidential nominations under the convention system. The in-party cases of Martin Van Buren in 1836, William Howard Taft in 1908, Herbert Hoover in 1928, and Richard Nixon in 1960 are the clearest examples of the type. Henry Clay's second nomination in 1844, although classified here as an in-party case, was not greatly different from his first nomination in 1832, in view of the circumstances prevailing during the Tyler administration. Al Smith's nomination in 1928 was similarly the result of high availability in an out-party situation where no other powerful figure was willing to contest the nomination.

INNER GROUP SELECTION

Processes of inner group selection can be said to occur at times in American national parties, but only if the term "inner group" is given a rather special meaning. As noted earlier, the American parties do not ordinarily have any single or genuinely cohesive inner group that is dominant for all party affairs, except in the party in power when leadership has become firmly centered in the President. But there have been occasions when the dominant leaders of the various party factions have seemed disposed to work together informally on a sort of federated basis in reaching agreement on the next nomination—with the "federation" not usually lasting long when the convention is over, and especially if the candidate loses.

Only two cases have been identified as reflecting inner

TABLE 6. PATTERNS OF LEADERSHIP SUCCESSION THROUGH
NOMINATIONS IN NATIONAL PARTY CONVENTIONS[a]

Inheritance	Inner Group Selection	Compromise in Stalemate	Factional Victory
PARTY IN POWER			
Van Buren (D), 1836	Cass (D), 1848	Hayes (R), 1876	Scott (W), 1852
Clay (W), 1844	Grant (R), 1868	Garfield (R), 1880	Buchanan (D), 1856
Taft (R), 1908			Douglas (D), 1860
Hoover (R), 1928			Blaine (R), 1884
Nixon (R), 1960			Bryan (D), 1896
			Cox (D), 1920
			Stevenson (D), 1952
PARTY OUT OF POWER			
Clay (NR), 1832	Frémont (R), 1856	Polk (D), 1844	W. H. Harrison (W), 1840
Smith (D), 1928	McClellan (D), 1864	Pierce (D), 1852	Taylor (W), 1848
	Greeley (D), 1872	Seymour (D), 1868	Lincoln (R), 1860
	Hancock (D), 1880	Harding (R), 1920	Tilden (D), 1876
	Cleveland (D), 1884	Davis (D), 1924	B. Harrison (R), 1888
	Parker (D), 1904		McKinley (R), 1896
	Hughes (R), 1916		Wilson (D), 1912
	Landon (R), 1936		F. D. Roosevelt (D), 1932
			Willkie (R), 1940
			Dewey (R), 1944
			Eisenhower (R), 1952
			Kennedy (D), 1960

[a] The symbols after each name indicate the party making the nomination: Democratic (D), Republican (R), National Republican (NR), Whig (W). For full names of all candidates, see pages 358-359.

group selection in a party in power. The nomination of Lewis Cass in 1848 was close to a case of inheritance, but the incumbent Polk administration was not willing to show its hand clearly and there was considerable conflict at the convention. The Grant nomination in 1868, like Clay's in 1844, was only technically the nomination of a party in power, with Andrew Johnson still in the White House after the unsuccessful Republican attempt to impeach him. Both parties were disorganized, but Grant won the election in a close vote.

Most of the cases identified as inner group selection occurred in a party out of power, and most of these out-party cases took place under conditions of some party weakness. John C. Frémont was the first candidate of the newly organized Republican party. The Democratic nominations of Horace Greeley and Alton B. Parker occurred under conditions in which the party prospects looked nearly hopeless; this was less true of the nominations of George B. McClellan, Winfield S. Hancock, and Grover Cleveland. The only election winner among the out-party nominees was Cleveland, and his nomination involved more of a struggle than most of the cases in the inner group category. Charles Evans Hughes was the choice of the Republicans in 1916 as they tried to heal the split of 1912; Landon was chosen in 1936 as they tried to recover from the disaster of 1932.

Despite the relative success of Grant and Cleveland in winning elections, and the eminence and near-win of Justice Hughes, it appears evident that the pattern of inner group selection, as employed by the American parties, has been remarkably unsuccessful in recruiting candidates who could win elections or provide party leadership. This may be, however, mainly a sign of the conditions under which this pattern of nominations has occurred.

COMPROMISE IN STALEMATE

Seven compromise candidates have been chosen in stalemated conventions, four Democrats and three Republicans. Two of the seven—Rutherford B. Hayes (1876) and James A. Garfield (1880)—were the nominees of a party in power; both won. In each case, the incumbent President refrained from making any noteworthy effort to influence the succession and the convention was badly split, with the strongest faction supporting a front-runner who fell short of a majority.

In each of the other five cases, all in a party out of power, the eventual compromise candidate was acceptable to all of the major factions represented in the convention. The nomination was thus a major act of interfactional conciliation. James K. Polk (1844) and Franklin Pierce (1852) were each nominated after attempts to renominate the previous titular leader had reached a stalemate; both won election. The other three nominations all occurred in factional situations where the previous titular leader had lost all standing or had specifically taken himself out of the running. Only Warren G. Harding won election.

Most of the seven have been considered "dark horse" nominees, that peculiar appellation of American politics. There is no generally agreed definition of what constitutes a "dark horse," but on its face, the term seems to imply an unanticipated or minor candidate whose victory was a surprise. Sidney Hyman, writing in the *New York Times* in 1955, held that in the oral tradition of American politics the authentic dark horses were but five: Polk, Pierce, Hayes, Garfield, and Davis, to whom he would add Harding and Wendell Willkie. But since Willkie had been campaigning vigorously for several months before the convention and was the avowed

candidate of an important aggregation of party supporters, he would seem the most highly illuminated dark
horse in history. In any event, he was not a compromise
candidate in a situation of convention deadlock, as were
Harding and Horatio Seymour, both of whom have
often been regarded as dark horse candidates.

FACTIONAL VICTORY

Factional victory can occur in a party in power when
there is a successful attempt to deny renomination to an
incumbent President, or when a retiring President is defeated in an attempt to control the succession, declines
an active role, or finds no satisfactory candidate to back,
thus leaving the way open for what is called an "open"
convention.

Among the cases classified here as reflecting factional
victory in in-party situations, those of Winfield Scott,
James Buchanan, and James G. Blaine represented defeat for an incumbent President who was seeking renomination. Stephen A. Douglas was nominated despite
the opposition of the incumbent President, Buchanan,
who was not himself running for renomination; William
Jennings Bryan was the nominee of the forces most
opposed to the Cleveland administration. James M. Cox
was nominated in a situation in which the administration had deliberately adopted a hands-off policy, Adlai
E. Stevenson in one where the administration had been
unable to find an adequate candidate before the convention, with Stevenson originally refusing to serve as an
understudy to President Truman. Among the seven in-
party cases, Buchanan was the only election winner.

Factional warfare is especially common in out-party
situations, where it has led to compromise after stalemate in about one third of the cases. Where the struggle
has led to factional victory, it has sometimes involved
a form of insurgency in which renomination was denied

a titular leader. More often, the victory has simply been the outcome of a contest among coordinate factions, no one of which was clearly in control of the party leadership.

Twelve cases have been classified as representing factional victory in the choice of an out-party nominee —the largest single group of cases in Table 6. William Henry Harrison and Abraham Lincoln were both the nominees of new political parties in which there was ample scope for coordinate factionalism. Zachary Taylor's nomination in 1848 involved a defeat for Henry Clay, as had William Henry Harrison's in 1840, but in 1848 Clay was somewhat more clearly cast in the role of titular leader. Samuel J. Tilden was the nominee of a party whose last previous nominee had died before the electoral votes were counted. Benjamin Harrison, McKinley, Wilson, Willkie, Eisenhower, and Kennedy were each candidates of an out-party whose previous nominee was generally regarded as out of the running. Roosevelt in 1932 and Dewey in 1944 were both successful in winning nominations against titular leaders. Nine of the twelve nominees won their elections; the three losers, Tilden, Willkie, and Dewey, were all strong candidates.

The candidate who wins a nomination in a factional contest may himself be a factional leader; he may be an outsider; he may be a subordinate leader or a relatively inactive member of the faction. McKinley, Wilson, and Dewey were factional leaders: there was no one more important in their faction nor more representative of its aims. William Henry Harrison, Taylor, and, at least in the early stages of his candidacy, Eisenhower, were outsiders recruited by a faction in search of a winner.

A recognized factional leader generally takes an active part in the strategy. He must fight openly against the field, and is usually limited to first-choice votes, for he will usually have at least one unbending opponent. An outsider is a passenger on a band wagon operated by the faction. He has a better chance to pick up second-choice votes at the convention, and to court the independent voters in the election campaign.

Continuity and Change in the Patterns of Nomination

If the sixty-five nominations are recapitulated as for the periods 1832-1892 and 1896-1960, first by major party, then by in-power and out-power status, as in Tables 7 and 8, the patterns that emerge have special

TABLE 7. PATTERNS IN MAJOR-PARTY PRESIDENTIAL NOMINATIONS SINCE 1832; BY MAJOR PARTIES[a]

Type of Nomination	Democratic		Republican[b]		Major-Party Total	
	1832-1892	1896-1960	1832-1892	1896-1960	1832-1892	1896-1960
A. Confirmation	4	8	3	7	7	15
B. Inheritance	1	1	2	3	3	4
C. Inner Group Selection	5	1	2	2	7	3
D. Compromise in Stalemate	3	1	2	1	5	2
E. Factional Victory	3	6	6	4	9	10
Total	16	17	15	17	31	34

[a] Data from the previous tables.
[b] Includes National Republican and Whig.

interest in connection with the study of long-term changes in the nominating process and the party system. The periods divide the total experience under the convention system of nominations into two nearly equal portions, the breaking point coinciding with the critical election year of 1896.

TABLE 8. PATTERNS IN MAJOR-PARTY PRESIDENTIAL
NOMINATIONS SINCE 1832; BY IN-POWER
AND OUT-OF-POWER STATUS
OF THE PARTIES[a]

	Party In Power		Party Out of Power	
Type of Nomination	1832-1892	1896-1960	1832-1892	1896-1960
A. Confirmation	6	11	1	4
B. Inheritance	2	3	1	1
C. Inner Group Selection	2	0	5	3
D. Compromise in Stalemate	2	0	3	2
E. Factional Victory	4	3	5	7
Total	16	17	15	17

[a] "In-power" and "out-power" status was determined in accordance with whether the currently incumbent President had been elected on the party ticket. The result is anomalous to the extent that it classifies the Whig party as holding power during John Tyler's administration, and the Republican party during Andrew Johnson's; but the result would be even more anomalous if the Democratic party were regarded as holding power in those instances.

THE PATTERNS OF THE FUTURE

In all analytical work based upon small numbers of cases it is necessary to guard against inferences that may have no basis other than purely random variations in the numbers. There is also danger in projecting into the future the observed trends of the past, however well ascertained. A projection of trends on the basis of the figures of Tables 7 and 8 alone would be hazardous indeed, but, in the total historical context, the figures mainly have the effect of clarifying and solidifying what would otherwise be much more vague.

Probably the simplest prediction that can be made is that first-term Presidents who have been elected directly to the office will, when willing and available, continue to secure party renominations with a high degree of unanimity, as they have since 1864, and will continue to be extremely strong election contenders. The second part of the prediction is not as safe as the first, since re-election implies eight years of continuous tenure by the same political party, and, as noted in Chapter 4, the United States may be moving into an era of closer party balance and more frequent party overturn.

Vice Presidents who succeed to the Presidency through death of the incumbent will probably continue to secure nomination for a second term with little difficulty, as they have since 1904. Succession by the death of the President will cause less disruption of party and governmental affairs in the future, to the extent that increasing attention is given to factional and personal compatibility between the presidential and vice-presidential candidates of each party. However, the new doctrine on the selection of Vice Presidents has not yet been fully accepted. (See Chapter 5.)

The future of the titular leaders as candidates for the Presidency is full of uncertainties and imponderables. It seems likely that the position of the titular leadership will continue to be strengthened, and this may be favorable to continued success in the pursuit of the party nominations. But these tendencies could be delayed or even reversed unless some titular leader eventually wins election as well as renomination.

In making predictions about the choice of new leadership the situation of the in-party must be distinguished from that of the out-party. Factional conflict over the nomination, with a struggle and a divided vote, has become much less common in the party in power than in the party out of power. But conflict over the succession will probably continue to occur from time to time even in the party in power, as long as the Democratic and

Republican parties are no more internally cohesive than they are at present.

Factional candidates in a party out of power will probably continue to achieve nominations with considerable frequency, unless the titular leadership is greatly strengthened, and perhaps even if it is. The successful candidates who drive through to out-party factional nominations within ten years or less after they first become prominent have a type of glamour that can be extremely useful. If the factional infighting does not become too severe, the contest may serve to demonstrate party vitality and to publicize the eventual candidate. Such candidates should continue to have good chances for electoral victory.

Inner group nominations will probably be much less heard of in the future, unless there is a return to a party imbalance so extreme that the out-party becomes a minority in which the recruitment of suitable candidates is difficult.

The compromise or dark horse nominees have been reserved for final treatment because they are, as a group, perhaps the most interesting, and also the most crucial when the nominating process is being appraised. It is the group that is most generally cited when the convention system is under attack. The fact that even one Harding could be nominated under the convention system is to many critics a sufficient argument for substituting a national primary as the nominating instrument.

But all the other compromise candidates except John W. Davis, who was defeated, are figures of ancient party history. It is easy to argue that they were the only possible solution—the price of union—at a time when politics was fiercely sectional and factional passions ran high. Yet the parties may thereby have missed performing an essential function—that of giving the voters alternatives through which national issues could have been solved. Be that as it may, dark horse candidates seem to be a vanishing type, just as most of the conditions conducive to their candidacies have disappeared.

The nominating habits of the major parties have developed over the years under the impact of changes in the structure of government, and in the kind of political issues at stake—and sometimes under the impact of personalities and personal decisions. The main purpose of the convention system from the first has been to select candidates in such a way as to unite the party for the election.

The nominating patterns identified in this chapter represent the tactics variously chosen by political leaders who sought both to press for the results they desired and to avoid breaking up the party.* Usually a consensus has been achieved. Those who were disappointed were not so bitter as to walk out; the party held together; and the chance of victory in the election was not thrown away. On other occasions the consensus failed and the party was split—whereupon the voters took a hand in the election and taught the warring political leaders the value of compromise, unity, and the integrity of the two-party system.

* The patterns are examined further in Chapter 14, in regard to consensus in the convention. They are also applied to the analyses of Chapter 15.

8

The Candidates

■

Along the way to the final nominating decision every leading contender is, for a time at least, regarded as being "available," in some sense of that intangible quality. In each case certain aspects of ability, experience, and background must obviously be responsible for this estimate, although the extent to which such characteristics influence the choice as finally made will probably always be as difficult to pin down as the concept of availability itself. Nevertheless, even meager descriptive information on the backgrounds of the individuals who have been seriously considered for the Presidency and the Vice Presidency does throw some light on both the nominating process and on various aspects of government.

From convention to convention the number of names under consideration has fluctuated widely. An incumbent President has sometimes been renominated without any competing name being placed before the convention; at the other extreme, in the 103-ballot Democratic convention of 1924, 60 candidates received votes. From 1832 through 1956 approximately 300 persons were found to receive 3 per cent or more of the convention vote for a presidential or vice-presidential nomination. (The aspirants who polled less than 3 per cent are excluded from this total as not meeting the definition of "candidates seriously considered"; usually they were proposed merely as a courtesy gesture or for some other reason of short-lived importance.)

For each of the 300, biographical information was assembled during the research for the unabridged edition of this book and was reported more fully there. This background material was helpful in reaching the assessments of the present chapter, which reports mainly on the candidates who were actually chosen for the presidential and vice-presidential nominations of the two major parties.

The Geography of Ticket Selection

Political analysts in theorizing about the importance of geography in the selection of presidential and vice-presidential candidates have commonly held three principles as basic:

• • • A presidential candidate should be selected from a large state, thus helping to secure the state's large vote in the electoral college.

• • • The state should be politically a doubtful one, since otherwise the nomination could not be used to pull a doubtful state into the winning column in the election.

• • • After the presidential candidate has been picked, the vice-presidential candidate should be selected so as to balance the ticket geographically. (Rudiments of this principle were imbedded in the Constitution by requiring the presidential electors to vote for two persons, "of whom one at least shall not be an inhabitant of the same State with themselves.")

When the geographic combinations of major-party

tickets from 1832 to 1960 are examined and then coded for the regional balance of the two nominations, it becomes apparent that certain regional combinations are much more common than others. This can be seen clearly for the four periods and the two parties when the combinations are recapitulated as follows:*

Democratic	Republican	Democratic	Republican
1832-1860		*1896-1924*	
3 N-S	3 S-N	3 N-M	5 M-N
2 S-N	1 M-S	2 M-N	3 N-M
2 M-S	1 S-S	2 M-M	
1 N-X	1 W-N	1 N-N	
	1 M-N		
1864-1892		*1928-1960*	
8 N-M	6 M-N	4 N-S	4 N-W
	1 N-M	2 N-M	2 W-M
	1 M-S	3 M-S	1 M-M
			1 N-M
			1 W-N

The groupings show the South's importance as a source of presidential and vice-presidential nominees before the Civil War, and its lack of importance thereafter until 1928. In the 1864-1892 period the tickets of both parties were remarkably unvaried in their balance, but in the most recent period diversity returned.

In five instances among the sixty-five pairs, both nominees came from the same region; all of these tickets were defeated in the elections. In each case the inability or failure to compose a regionally balanced

* Coding is by major region: Northeast, N; Middle West, M; South, S; West, W. X indicates no vice-presidential nominee was chosen (Democrats, 1840). For assignment of states to regions, see explanation and listing at end of Chapter 4.

ticket was undoubtedly related to aspects of party weakness, including sectional antagonisms within the party. For instance, when midwesterner Landon was nominated in 1936 by the Republican convention his running mate was Frank Knox, another midwesterner; the Republicans had already been swept out of office in most of the northeastern region, and eastern Republicans of political note had little desire to run for Vice President in a year of almost certain national defeat.

Presidential nominations have been increasingly concentrated in a small number of states. Between 1832 and 1892, when the number of states was smaller than it is now, the twenty-three first-time nominees were drawn from thirteen states (New York, Ohio, Illinois, California, New Jersey, Pennsylvania, Virginia, Tennessee, Indiana, Maine, New Hampshire, Michigan, Kentucky), with at least two from each of five states (New York, five; Illinois, three; Ohio, three; Pennsylvania, two; Virginia, two) and no more than five from any state. Since 1896, the nineteen first-time nominees have been drawn from nine states only (the first five states named above for the earlier period, plus Kansas, West Virginia, Nebraska, and Massachusetts), with more than one from only New York, Ohio, and California, and with seven from New York alone.

In the 1928-1956 period a single state was for the first time predominantly the source of presidential candidates in both major parties—New York, the state of residence for the men receiving five of the eight Democratic nominations and renominations, and four of the eight Republican. The great size of the state and the importance of New York City as the leading metropolis of the nation were probably not alone responsible; undoubtedly, the return to a close competitive balance in state politics during that period, after a lengthy period when the governorship had generally been won by Republicans, had much to do with the phenomenon.

With changes in population and political currents, this predominance of New York may disappear. California, Pennsylvania, Ohio, Illinois, Michigan, and Texas have all become major fighting grounds in state and national elections, with governors and senators who find many opportunities to reach national prominence as party leaders. In 1962, California became the largest state in the Union, passing New York.

The Age Factor

Information on age is readily available for most high-ranking political figures. The importance actually attached to age in the making of nominations is much more difficult to discover, and the question of what importance *should* be assigned to it entails complex practical and philosophical issues.

In both parties the average age of first-time presidential nominees has been relatively young from the beginning—54.5 years before 1896, 50.6 since. The concentration in the most recent period has been in the bracket of 50 to 54 years, as the following distributions show:

Age	Democratic 1832-1892	Democratic 1896-1960	Republican 1832-1892	Republican 1896-1960	Both Parties 1832-1892	Both Parties 1896-1960
35-39	1	1	—	—	1	1
40-44	—	1	1	1	1	2
45-49	4	—	2	3	6	3
50-54	1	5	3	4	4	9
55-59	2	2	2	1	4	3
60-64	2	—	1	1	3	1
65-69	2	—	2	—	4	—
Total	12	9	11	10	23	19

The 1960 nominations reduced the averages; Kennedy was 43 when nominated, Nixon 47.

The average age of vice-presidential nominees has gone up since 1896, and especially so in the Democratic party. Although in 1952 and 1956 both parties selected relatively young vice-presidential candidates, the Republicans since 1896 have nominated four candidates over age 60, the Democrats eight. As the junior of the two offices and because it might lead to the senior office by constitutional or electoral succession, the Vice Presidency presumably should be filled by an incumbent young enough to serve effectively as President—if called upon to do so—for additional periods of at least four years and possibly eight. Evidently neither party has been disposed to worry much about the factors of vice-presidential age, especially when the presidential candidate was relatively young. There have also been three instances—all in the Democratic party—when both members of the ticket were over 60: 1916, Wilson and Marshall; 1944, Roosevelt and Truman; 1948, Truman and Barkley.*

The death of President Franklin D. Roosevelt at age

* Since it seems clear that the characteristics of availability for the presidential nomination are likely to differ from those for the vice-presidential, it is important to keep the two groups as distinct as possible. In the further analyses in this chapter, therefore, T. Roosevelt, Coolidge, and Truman are omitted from the categories of first-time presidential nominees, since they were originally elected as Vice Presidents. Fillmore, Johnson, and Arthur are omitted from the "other contenders" for the presidential nomination, since they were incumbent Presidents who had been elected as Vice Presidents. Jackson is also omitted, because he was an incumbent President when the convention system was instituted.

Henry Clay is counted as a first-time nominee in his National Republican nomination of 1832, but not in his Whig nomination of 1844. The forty-two first-time nominees of this chapter are otherwise identical with the forty-three classified in Chapter 7 under the four nominating patterns of leadership succession (Table 6).

63 and the heart attack suffered by President Eisenhower at age 65 sharply highlighted the problems of
age and mortality in the nation's highest office. The
oldest presidential candidate ever nominated was William Henry Harrison, age 67; he died in office at 68.
Men much older have often served in the chief executive positions of other countries, but the United States
Presidency is unique both in the burdens it imposes on
the incumbent and in the amount of governmental confusion, and possibly actual danger to the nation, that
may arise when its incumbent dies or becomes incapaci-
tated during his fixed term of office.

The eleven first-time Presidents serving between 1832
and 1892 who escaped assassination lived to an average
age of 68.6 years. For the six deceased Presidents of
the 1896-1960 period (as of 1962, and omitting Cleveland, whose term ended in 1897, and McKinley, who
was assassinated) the average age at death was 63.2.
Two independent actuarial studies made in 1940 and
1946 seemed to suggest a considerable curtailment since
1900 in presidential life expectancy—possibly due to
the increasing stress inherent in the office. On the other
hand, it is likely that recent Presidents have been better
protected from assassination and have been getting
better medical care than their predecessors. Of the three
former Presidents still living in 1962, Herbert Hoover
was 88 on August 10 of that year, Harry S Truman
was 78 on May 8, and Dwight D. Eisenhower was 72
on October 14.

A political party, like any organization, must give
thought to the age of its leaders if it is to retain vitality
in a rapidly changing world. Yet parties often have more
difficulty than other organizations not only in retiring
the superannuated but also in providing rapid advancement for the able young. The two-term tradition, and
now the Twenty-second Amendment, have imposed a

limit on service in the Presidency, once a man is elected, but there is nothing to prevent aged candidates from being nominated for President and Vice President. There are many sectors of the American political system from which such candidates may come; an observer of any important state or national political meeting can find a substantial quota of persons of advanced years, many of whom are still considered potential candidates.

There is little evidence that the parties give much thought, under ordinary conditions, to the age of their candidates one way or the other. The number of first-time presidential nominations in the 50 to 54 year bracket seems primarily to be the by-product of the career channels that bring men to the point of active consideration for the Presidency. That the career patterns normally most successful in producing presidential candidates also produce them at a relatively young age is a special feature of the American political system.

Backgrounds in Private Life

All of the ten Republican first-time presidential nominees from 1896 to 1960 and seven of the nine Democrats had received some college training; sixteen of the total nineteen had also gone to law school. The other contenders differed little from the nominees in this respect. Of the vice-presidential nominees, thirteen of the fourteen Republicans and eleven of the fourteen Democrats had also received college training, with a total of twenty attending law school. As might be expected, for the 1832-1892 period the proportion of college training was somewhat less. The law school proportion was greatly less, but this undoubtedly reflects the greater extent to which legal training in recent decades has been provided in law schools, instead of by the older custom of reading law in an attorney's office.

Postgraduate education in fields other than law has been extremely rare. Woodrow Wilson was the only nominee of either party with an earned doctorate in political science—or in any other subject. In general, the educational preparation of the presidential candidates compares favorably with that of the state governors and of members of the Senate, but has not been conspicuously higher.

When the principal occupations in private life are examined, the overwhelming importance of the practice of law as a background is apparent. For both parties and both periods, twenty-five of the forty-two presidential candidates and forty-five of the fifty-eight vice-presidential candidates had been lawyers at some time. Publishers and editors, business proprietors and executives, and the professions other than law occasionally find representation among the nominees and among the other aspirants, but even collectively all the other occupations are outnumbered by the practice of law.

Mainly, all of these occupations have in common a moderately high social and economic status, providing a base of operations from which to campaign for high public office and to which to return when necessary. As an occupation, law is especially suited to the combining of public and private careers; fortunately, it also ranks high in the kind of preparatory training it can give for public office.

Governmental Experience

In parliamentary forms of government, it is usually necessary to be a member of the legislature in order to be appointed to a junior cabinet post; and only when a new political party is coming to power for the first time is anyone likely to become prime minister without having previously served for some years as a prominent member of the cabinet—and at the same time of the parliament. There is a strong presumption that such experience has value as training for those who eventually reach the top; but service in office also gives the individual a status from which to compete more effectively for higher posts on the political ladder.

The American political system is much more open than most others, and its channels of political advancement are less rigid. Many roads may lead to the Presidency. In the competition for the office, an existing position as a governor or senator, for instance, is more likely to be regarded as a power base from which to campaign than as an opportunity to obtain a type of qualifying experience; but both aspects of the situation are important.

Examining the previous governmental experience of the candidates, we find that most of the presidential nominees, as well as the contenders, had previously occupied at least two, sometimes three, different governmental positions before being actively considered for the Presidency. In both parties for both periods only Wendell Willkie, of the nominees, and only four of the other contenders had had no governmental experience. Willkie was a career executive in big business, although he had started as a lawyer; as a successful candidate for a major-party presidential nomination, he was unique. Not one vice-presidential nominee lacked governmental experience; among the other contenders, only five lacked it.

In careers leading to the nominations, local government channels have not been of major importance. Of the forty-two first-time presidential nominees, nine had experience in local government, of the fifty-eight vice-presidential nominees, twenty-two. Big-city mayors are local political figures of unusual importance, but no mayor or former mayor of a city of 500,000 population or more ever polled over 3 per cent for either Republican nomination, and the Democratic cases include only three minor contenders. Without doubt, this reflects the long-persisting rural bias in all American politics other than those of the big cities themselves, but it seems unlikely that this bias can continue indefinitely. The 212 metropolitan areas with a central city of 50,000 or more now contain 63 per cent of the total population of the United States.

In modern times the state legislatures are seldom beginning points for either presidential or vice-presidential careers. For all nominees and for other contenders the trend was sharply downward from the 1832-1892 period to the later period—in most cases a drop of about one half. Executive positions—other than governor—in state governments have provided a stepping stone to a few Republican presidential and vice-presidential nominees since 1896, but to none of the Democrats.

With its many members the House of Representatives could be expected to be a point of entry for all types of national political talent, but it has never been a gate through which all presidential and vice-presidential candidates must pass. About a third of the first-time presidential nominees from 1896 to 1960 had served in the House, including both nominees of 1960. The Senate has become increasingly important in recent decades as part of the career pattern of those seeking the top nominations. Frequently the senatorial candidates have settled for the second position after reaching for the first, but Kennedy made it all the way in 1960.

Of all the high civil executive positions, the office of governor has traditionally been the most important source of presidential candidates. Since 1896 nearly half of the presidential nominees and about one third of the vice-presidential have been incumbent governors or former governors. Among the other contenders for both nominations governors have also been prominent, but not so much as might be expected—the implication being that, in a field of contestants, governors do not run without success as often as others.

Federal appointive office is a type of experience possessed by less than one third of all presidential and vice-presidential nominees since 1832, and has had about equal weight in the careers of the other contestants. The proportion among presidential nominees of both parties has been remarkably stable since the beginning. In the Democratic vice-presidential nominations, however, the figures for recent years show a marked decline.

For the whole convention period, six generals of the regular army were nominated for President, five of them before 1884: Zachary Taylor (W, 1848), Winfield Scott (W, 1852), George McClellan (D, 1864), Ulysses S. Grant (R, 1868), Winfield Scott Hancock (D, 1880), and Dwight D. Eisenhower (R, 1952). The other contenders furnished a sole but important example, General Leonard Wood, who polled 32 per cent of the vote on the fourth ballot in the Republican convention of 1920. For Vice President, no general ever received the nomination, and General James Harbord (R, 1932) was the one contender to pass the 3 per cent level.

Judicial experience in federal or state courts has been the background of four presidential nominees in the two periods, including William Howard Taft and Charles Evans Hughes. Of the other contenders, three Supreme Court Justices, all before 1880, were active but unsuccessful candidates. Since then a tradition has gradually strengthened that men becoming high court judges should leave politics behind them, although preconvention speculation in recent years has involved several incumbent members of the Supreme Court.

When the governmental experience of all candidates for the two time periods is compared, it is apparent that, from the earlier period to the more recent, the average number of government positions previously held has declined from about 2.9 positions per candidate to 2.2. Circulation of officeholders among the various types of public office was apparently both more rapid and more extensive (in terms of variety of experience) in the early period. In either house of Congress, long tenure was relatively rare, and a period of federal service was often followed by a return to state office. Henry Clay saw no loss of dignity in returning to his state legislature after a term in the U. S. Senate. James K. Polk went home to Tennessee to run for governor after fourteen years in Congress, served one term as governor, then was defeated twice for renomination. In 1844 he was nominated for the Presidency and elected—the only ex-Speaker of the House ever to become President.

THE CHANGE IN CAREER PATTERNS

In recent decades political career patterns have changed. Election to the House of Representatives without prior governmental experience is now relatively common. From there the road leads mainly to the Senate, only rarely back to a state governorship and only occasionally into the President's Cabinet. A governor now typically arrives at the State House without prior federal experience, is rapidly rotated out of office under tenure limitations, then moves either to the Senate or back into private life, after a possible brief interlude of consideration along the way as a presidential hopeful.

Senators hate to go back home, even to run for governor, although they occasionally do both. Seemingly they are increasingly reluctant to enter the President's Cabinet or else they are less often invited, or both. An incumbent senator who could appropriately be considered for the Cabinet would, if he accepted, almost invariably suffer a marked loss in seniority and security without any countervailing gain for a long-term future. Recent Cabinet members have seldom been considered seriously for the top nominations, but some have been appointed to the Supreme Court and others have won election to the Senate. The Cabinet has become a means of entering the Senate, rather than the other way around.

The most important change in career patterns, however, has been the increasing emphasis upon incumbency in high elective office as a qualification for either of the top nominations.

In the early period, nine of the twenty-three first-time presidential nominees and fourteen of the thirty vice-presidential were occupying no government post at the time of nomination. After 1896 only three nominees for the Presidency were not incumbents of some government office—Bryan (D, 1896), Davis (D, 1924), Willkie (R, 1940). All were defeated. Of the various vice-presidential nominees after 1896, only seven did not currently hold government offices. There can be no doubt that incumbency—and often in high office—by comparison with similar previous governmental experience, has recently become much more important to success in pursuing nominations for both the Presidency and the Vice Presidency.

From the total experience, it also seems clear that the career patterns of nominees for the Vice Presidency have on the whole been much more "political," in the term's derogatory sense, than those of the presidential nominees. A party war horse or a party hack has rarely if ever been nominated for President even when a party could reasonably be expected to lose—but often, under such circumstances, for Vice President. And patronage considerations, which have seldom influenced a presidential choice, have often been of the essence in a vice-presidential nomination, especially when a party in power was filling a vacancy on a prospectively winning ticket.

Electoral Success

What political offices have been most important as the final stepping stone to a presidential nomination? To success in the election that followed? If the information basic to these questions is organized for the two time periods on an in-party, out-party basis, as in Table 9, the result is at least thought-provoking, even though the figures to be considered are too few and too small to provide statistical evidence of any simple pattern of one-way, one-factor causation.

One striking feature is the small total number (six) of first-time nominees for President from 1896 to 1960 in the party in power, and the even smaller number (two) of these who won election. The two winners— William Howard Taft and Herbert Hoover—came directly out of the administration of the party in power; when an in-party administration went outside of its own ranks for a new nominee (Cox and Stevenson) or was unable to control the choice (Bryan), it lost the election and went out of power. One can speculate that a party too weak or too divided internally to deal smoothly with the problems of succession in the headship will also find its competitive problems difficult until its leadership situation has again become stabilized.

For the out-party the relative predominance of governors among the thirteen first-time nominees of the period 1896-1960 is clear. Six out-party governors won nomination; three won election (McKinley, Wilson, and F. D. Roosevelt), three lost (Smith, Landon, and Dewey). In the earlier period the out-party nominated only two governors; one was elected.

The record of the six generals in winning election was merely average. Of the in-party nominees, Grant won and Scott was a spectacular loser. Hancock lost as the out-party nominee, as did McClellan. The out-party winners were Taylor and Eisenhower, one in each period.

All the incumbent senators nominated for President prior to 1896 lost their elections (Clay, Cass, and Douglas). In the period 1896-1960, the two senators nominated (Harding and Kennedy) were both out-party winners.

As for candidates holding no governmental position when first nominated, the respective in-parties lost elections with Blaine in 1884 and Bryan in 1896, and thereafter made no such nomination. Out-parties did relatively well before 1892 with former holders of public office (the two Harrisons, Polk, Pierce, and Lincoln). Between 1896 and 1960 an out-party candidate with only previous governmental experience (Davis) and one with no government experience (Willkie) lost; the showing further illustrates the apparent need for incumbency in some high office in seeking the Presidency under modern conditions.

Is There a Type That Emerges?

Popular writing in every presidential election year always includes efforts to define the personality characteristics and other qualifications of "the perfect President" or "the ideal nominee." The data we have presented do not lend themselves easily to this kind of

TABLE 9. SOURCES OF FIRST-TIME NOMINEES AND
THEIR ELECTORAL SUCCESS, BY PARTY STATUS,
1832-1892 AND 1896-1960[a]

Governmental Position of Nominee	Party In Power		Party Out of Power	
	1832-1892	1896-1960	1832-1892	1896-1960
PRESIDENTIAL NOMINEES				
Governor	1/1	0/2	1/2	3/6
Federal Official[b]	1/1	2/2	—	—
Army General	1/2	—	1/3	1/1
Senator	0/2	—	0/1	2/2
Other[c]	2/2	0/1	—	0/2
None	0/1	0/1	5/8	0/2
Total	5/9	2/6	7/14	6/13
VICE-PRESIDENTIAL NOMINEES				
Senator	1/3	4/5	2/3	2/5
Representative	3/3	1/1	0/1	1/1
Governor	—	1/1	1/2	2/5
Federal Official[b]	1/2	1/3	0/1	—
Other[d]	0/1	—	1/1	—
None	3/6	2/3	4/7	1/4
Total	8/15	9/13	8/15	6/15

[a] In each cell of the table, the denominator is the total number of nominees in the category and the numerator is the number who won in the ensuing general election.
[b] Appointive officials in the Executive Branch.
[c] Two Vice Presidents, one representative in Congress, and two judges.
[d] One army general and one state official.

judgment—except to suggest that there *is* no single pattern of characteristics that the conventions will invariably choose. A convention may be guided to some extent by an unconscious ideal that has already screened out those clearly unavailable, but it is mainly seeking to choose among those who are still available. The system seems to throw up a wide range of types for choice, although not always very wide in any one year.

The early Presidents from Washington to John Quincy Adams were all well known from their previous participation in national affairs, and had many qualities in common. The congressional nominating caucus in most cases stayed within the circle of its own observation and acquaintanceship. When Andrew Jackson came to power as a people's hero, the earlier channels of advancement were disregarded and the convention system soon effectively prevented their restoration. Within a decade the field was open to state officials as well as federal, to legislators as well as executives, and to persons with no governmental experience who had somehow developed that intangible quality known as availability.

A sort of cumbersome "natural selection" has always gone on in the determination of initial availability—resulting in various standards that are essentially negative, but that sometimes change as national or sectional mores change. For instance, up to 1960 all women were still excluded and all Negroes, and aspirants with conspicuous marital difficulties or with close identification to a specific economic interest group were essentially excluded. These and eleven other categories of such semiautomatic exclusions are summarized by Sidney Hyman in his book *The American President,* with this conclusion:

> If these rules . . . are applied to the entire population—with millions lopped off at each turn—the

minority that can pass all these tests at any one time is probably in the neighborhood of one hundred men.

Whether this residue is one hundred or fifty, the conventions have not easily solved the problems of defining the standards for final choice among the still fewer aspirants who will be actual candidates. For the observer, the patterns of preference from convention to convention are difficult to understand. Largely as a guide to what has been clearly untypical and to what is perhaps becoming more typical, the information in this chapter may be helpful in suggesting the kind of person a party is more likely to nominate.

Among the eight first-time Democratic nominees for President from 1896 through 1956, for instance, Bryan, Parker, and Davis all seem notably untypical in major respects. Bryan was young, inexperienced, and from a small, predominantly Republican state. Parker, a high court judge long withdrawn from active politics, was a vigorous supporter of the gold standard opposed earlier by majorities of his party. Davis was a Wall Street lawyer, who had previously been elected twice to the House of Representatives from West Virginia and held appointive positions under Wilson.

Each of the other Democrats—Wilson, Cox, Smith, F. D. Roosevelt, and Stevenson—was the active and able incumbent governor of a populous, hard-fought, two-party state. Their ages respectively were 55, 50, 55, 50, 52. Relatively new to the national scene, each had already achieved distinction in a public-service type of career. Cox was somewhat untypical in being a businessman and publisher, and Smith was certainly untypical in being highly urban and of the Roman Catholic faith. But all five were typical of much that has seemed best in the American political system: the rapid elevation, through elective executive office in states where politics is vigorous and competitive, of able leaders still in the prime of life who have not necessarily yet taken on the characteristics of a "father image." This appears to be the type recently preferred by the Democratic party in its first-time presidential nominations, when the type was available. And the two elected—Wilson and Roosevelt—were highly exemplary of that preference.

The Republican party seems to have had a fondness for "untypical" nominees—of whom Willkie was probably the most outstanding example, with his total lack of governmental experience. Eisenhower, with his eminence as a five-star general, was a reversion to an earlier pattern of American politics—and thus one of the most untypical of the choices offered. Hughes, remote and Olympian, was untypical—despite his experience as a successful governor of New York State— as the only Supreme Court Justice in history nominated for President. Harding, the only nominee from the Senate between Douglas in 1860 and Kennedy in 1960, was untypical in a sufficient number of other respects.

Of the other five Republican nominees of 1896-1956, McKinley, Landon, and Dewey were incumbent governors, and Taft and Hoover served in the Cabinets of the Presidents that they succeeded. They seem to offer a composite pattern of the Republican preference in first-time presidential nominees. All were able executives, well known to be closely affiliated with the business community. Their ages respectively were 53, 49, 42, 51, and 54. Their careers had included distinguished public service and evidence of capacity to cultivate the electorate. With the exception of Landon, their origins were the populous, two-party states that often decide presidential elections. None of them, except perhaps Dewey, was characterized by the kind of dynamism in approaching public problems that appeared to be a collective characteristic of the five Democrats deemed typical. They were therefore less likely to become the kind of "strong" President that, since Lincoln, seems to have been regarded by the Republican party as objectionable in the White House.

The type that has been most frequently preferred by the conventions of the two parties when they had an adequate opportunity for choice has provided the more successful Presidents of recent decades—Wilson and F. D. Roosevelt, McKinley, Taft, and Hoover. In a poll of fifty-five historians conducted in the late 1940's by Arthur M. Schlesinger, the two Democrats were rated as "greats," the three Republicans as at least average. The poll rated the only "untypical" nominee of either party to win election—Harding—as an outright failure as President. The set of ratings (published in *Life* in 1948) is here classified in Table 10, according to the political party of the Presidents and the system which nominated them. (The ratings express one form of authoritative opinion. The reader may disagree with some of them—as do the authors of this book.)

One must remember that either party at any given time can choose only from among those who are available. If the preferred type, especially in a party out of power, is a vote-getting governor with a distinguished record in an important two-party state the number is seldom large. There have been times in out-party history when no such candidate was available, and some of the odd nominations that have been made were the result.

The picture given in this chapter has been one based mainly on the long historical record. It remains to be seen whether the nominations of 1960 reflect some permanent change. Kennedy was an incumbent senator when nominated, as Nixon had been before becoming Vice President. Neither had ever been a governor and neither had ever headed a large executive organization. In other respects, however, both men conformed

TABLE 10. THE PRESIDENTS UP TO 1945
AS RATED BY HISTORIANS[a]

(adapted here to categories of nominating
systems and political parties)

Category Assigned by Poll of 55 Historians	Presidents Selected Prior to Convention System	Presidents Nominated in National Party Conventions	
		Democratic	Republican[b]
Great	2. G. Washington 5. T. Jefferson 6. A. Jackson	3. F. D. Roosevelt 4. W. Wilson	1. A. Lincoln
Near Great	9. J. Adams	8. G. Cleveland 10. J. K. Polk	7. T. Roosevelt
Average	11. J. Q. Adams 12. J. Monroe 14. J. Madison	15. M. Van Buren	13. R. B. Hayes 16. W. H. Taft 17. C. A. Arthur 18. W. McKinley 19. A. Johnson 20. H. Hoover 21. B. Harrison
Below Average		26. J. Buchanan 27. F. Pierce	22. J. Tyler 23. C. Coolidge 24. M. Fillmore 25. Z. Taylor
Failure			28. U. S. Grant 29. W. G. Harding

[a] Arthur M. Schlesinger, "The U.S. Presidents," *Life* (Nov. 1, 1948). Professor Schlesinger explained that he conducted the poll informally among his "colleagues in American history and government. . . . There was a large measure of agreement among the 'experts' within the important categories of great, near great, and failures. The six greats . . . had no close runners-up, although Lincoln was the only one to get all 55 votes for the top rank." Harrison and Garfield were omitted because of the brevity of their life in office. Truman was omitted because his record was not complete at the time. (Rating material used by courtesy of Professor Schlesinger and *Life*.)

[b] Includes Whig (Tyler, Fillmore, and Taylor) and War Democrat (Johnson).

to the type that has been identified: both had risen rapidly and with great distinction in a public service career, both were relatively young—43 and 47—and each was the product of vigorous competition in the campaigns and elections of a populous, two-party state.

It is possible that the Senate may become the most important source of presidential candidates in the future; the growing importance of the issues of national policy and of American involvement with the world at large are shifting the political spectrum in that direction. But it is much too early to conclude that governors are finished as presidential candidates, and especially so on any permanent or long-term basis.

9

Apportionment and
Voting Structure

■

The most basic of all convention rules are those that apportion the number of votes each state delegation shall have when it reaches the convention hall, for they determine where units of power will be located and therefore influence every decision. They are, however, only one part of the system of rules—some of them precise, some diffuse—whereby each party establishes the distribution of voting power and how the vote shall be counted. Surrounding and interweaving with the whole system is the complex informal network of personalities and practices that can at times modify rigid formulas in a way the formal structure cannot or will not do.

Evolution of Apportionment Rules

At the beginning of the convention system, voting power was allocated on the basis used in the electoral college—equal to the total of senators and representatives from each state. When the constitutional structure of the United States Congress was being designed in 1787 the principle of allowing all states two votes in the Senate in recognition of their equal sovereignty, plus a number in the House of Representatives proportionate to the population of each, had been thoroughly debated and finally agreed upon, and it was carried over into the national party organizations without question. Major elements of this system still survive in the conventions, with regular delegates at large who correspond to the senators, and congressional district delegates who correspond to the House members; in the conventions they all vote together.

Along the way, the validity of allotting convention votes without regard to party strength was often questioned. There was a clear anomaly whenever the party concerned was giving representation to states where it had few votes or none.

The conventions have always held the right to apportion voting strength among the states, but in general each party in a state has retained the right, subject at times to state laws, to select its delegation. The size of delegations sent to the conventions has therefore often varied with little regard to the number of votes allotted, because of local pressure to provide seats for all the influential party members who desired to attend; as a result the delegates have often had fractional votes.

THE REPUBLICANS' CENTURY OF CONTROVERSY

The history of Republican apportionment rules has been long and complex. The convention of 1856, the first for the newborn party, was entirely northern in composition, but in 1860 delegations came from Virginia and Texas. Texas was challenged, since the party had no significant membership there. The credentials committee suggested seating the Texans, with a reduction in voting strength, and this was approved—the first instance of recognition that lack of party strength did not require total exclusion but might involve an apportionment penalty.

During Reconstruction and thereafter all the southern states sent delegations, and were given their full apportionment. With the emergence in 1880 of the Solid South controlled by white Democratic majorities, the "rotten borough" Republican delegations, often composed mainly of federal officials when the party was in power, were an embarrassing feature of the conventions. The problem was repeatedly discussed, but suggestions for changes generally had the overtones of political maneuver that voting and seating matters are so likely to acquire.

At the convention of 1908, a minority of the rules committee proposed that a system be adopted for 1912, whereby each state would have four delegates at large plus an additional delegate for every 10,000 Republican votes cast in the last preceding presidential election, with no district delegates as such. This was defeated, the bulk of the opposition naturally coming from the southern states—whose percentage of representation in the 1912 convention would have been cut in half had the ruling been passed. In 1912 eleven formerly Confederate southern states held 23 per cent of the convention voting strength—though they had supplied only 7 per cent of the Republican popular vote in the 1908 election. Their disproportionate convention strength was a major element in the test votes—won by President Taft—that resulted eventually in the convention bolt by Roosevelt and the Progressives and the election debacle for the party.

Reacting to the disaster, the Republican national committee offered a plan for cutting representation in the 1916 convention to be approved in advance by state conventions in states having a majority of the electoral votes. The plan was ratified; seventy-eight delegates were lost by southern states in 1916, seven more in 1920.

A system of bonus votes for states the party carried in the presidential election was adopted in 1924 and has since been repeatedly expanded. Effective in 1944, a state which the party failed to carry could still have its three bonus votes if it elected a Republican senator in the following off-year election. Effective in 1952, the number of bonus delegates for party victory in a state was raised from three to six and the bonus was given for success in the last preceding presidential, senatorial, or gubernatorial election.

RECENT CHANGES IN DEMOCRATIC APPORTIONMENT RULES

Fractional votes and oversized delegations have been characteristic of Democratic conventions through most of their history, but bonus votes were late arrivals. Effective in 1944, two bonus votes were allotted to each state going Democratic in the last preceding presidential election. The call for the 1948 convention included an increase in the bonus to four votes; this was unchanged in the 1952 convention, but the national committee adopted a special ruling that assured no loss of votes to any state by reason of the 1950 congressional reapportionment.

For the 1956 convention the national committee provided that every state should receive all of the votes allotted in 1952 and four additional votes if it had either cast its electoral votes for the Democratic nominees of 1952 or had elected a Democratic governor or senator on or after November 4, 1952. Many states thus received a total of eight bonus votes, and a precedent was established for the accumulation of bonus votes from convention to convention. States were also authorized to send either one or two delegates for each vote, thus putting most of the delegates on a half-vote basis.

Preparing for the 1960 convention, national committee Chairman Paul M. Butler led an effort to end the bonus system, which he said had "grossly distorted representation" at the 1956 convention. His initial plan would have compensated many of the states for their loss of bonus votes by increasing the number of regular votes, although fifteen states would have lost some of their total number. A meeting of the national committee in September 1959 adopted compromise rules that retained elements of Butler's plan, but also provided that no state should suffer any reduction of the votes received in 1956. National committee members for the first time were to be seated as ex officio delegates, with one half vote each; their additional votes would not be charged against the regular quota or the bonus votes carried over from 1956, with the result that every state received at least one more vote than previously. In total, votes were increased to 1,521 with the states again authorized to send either one delegate or two for each vote; approximately 3,000 delegates attended the 1960 Democratic convention.

Apportionment in 1960

The practical effect of the apportionment rules as they stood in 1960 is demonstrated in Tables 11 and 12, in which the states are listed in the standard regional pattern described in Chapter 4. Among the major regions, the Northeast, Middle West, and South were comparable in total population; they were accorded approximately the same voting strength in the 1960 conventions of both parties. The Republican South, however, was in this position because it had profited greatly from its previous increases in Republican presidential voting.

In total population, the West is the smallest of the regions, but it has been growing much more rapidly than the others, and in recent years its voting strength in each party convention has been helped considerably by bonus votes. Since 1959, moreover, its influence has been increased by the new states, Alaska and Hawaii.

Voting Power Under the Apportionment

In actual convention votes in 1960, the state delegations ranged between 9 and 114 in the Democratic convention, 6 and 96 in the Republican. The variations are accentuated by the tendency of delegation members to vote together—in some cases as required under state law or party rules, in others simply because a considerable amount of cohesion is normal.

Cohesion in delegation voting inevitably emphasizes the conspicuous position of the larger delegations, notably those of New York, Pennsylvania, Ohio, Illinois, California, and Texas. The suspicion that these states exercise overwhelming power is a continuing source of frustration to the smaller delegations. Yet in some situations small delegations can have a power advantage. In the Republican convention of 1952, when two strong voting coalitions of nearly equal size were supporting the respective candidacies of Taft and Eisenhower, disproportionate amounts of the power balance were held by the uncommitted delegations, and relatively small ones, like Maryland and Minnesota, were of critical importance.

In general, the power of large states is probably not disproportionately greater in contested situations than their manifest voting strength. Almost by definition, (Text continued on page 176)

Table 11. Voting Strength in the Democratic National Convention of 1960, by States and Regions

	1960			
	Basic Allotment		Hold-over Bonus Votes[b]	Total Votes
Region and State	Regular Votes	Nat. Com. Votes[a]		
Northeast				
Maine	13	1	1	15
New Hampshire	10	1	—	11
Vermont	8	1	—	9
Massachusetts	40	1	—	41
Rhode Island	10	1	6	17
Connecticut	20	1	—	21
New York	113	1	—	114
New Jersey	40	1	—	41
Delaware	8	1	2	11
Maryland	23	1	—	24
Pennsylvania	80	1	—	81
West Virginia	20	1	4	25
	385	12	13	410
Middle West				
Ohio	63	1	—	64
Michigan	50	1	—	51
Indiana	33	1	—	34
Illinois	68	1	—	69
Wisconsin	30	1	—	31
Minnesota	28	1	2	31
Iowa	25	1	—	26
Missouri	33	1	5	39
North Dakota	10	1	—	11
South Dakota	10	1	—	11
Nebraska	15	1	—	16
Kansas	20	1	—	21
	385	12	7	404
South				
Virginia	30	1	2	33
North Carolina	35	1	1	37
South Carolina	20	1	—	21
Georgia	30	1	2	33
Florida	25	1	3	29
Kentucky	25	1	5	31

TABLE 11 (*continued*)

Region and State	1960			
	Basic Allotment		Hold-over Bonus Votes[b]	Total Votes
	Regular Votes	Nat. Com. Votes[a]		
Tennessee.............	28	1	4	33
Alabama.............	28	1	—	29
Mississippi...........	20	1	2	23
Arkansas.............	20	1	6	27
Louisiana............	25	1	—	26
Oklahoma............	20	1	8	29
Texas................	60	1	—	61
	366	13	33	412
West				
Montana.............	10	1	6	17
Idaho................	10	1	2	13
Wyoming.............	8	1	6	15
Colorado.............	15	1	5	21
Utah.................	10	1	2	13
Nevada..............	8	1	6	15
New Mexico..........	10	1	6	17
Arizona.............	10	1	6	17
Washington..........	23	1	3	27
Oregon..............	15	1	1	17
California...........	80	1	—	81
Alaska..............	8	1	—	9
Hawaii..............	8	1	—	9
	215	13	43	271
Non-State Areas				
District of Columbia...	8	1	—	9
Puerto Rico...........	6	1	—	7
Virgin Islands........	3	1	—	4
Canal Zone..........	3	1	—	4
	20	4	—	24
Total.............	1,371	54	96	1,521

[a] Votes for national committee members serving ex officio as members of state delegations.

[b] Votes authorized to prevent reduction from the number of votes held in 1956, exclusive of the added vote for national committee members, and which thus in effect continued most of the bonus votes of previous years.

TABLE 12. VOTING STRENGTH IN THE REPUBLICAN
NATIONAL CONVENTION OF 1960, BY
STATES AND REGIONS

| | 1960 | | |
Region and State	Regular Votes	Bonus Votes	Total Votes
Northeast			
Maine.................	10	6	16
New Hampshire........	8	6	14
Vermont..............	6	6	12
Massachusetts.........	32	6	38
Rhode Island..........	8	6	14
Connecticut...........	16	6	22
New York.............	90	6	96
New Jersey............	32	6	38
Delaware.............	6	6	12
Maryland.............	18	6	24
Pennsylvania..........	64	6	70
West Virginia.........	16	6	22
	306	72	378
Middle West			
Ohio.................	50	6	56
Michigan.............	40	6	46
Indiana..............	26	6	32
Illinois..............	54	6	60
Wisconsin............	24	6	30
Minnesota............	22	6	28
Iowa.................	20	6	26
Missouri.............	26	—	26
North Dakota.........	8	6	14
South Dakota.........	8	6	14
Nebraska.............	12	6	18
Kansas...............	16	6	22
	306	66	372
South			
Virginia..............	24	6	30
North Carolina........	28	—	28
South Carolina........	13	—	13

TABLE 12 (*continued*)

Region and State	1960 Regular Votes	Bonus Votes	Total Votes
Georgia...............	24	—	24
Florida...............	20	6	26
Kentucky..............	20	6	26
Tennessee.............	22	6	28
Alabama..............	22	—	22
Mississippi............	12	—	12
Arkansas..............	16	—	16
Louisiana.............	20	6	26
Oklahoma.............	16	6	22
Texas................	48	6	54
	285	42	327
West			
Montana..............	8	6	14
Idaho................	8	6	14
Wyoming.............	6	6	12
Colorado.............	12	6	18
Utah.................	8	6	14
Nevada...............	6	6	12
New Mexico...........	8	6	14
Arizona..............	8	6	14
Washington...........	18	6	24
Oregon...............	12	6	18
California.............	64	6	70
Alaska...............	6	—	6
Hawaii...............	6	6	12
	170	72	242
Non-State Areas			
District of Columbia....	8	—	8
Puerto Rico...........	3	—	3
Virgin Islands.........	1	—	1
	12	—	12
Total..............	1,079	252	1,331

when there is a contest the big state delegations will be found in opposing groupings. In each group the big delegations may provide much of the leadership, tactical skill, and sheer mass for the battle; but they nonetheless tend to offset each other, thereby offering the power of decision to the uncommitted delegations, whether large or small. However, when the large states do happen to agree, there can seldom be a contest unless the other states unite closely in opposition, as rarely happens.

Apportionment Issues

Apportionment rules are seldom praised and often criticized. Their alleged deficiencies involve the problem of defining a just distribution of voting power—a problem not easily solved. As Alfred de Grazia has pointed out, "No system of apportionment and no system of suffrage, balloting, or counting is neutral. The process of apportionment is . . . a point of entry for preferred social values [and] institutionalizes the values of some group in society." *

EQUAL REPRESENTATION OF SOVEREIGN STATE UNITS

The principle of equal representation of sovereign states rather than of human voters is usually the only basis on which relatively weak but independent units of government can be persuaded to join with more powerful units in a voting system. It is currently reflected in the General Assembly of the United Nations, where every member nation has one vote, and in the Senate of the United States, where each state has two votes, although represented in the other House on the basis of population.

* "General Theory of Apportionment," in *Law and Contemporary Problems,* Vol. 17 (Spring 1952), p. 257.

As used in convention apportionment, the equal quota of regular delegates at large for every state as a part of its total apportionment has seldom been questioned, and never impaired, except as it has been muddied by the unequal addition of bonus votes. Most political leaders would probably say that its continued use is possibly desirable and in any case inevitable, in view of the established power relationships among the states.

Some political scientists contend, nonetheless, that recognition of state sovereignty in a national political convention is specious. Certainly the resemblance between a sovereign state and the state organization of a political party grows thin when the state party is weak or practically nonexistent. Logic points toward giving no sovereignty votes when a state shows no foreseeable prospect of contributing electoral votes to the party's national ticket. Nevertheless, the principle of state sovereignty in convention apportionment could still be useful as part of the total formula, if the major parties can become and remain sufficiently competitive through loyal state party organizations to justify giving the same kind of recognition to every state in the national conventions.

APPORTIONMENT RELATED TO THE
PARTY VOTE

The extent to which existing systems of apportionment have departed from the principle of equal representation of party voters is indicated by the following examples from the 1956 conventions. Nevada Democrats were more heavily represented proportionately than the party voters of any other party or state, with 11 votes in the convention for every 25,000 party voters in the 1952 presidential election. Wyoming Democrats placed next, with 7 votes for every 25,000 party voters, and

Nevada Republicans third, with 6 votes per 25,000. The most under-represented voters were the New York, Illinois, and California Republicans, with 6/10 of a delegate vote for every 25,000 party voters.

In general, the apportionment rules tend to over represent the small states and under represent the large. They also over represent the areas of low voter turnout and under represent those of high voter turnout. In states where one party is much stronger than the other, the rules tend to over represent the weaker party and under represent the stronger.

A formula to give equal representation to party voters in all states could be devised without too much difficulty, since this is the system used in most states for state party conventions. The respective national committees could be directed to apportion the votes for the next convention on the basis of the party vote as last recorded. Conventions of approximately the present size could be produced by giving each state a delegate vote for every 25,000 or 30,000 party voters in the previous election. The smaller states—Nevada, Wyoming, Vermont, and Delaware, for example—would have no more than three or four delegates apiece in the respective conventions. Regions with low voter turnout would also be penalized in both parties, and the change in power relationships within the conventions would be drastic.

A less disruptive plan could be based on a combination of equal representation of each state and equal representation of party voters—giving each state a quota of votes at large and also an allocation based on party vote, as was proposed in the Republican convention of 1908. Such a formula would reduce the representation of the small states now receiving bonus votes, increase that of most large states, have little effect upon states of average size and voter turnout, and substantially reduce the representation of the states in which voter turnout is low. All southern states would lose votes in both conventions, unless they took steps to increase turnout rates.

REWARD AS A CRITERION

Probably every partisan would agree in principle that the system of representation should encourage party growth and success—in any event not discourage it. But the recent systems of bonus votes are highly deficient as procedures for providing rewards and incentives, although presumably so intended. They give easy rewards where victory is automatic, as in the dominant party in a one-party state, and frequently fail to provide rewards where they are deserved, as in heavily contested states where national political tides may bring defeat regardless of devoted local party effort. By 1956 each party had relaxed the requirements so much that the incentive feature of the bonus votes had virtually disappeared.

The system is arbitrary and unsatisfactory in giving a uniform reward for victory in a small or large state, thus adding to the over representation of the small states. In 1956 bonus votes equaled or exceeded other votes in Rhode Island, Montana, Wyoming, Nevada, New Mexico, and Arizona (Democratic); Vermont, Delaware, Wyoming, and Nevada (Republican). The extent to which, in 1960, small states were over represented, and large states under represented, is shown in Table 13.

If bonus votes are to be given at all, form should be brought into accord with reality. There is nothing inherent in the concept of such votes that requires the same number to be given to all states that qualify. A bonus vote could be given, for example, at the rate of one vote for every three electoral votes contributed by the state party in the presidential election; on that basis in 1956 a small state with three electoral votes could

TABLE 13. VOTING STRENGTH OF THE STATES IN
1960, BY POPULATION GROUPINGS
(in percentage of total)

States by Population Groupings	Population, 1960 Census[a]	Electoral College Vote	Democratic		Republican	
			Popular Democratic Vote[b]	Convention Votes	Popular Republican Vote[b]	Convention Votes
Twelve Most Populous States	58.5%	50.8%	64.5%	46.4%	62.9%	46.1%
Twenty-six Middle States	36.2	41.4	31.6	42.6	33.0	41.7
Twelve Least Populous States	3.5	7.8	3.9	9.8	4.1	11.3
Non-State Areas	1.8	—	—	1.2	—	.9
Total	100.0	100.0	100.0	100.0	100.0	100.0

[a] Population of United States including District of Columbia, plus outlying areas represented at national party conventions: Puerto Rico, Virgin Islands, Canal Zone.
[b] Major-party popular vote for President in 1960.

have received one bonus vote, while New York, with its forty-five electoral votes, could have qualified for fifteen. The bonus basis could also be limited to presidential elections, the ones of greatest relevance to the functions of a national convention.

Apportionment Within States

There are many different ways in which a state's quota of votes can be assigned or distributed *within* the state, and there is a further issue in the extent to which the state parties are allowed to exercise authority in the matter. The Democrats have always been more inclined than the Republicans to leave freedom to the state parties in these matters.

The bonus systems introduced a substantial element of uncertainty and fluctuation in the assignment of convention seats—met almost invariably by permitting the number of delegates at large to fluctuate while holding the number of district delegates constant. The places for delegates at large are frequently assigned to distinguished party members as a special form of patronage and recognition. In many states the number of individuals with claims for recognition has been so great that there has been constant pressure to increase the number of places for such delegates. This has undoubtedly been a major reason for the development and misuse of the bonus votes.

ALL-OR-NONE VS. PROPORTIONAL REPRESENTATION

In convention experience, it soon became apparent that apportionment of delegates to congressional districts was of little importance if state delegations were to be voted as units without regard to the district constituencies. As a question of policy, the issue has often been argued at state party conventions: should delegates be committed to a single candidate, giving no representation to the minority choice, or should there be some informal proportionate distribution of delegateships among all candidates that have appreciable support in the state?

The issue was especially acute in the Republican party in 1952. Party leaders in several states were deeply stirred over whether the party's inner conflicts on Taft vs. Eisenhower should be fought out on a winner-take-all basis or should be compromised by awarding delegate seats to each faction on an agreed basis. In many states where either Taft or Eisenhower supporters could hope to dominate the proceedings through solid working majorities at district or state levels, the natural impulse was to exploit their advantage to the fullest in view of the prospective close division at the national convention. But all-or-none tactics on behalf of one candidate, in a situation where he was winning, tended to provoke similar tactics on behalf of the other, where *he* had the upper hand, as was documented time after time in the unfolding chronology of the struggle. There were some states, however, where both candidates were short of a majority and uncommitted elements occupied a strategic position. In such cases a proportionate distribution was a frequent result.

In the multiple candidacy situations that are more usually typical of nominating contests, state parties, by composing a balanced slate of delegates, are able to avoid committing their entire strength. They also thus avoid staking all of their interests on a single outcome at the convention and can maintain potentially friendly relations among opposing factions in preparation for the later election contest—where in union there is strength.

Contests for delegate support on a state-wide, all-or-none basis, as in the California primary, intensify the burden of a candidate going into a state to campaign, and thus the weak contenders (other than favorite sons in their own states) are generally frightened off. If the system were used in many states, the number of contestants might narrow down by alliance or defection until only two or three, possibly only one, remained for choice by the convention. This might expedite decision in the convention, but would also seem likely to embitter the divisions within the parties and obstruct the restoration of party unity for the election campaign.

The selection of district delegates through procedures that maintain district autonomy permits a series of small all-or-none contests, whether in primaries or party conventions, without necessarily leading to rigid commitments that may be costly later on. Separate district elections provide direct representation for relatively small units of party opinion and occasionally result in the election of mixed delegations made up of supporters of two or more different candidates. Such elections in the districts are thus in effect intermediate between all-or-none and proportional representation systems for the state as a whole.

The Unit Rule

In one form or another, the unit rule has been used to some extent in the Democratic party throughout its history. It has been a perennial source of conflict within individual delegations, with requests for rulings by the chair at almost every convention. The Republican party never adopted it as a part of its national rules, though it was an issue for a time. In the Democratic party, it was held after the advent of the presidential primaries that the unit rule could not be enforced for any state that elected delegates in a primary. For this and other reasons, fewer than half of the Democratic delegations have used the rule in recent years.

To both parties the unit rule was for a time an expression of the difference between them in regard to states' rights versus convention rights. At the Democratic convention of 1884 a move to abolish the rule was sparked by the minority within the New York delegation that opposed Grover Cleveland's nomination, but its retention was sustained after an extended debate in which the states' rights position was summed up by a Wisconsin delegate:

> I know, Mr. President, that in the Republican party—a party which believes that Congress and the Federal Government have every power which is not expressly denied, and that the States have hardly any rights left which the Federal Government is bound to respect—they can adopt in their Convention this idea that the State does not control its own Delegation in a National

Convention. Not so in the Convention of the great Democratic party. We stand, Mr. President, for the rights of the States. We do not, by declaring ourselves in favor of the rights of the States, declare that the Federal Government has not its rights also; and the Federal law and the Federal Constitution have provided that the votes for President shall be by States, and the voice of the State shall be obeyed by its Delegates.

In the Republican convention of 1876, the Pennsylvania delegation arrived with unit voting instructions. When the vote was challenged, the chair ruled "that it is the right of any and of every member equally, to vote his sentiments in this convention." The ruling was sustained. During the course of the debate a Kansas delegate stated the theory behind the Republican practice:

> The principle which is involved in this controversy, is whether the state of Pennsylvania shall make laws for this convention; or whether this convention is supreme and shall make its own laws. We are supreme. We are original. We stand here representing the great Republican party of the United States, and neither Pennsylvania nor New York nor any state can come in here and bind us down with caucus resolutions. More than that . . . the great principles of the Republican organization demand that each man shall have his vote himself, and not be bound up by some party or power that is behind him. . . . The convention . . . has the right, and it is its duty, its beholden duty, to let each delegate here represent the sentiments of his constituents, and not compel him to vote as anybody shall dictate.

MERITS AND CONSEQUENCES

The merits of the unit rule have been argued in terms of theories of federalism, of party organization, of representation, and of majority rule. In theory at least, the rule gives effect to majority sentiment within a state party and helps maintain the federal nature of a national party organization; it is also said to help maintain the integrity of a state party, since a majority can simply override dissident elements, without resort to other forms of pressure and persuasion.

Delegates with a direct relationship to a district constituency argue against the rule, insisting that mandates originating in smaller territorial units are closer to the popular will and more likely to be expressive of popular sentiment within the party. Minority factions in unit rule delegations argue that fair play, willing consent, and freedom to vote as they see fit would be more conducive to harmony in state party organizations than a rule that binds delegates against their will. This reasoning has apparently been persuasive in a number of states where the rule has been abandoned.

A state party has undoubtedly often imposed a unit rule on its delegation to keep intact the greatest possible voting weight in the convention voting. When a delegation is allowed to divide its vote, part of the delegation merely cancels the other part. The state's influence on the nominating decision is visibly reduced, and its bargaining position in national party councils weakened. Use of the rule can either almost double or entirely eliminate the influence of a faction within a delegation; thirteen votes, for example, may decide how the entire twenty-five votes of a delegation shall be cast, each of the twelve votes submerged by the majority being worth exactly zero. The constituency of one delegate then finds its mandate multiplied, another finds its mandate dissipated. The submerged minority votes may possibly mean the difference between victory and defeat for a candidate.

The charge has been made repeatedly that the unit

rule can intentionally be used to nominate candidates with a minority of the delegates. To estimate the actual consequences is in fact an extremely difficult matter, because sufficient information is usually lacking. For the 1952 and 1956 Democratic conventions, however, a fair amount of information is available—and it indicates that the winning candidates received fewer unit rule votes than their opponents.

The rule has been chiefly used in recent years to concentrate the voting strength of the southern faction that has been in chronic disagreement with the rest of the Democratic party. It seems reasonable to suspect that the rule has been allowed to survive mainly as a concession to the southerners. In any event, with the rule no longer available in states such as New York, Pennsylvania, and Illinois, and with its voluntary abandonment in other states, its retention where it still exists seems unfair and should no longer be permitted.

The Two Thirds Rule

The nominating procedures of the Democratic party were governed for more than a century by variations of the rule adopted in 1832—"that two thirds of the whole number of votes given be required to a nomination." The Jacksonians who so readily took the idea from the Antimasons were remarkably blind to its strength as a weapon their factional opponents could also use.

The consequences of the rule were clearly apparent on many occasions. In 1844, as noted in Chapter 3, it was a direct cause of Martin Van Buren's failure to secure the presidential nomination; he polled a majority for seven ballots, but without attaining the necessary two thirds, before the convention shifted to Polk. In

1852, the rule probably prevented a renomination for Lewis Cass, the titular leader; Franklin Pierce won on the forty-ninth ballot. In 1856, it was apparent that Pierce could not be renominated under the two thirds rule (or perhaps any other rule); Buchanan was nominated on the seventeenth ballot. The record from 1832 to 1860, taken as a whole, suggests that the rule was a major factor in producing the weak executive leadership of the period, since its effect was to eliminate anyone of sufficient character to arouse serious opposition.

Efforts to abolish the rule accompanied its use through the years. The finally successful effort began as part of the preconvention campaign for Franklin D. Roosevelt's nomination in 1932. Four days before the convention opened, a meeting of some 150 Roosevelt supporters adopted a resolution presented by Senator Huey Long, pledging them to do all within their power to abolish the rule. The other contenders for the nomination, among them Al Smith, were vehement in their protests; as a strategy, the abolition would obviously make front-runner Roosevelt harder to block. Sam Rayburn warned James A. Farley that if Roosevelt wanted to win the nomination he would have to play according to the rules of the game. Opposition to the move came even from some of Roosevelt's own supporters, who deplored the timing of the effort as unfair. On the second day of the convention the Roosevelt forces accepted defeat. The rules committee then recommended a resolution to consider changing the rule in 1936; the resolution was adopted by a convention voice vote.

In 1936, nearly 900 delegates came to the convention committed to changing the rule. The opposition to repeal was led by Texas Governor James V. Allred, Representative Eugene E. Cox of Georgia, and Senator

Harry F. Byrd of Virginia. When the committee's report finally came to the floor of the convention, the repeal of the rule was moved by Senator Bennett Champ Clark of Missouri, whose father had lost the nomination to Woodrow Wilson in 1912 through the operation of the rule. The action was then taken by voice vote and without a floor fight—a strangely mild end for a device that had caused conflict for a hundred years.

Proposals to restore the rule have been a favorite rallying cry in the South ever since—and it is hard to tell which, if any, have been put forward for more than trading purposes. But the values that men live by have always been deeply involved in both sides of the historic controversy over the rule. As a means of accommodating the views of respectable minorities, it was and is defended by many public-spirited men. But it could also permit an embattled minority to frustrate the will of a respectable majority, although nominating decisions must be made, or a party dies. When accommodation proves impossible, the only alternative to majority rule is minority rule. In the Republican party, which has been rather clearly bifactional throughout much of its history, the two thirds rule would probably have endangered if not prevented the nominations of Lincoln and Eisenhower, and would have made decision difficult in many other cases.

It seems clear that the Democratic minority who still advocate a return to the rule desire to frustrate the majority within the party. So used, the effect would be to favor again the nomination of weak men for the Presidency, in the face of the evident preference of the American public for a strong executive. Since the Democratic majority is fully aware of the frustrating effects of the rule, it seems unlikely to be readopted, despite agitation to that end that may continue for another generation.

Massive Size and Its Consequences

A national party convention was originally intended to approximate the size of the Senate and House of Representatives in joint session; this would have produced a convention of 535 members in 1964. Even that number would have produced many awkward problems —but the conventions have repeatedly moved in the direction of even greater numbers. In the 1960 Democratic convention this reached an extreme of about 3,000 seated delegates, with an authorized voting strength of 1,521. The Republican convention seated 1,331 delegates, all on a full-vote basis. The authorized alternate delegates for each convention numbered more than 1,300.

Size was further swelled by the many non-voting but important participants who have been a notable feature of all recent conventions—among them the convention officers, the outgoing national committee members, and the innumerable guests who are distinguished enough to claim special recognition, such as present and former party governors and senators who failed to achieve convention status. The representatives of the special interest groups that attempt in some way to influence convention action usually number several hundreds. The staffing of press, radio, and television operations in 1956 brought an estimated 1,700 persons to the Republican convention, 2,500 to the Democratic convention, and more in 1960.

With these groups, and many others of less determinate identity, the total mass of involved persons in the immediate environment of recent conventions has usually exceeded 5,000—and at the Democratic convention of 1960 was undoubtedly well above 10,000.

The consequences of such massive size influence

every aspect of convention action. The choice of meeting place is in the first place limited; very few cities can provide the facilities such numbers require. The state delegations are hampered in all of their operations, both by lack of privacy and by the unwieldy proportions to which many of them have grown. On the convention floor, every formal procedure is distorted by the confusion and noise that are in part factors of size. Speeches from the rostrum and the give-and-take of debate from the floor, beating against the background disorder, are seldom closely followed by anyone. Communications between floor leaders and the rostrum often break down; signals are then resorted to, or messages sent by runner. When votes are taken, the voice vote becomes an extremely hazardous instrument for decision. Both routine matters and those not so routine are sometimes gaveled through one after the other, with no one voting or even actually listening. Roll call votes remain as the final recourse, but they too are made immensely more difficult to achieve accurately.

And yet all of the individuals who collectively are responsible for this monstrous meeting have some legitimate personal or institutional reason for being there. Probably nearly every one of them contributes in some degree to the operations of the party system and the nominating process. The conventions and the preconvention activities require the work of so many people so directly that it is difficult to see how massive size can be prevented.

Admitting this, it is evident that in recent years both conventions have pushed close to the limits of operational feasibility. In 1960, the Democratic convention would have been in great danger of total breakdown if it had encountered controversies as difficult as those debated and voted on in 1952.

The parties need to give thought to all means by

which they might clarify representation, while improving the meeting's internal structure as a working organization. Such means might include the following proposals:

1. Authorize each delegation to appoint from three to five knowledgeable delegation consultants capable of giving advice when needed.
2. Return the Democratic convention to a delegate strength no larger than the authorized voting strength by eliminating all fractional votes.
3. Eliminate alternates except as replacements for delegates-elect who fail to appear at the convention, and allocate the space thus gained to the delegates for use by their official visitors.

In a national party there is inevitably a discrepancy between the requirements for long-term integrity and survival and the pressure of expediency and short-range gains. The discrepancy has recently been growing in both parties, with expediency taking the upper hand—and the dangerous over representation of the conventions as the result. There are many arguments on the side of expediency: the importance of the convention as a campaign rally; the desirability of involving as many party workers and contributors as possible; the usefulness of having plenty of patronage available in the form of convention seats for the faithful; the benefits of compromising factional fights by seating both factions. But there are also limits beyond which the practical operation of the conventions cannot be impaired without endangering the success or even the survival of the parties they represent. Recently, the Republicans have done a better job than the Democrats in protecting the integrity of central party institutions; however, neither party's record deserves praise.

Most political institutions that survive develop a core

of elder statesmen who guard their traditions by reminding those with shorter memories of what has always happened when too many concessions are made to expediency. So far, the national parties have not developed the kind of farsighted and continuing leadership that stabilized the size of the House of Representatives at 435 members for nearly half a century, and again returned it to that level after admitting Alaska and Hawaii and adjusting for the census of 1960. The parties need such leadership.

10

Presidential Primary Systems

■

As representative institutions, the party conventions from the beginning were involved in the classic question of the relationship between a representative and his constituents. Is the delegate a mere agent, carrying an express mandate of detailed instruction to which he is firmly committed in advance? Or is he supposed to embody the conscience of a certain constituency, with an implied mandate to exercise his judgment in accordance with his own view of his constituents' best interests? If he finds himself in a minority position, at what point, if any, does it become permissible or obligatory to submerge the desires of his constituents, and possibly his own, for the sake of the unity of the whole body?

The presidential primary laws that began to appear in the early 1900's gave these issues a new and sharper form. Originating as an effort to bring the nominating process under the fullest measure of popular control, the elections that have come to be known as presidential primaries took on varying shapes in response to many conflicting motivations. Most of them provided for both the election of delegates to the conventions and an expression of preference among presidential candidates. The relationship between the two features was complex and variable.

The first known election of delegates in a public primary occurred in Florida in 1904, under legislation empowering any recognized political party to hold general primary elections; the Democrats used the opportunity to elect their national convention delegates, and continued to do so thereafter. In 1906, Pennsylvania provided for general primaries that included the election of district delegates, but the provision was not used until 1912.

The first law directed specifically at the election of convention delegates seems to have been the one enacted in Wisconsin in 1905. There was no provision for any form of presidential preference; nevertheless, under the new law the partisans of Senator Robert M. La Follette were able to elect a delegation in 1908 that fought hard for the Progressive credo. In 1910, Oregon enacted a measure that provided both direct election of all district delegates and a presidential preference vote for their guidance. The statute was hailed as part of the Progressive movement, and its formula was seized upon by the Progressive supporters of Theodore Roosevelt to aid their campaign to unseat President Taft. The result was a wave of legislation; by 1912 a total of fourteen states had authorized some form of presidential primary, and by 1916 the number had grown to at least twenty-two.

Thereafter the wave slowly declined, although there was a slight resurgence after World War II. Several states used their primary for only a few years, then repealed the law or let it fall into disuse. Since nearly half of the states in the country never enacted a presidential primary law, the movement's evolution has gone on mainly through amendments in the states where the idea started.

Existing primary laws differ one from the other so much that it is difficult to develop any satisfactory classifications under which to discuss them. As a first step, however, the systems in which delegate election is the major feature can be distinguished from those that emphasize a presidential preference poll.

Delegate Election Systems

Fifteen states and the District of Columbia elected convention delegates in presidential primaries in 1960. Mandates were obtained principally through the election process itself, except in one state—Oregon—where the mandate derived from a presidential preference poll. The following set of categories provides the most generally useful classification of the other systems used.

CATEGORY ONE: Ballot *must not* show the delegate's preference among candidates; delegates *must* run on a "no-preference" basis so far as the ballot is concerned.

New York, Pennsylvania, Illinois, West Virginia, Alabama, Nebraska.*

* The District of Columbia was included in this category in 1956. For 1960, however, the election board reinterpreted the law to permit two indirect presidential-preference questions on the ballots, whereby *voters* could instruct the winning delegates. Candidate names could appear only with consent. Thus the D.C. system in 1960 in effect fits none of the categories here (and may be subject to further change by 1964), although the Category One strictures still hold in regard to *delegates'* preferences. The Republicans did not use the device; the Democrats did use it, but their ballots carried only two names as presidential candidates—Wayne Morse and Hubert H. Humphrey.

CATEGORY TWO: Ballot *may* show delegate's prefer-
                 ence *if* the candidate consents;
                 delegates may also run on a "no-
                 preference" basis.
                 South Dakota, Massachusetts, New
                 Jersey.

CATEGORY THREE: Ballot *may* show delegate's prefer-
                 ence, whether or not the candidate
                 consents; delegates may also run
                 on a "no-preference" basis.
                 New Hampshire, Florida.

CATEGORY FOUR: Ballot *must* show delegate's prefer-
                 ence for a candidate who has given
                 consent; delegates *must not* run on
                 a "no-preference" basis.
                 California, Ohio, Wisconsin.

Within each category, the system of each state has differences from the others. The discussion below first notes these differences, then treats the general characteristics of the whole category as it operated in 1952, 1956, and 1960. Between 1960 and 1964 there were almost no changes in the laws. A California statute of 1961, however, authorized the filing of unpledged delegate states. Thus the California primary will in the future have the characteristics of Category Two Systems.

CATEGORY ONE

In this earliest form of presidential primary the would-be delegates cannot identify themselves on the ballot as supporters of a particular presidential candidate. In New York, Pennsylvania, and Illinois, the party organizations usually make the nominations for district delegate. The few contests that occur usually reflect local factionalism rather than attitudes toward the national candidates. The delegates arrive at the convention with mandates mainly derived either from their party organizations or from supporting factions. Thus in some cases they are firmly committed to a candidate, in others, firmly occupying a position of noncommitment. All delegates at large are named directly by the party organizations, and always include political figures of some note.

In Alabama, West Virginia, and Nebraska, the party organizations are relatively much weaker and have less control over delegate selection in the primaries. Contests are the rule in most districts, and often occur state-wide for the seats at large; a delegate wins his seat mainly as the result of personal and factional influences, and thus is largely on his own, with no express mandate.

In the District of Columbia in 1956 unofficial slate-making and distributions of sample ballots served to identify the would-be delegates and provided an opportunity to campaign for the presidential candidates. (The 1960 change has been noted earlier.) In the other cases of Category One, would-be delegates have seldom campaigned as announced supporters of a preferred candidate, since they may not state a preference on the ballot. The candidates, in turn, rarely take any direct part in the formation of delegate slates or in the delegate campaigns. Such mandates as may be created under such circumstances are usually implied rather than express, general rather than specific. To the extent that they become specific, they are apt to be negative—delegates know that certain candidates would not be acceptable to their constituency but usually have considerable freedom of choice among acceptable alternatives.

CATEGORY TWO

The South Dakota primary, unlike that of any other state except California, elects all delegates at large. The delegates are not voted on individually, so that its ballot is simpler than that of Massachusetts or New Jersey.

Contests between delegations supporting leading national candidates have been more welcome in South Dakota than in Massachusetts or New Jersey and have occurred more frequently.

In all three states, delegation commitment to a stand-in or favorite son candidate has been rare; the device is not needed, since "no-preference" ballots are permissible—and in any case none of the three has been productive of the type of candidate who is merely a favorite son. Massachusetts and New Jersey provide a separate presidential preference vote, which the party organizations in both states seem to tolerate only because the poll is purely advisory.

In practice, delegations from all three states are alike in usually carrying no more of an express mandate than a New York delegation. Only occasionally has there been an express mandate resulting from the election of delegates who indicated their preference on the ballot with the candidate's consent.

Since would-be delegates in the states of Category Two are not required to name a preferred candidate on the ballot and can do so only with his consent, "no-preference" delegations are frequently elected without a contest or with only scattered opposition. This may occur even when a lively convention contest is in prospect—if the state party organization prefers to send an uncommitted delegation with freedom to maneuver; if dissident factions see little reason to expect success with a contesting slate; if out-of-state candidates prefer to avoid being involved. In such cases, these systems operate in much the same way as those in Category One.

Under other conditions, Category Two can offer a focused contest between opposing slates and candidates. When thus challenged, even an ostensibly "no-preference" slate is likely to publicize its candidate preferences in the effort to attract votes. The voters are then given a meaningful choice, and the mandates, even if only implied, are likely to be affirmative and specific, and also likely to be executed with vigor at the convention.

CATEGORY THREE

In 1952 and 1956, New Hampshire, Florida, and Oregon permitted would-be delegates to identify their preferred presidential candidate on the ballot without his consent. In past years New Jersey and Wisconsin also used this type of primary. Oregon also provides for a separate presidential preference poll which commits the delegates without regard to their stated preference, a feature of such peculiar moment that the state is not discussed here but in the later section on mandatory preference polls.

In Florida in 1952, and in Wisconsin and New Hampshire over a long period of years, popular preferences were usually given effective expression through the delegate election, because the would-be delegates could identify their candidate preferences on the ballot. However, in New Hampshire and Wisconsin, whose primaries were held early in the election year, the delegates often had difficulty finding out whether their preferred candidates would be available.

A new system effective in Florida in 1956 greatly simplified the voter's task. Every would-be delegate was required to become part of an organized slate in order to get on the ballot; with the relationship between slates and their preferred candidates thus more apparent, voter attention was concentrated on the presidential candidates. The system was potentially a powerful instrument for popular choice, as demonstrated in the contest between Kefauver and Stevenson in 1956. In 1960, however, there was no contest in either party.

The Republican delegation was committed to Nixon, the Democratic to favorite son George Smathers, with Kennedy staying out. In all of the Category Three states, a preferred candidate can be named on the ballot without his consent. "No-preference" delegations have sometimes run and been elected, when candidate availabilities were not clear at the time of filing, or when the choice was viewed with apathy, but more usually the successful delegations are those that express their choice on the ballot. In open nominating situations, the primaries are usually contested, impelling would-be delegates to seek association with a popular candidate who will help them win. Candidates are encouraged to campaign, but no initiative has been required of those who were reluctant or unwilling—and even some of these have been handed the fruits of victory. In critical years, the voters have usually been offered a meaningful choice. The resulting mandates have been express, affirmative, and specific, and have been carried out at the conventions almost without exception.

CATEGORY FOUR

The mandating systems of the four states in this category in 1956—California, Ohio, Wisconsin, and Minnesota—differed distinctly in their formal aspects. (In 1959 Minnesota repealed its primary law and went back to the party convention system.) California required delegates to pledge in writing to support their candidate to the best of their judgment and ability. Ohio exacted no written pledge. Wisconsin and Minnesota both required written pledges that delegates would vote for their candidates, unless released, on the first ballot and thereafter until the candidate's vote dropped below 10 per cent of the total convention vote. However, under all of the systems in actual operation, the approval of a presidential candidate was required before delegate aspirants could get on the ballot.

In its separate origins in each state, this aspect of the system was less the result of clear and logical intentions than of conflicting motivations and accident. In any event, in all four states would-be delegates, for lack of a serious candidate willing to enter the primary, were often forced to run under the name of a stand-in or an undistinguished favorite son, who often won with little or no opposition. Delegates so elected were not likely to take their mandate seriously, since it did not validly reflect the views of the party voters. They might vote for their ostensible candidate at the convention when it was strategically desirable to do so on early ballots, as a holding operation; often, however, they voted for one of the serious candidates on the first ballot. Delegations pledged to favorite son candidates with enough strength to merit national attention were another matter; even when elected without a contest, they took their mandate seriously and rarely left their candidate until definitely released.

In the past, systems of this kind rarely placed more than one of the serious national contestants before the voters, because such candidates were usually reluctant to challenge a favorite son slate. In the future, however, the systems may be peculiarly susceptible to the effects of new styles of national campaigning. Willing candidates who are prepared to challenge a favorite son if necessary can find substantial opportunities in these states—as Harold Stassen, Estes Kefauver, and John F. Kennedy each demonstrated to the discomfiture of the favorite sons and party organizations concerned. And when one aggressive candidate is prepared to enter all available primaries, other serious candidates may have little choice except to do likewise. California, especially, may not often be allowed to lock up the great prize of its convention strength behind an unchallenged favorite son, unless he has genuine national strength.

Presidential Preference Polls

The term "presidential preference poll" is used to denote a vote on the candidates, separate from the election of delegates. (The California and Wisconsin primaries are not so termed, even though the voting is concerned almost entirely with candidates for presidential nominations, to whose names favoring slates of delegates are attached for election.) According to the intent of the statute creating a poll, the resulting mandate may be either advisory or compulsory. In either case, the delegates who receive the mandate may be elected in primaries or may be chosen by the party organization, usually in a state convention. In the early fervor of 1912, it was assumed that the outcome of a poll would control a delegation regardless of how the delegates had been selected. Disillusionment followed. The distinction between polls that are merely advisory and those intended to be mandatory was only gradually clarified in law and practice.

ADVISORY PREFERENCE POLLS

Seven of the states which elect delegates in primaries —New Hampshire, Massachusetts, New Jersey, Pennsylvania, West Virginia, Illinois, and Nebraska—have preference polls that are treated as advisory.

The validity of the advice given by any poll depends mainly on whether the voters have had a chance to express themselves on the candidates likely to be voted upon at the convention. The polls usually allow write-in votes, but there is often a problem in assessing their importance. The Massachusetts ballot, however, provides a designated blank space in which the voter may insert his choice of a presidential candidate for his designated political party. Since no candidate names appear on this part of the ballot, the device avoids the problems of filing dates, petitions, and candidate consent, thus facilitating assessment of the relative merits of the write-in vote. Under this system, Eisenhower was a two and one half to one choice over Taft in Massachusetts in 1952.

Any advisory poll always creates the possibility of conflicting mandates—one expressed by the poll, the other expressed or implied through the process of delegate selection. If its mandate is to be useful, the poll itself must express an informed popular judgment so clearly that it can be treated with respect, but this result has seldom been achieved. Kennedy's victory over Hubert H. Humphrey in the West Virginia preference poll in 1960 was a noteworthy exception. Even so, only 15 of the 25 West Virginia votes were cast for Kennedy at the convention.

MANDATORY PREFERENCE POLLS

In three states—Oregon, Maryland, and Indiana—polls were in effect in 1956 and 1960 that attempted specifically to control delegate action. The delegates were elected separately in the primary in Oregon, in party conventions in the other two states.

Oregon has revised its presidential primary laws repeatedly, attempting to find means for the greatest expression of the popular will. By various devices it has tried to place all principal candidates on the ballot, whether they are willing or not, and to make the outcome binding on the delegates elected in the same primary.

All three systems allowed the risk of giving instructions to delegates who might be not only indifferent but actually opposed to the mandate they were receiving—

the natural consequence of separating delegate selection from the mandating process. Delegates disliking their mandates have often sabotaged their ostensible candidates on procedural votes, even while dutifully voting for them on the first nominating ballots.

Open vs. Closed Primaries

Presidential primaries are usually open only to the registered voters of each political party concerned. Some states, however, notably Wisconsin and Minnesota, have used the so-called "open primary," which requires no party registration and permits voting in the primary of either party (but not both). This frequently leads to charges that voters of one party invade the primary of the other party for the alleged purpose of nominating the candidate who would be easiest to beat. However, the migration more probably happens because voters wish to support the kind of nominee offered by the other party but not by their own, and will vote for him in the general election if he is nominated, whether or not they have any intention of changing party affiliation permanently.

In Wisconsin in 1952 there was some evidence that Democrats moved into the Republican presidential primary in support of Warren against Taft. In the Minnesota primary of 1956, where Kefauver defeated Stevenson for most of the Democratic delegation at a time when there was no important Republican contest, Stevenson campaign leaders promptly charged Republican collusion—by which 125,000 voters had crossed party lines to stop the strongest Democratic candidate. The situation probably indicated both a substantial bona fide Republican farm vote for Kefauver and a considerable Republican crossover that appeared to be deliberately intended to confuse the issue for the Democratic party. Without the crossover, Stevenson might have won the primary by a small majority. All of these circumstances were widely discussed in Minnesota and undoubtedly had their part in discrediting the primary law, and hastening its repeal.

The "open" basis seems especially hazardous for presidential primaries that produce a focused race between candidates. When an exciting contest is going on in one party, voters of the other party may become almost equally involved emotionally, especially when their own party has no contest worth the name. They may then have strong incentives to migrate into the rival primary; this suggests that states insisting on an open primary for other purposes would do better not to attempt the more complex types of presidential primary.

Effects on Participants

PRESIDENTIAL CANDIDATES, ACTUAL AND POTENTIAL

THE PRESIDENT. Most of the primary elections initiated in 1912 had the immediate purpose of pulling down the incumbent first-term President, William Howard Taft, and he ran badly in them. Hoover also ran badly in the primaries occurring toward the end of his first term. President Coolidge, on the other hand, entered and won most of the 1924 primaries that were available, demonstrating his popular appeal at a time when he was not entirely confident of organization support. In 1940, President Roosevelt's waiting tactics on a third-term nomination were assisted by a series of primary victories, and in 1948, President Truman's primary record was impressive.

The party organizations usually enter a first-term President, unless he objects, in the available primaries expecting to use them as part of the mechanism for beating down dissident candidates and party factionalism. To a President who finds his political support in a massive popular following, the primaries can be helpful, but as instruments of the popular will they can harass an unpopular President.

OUT-PARTY TITULAR LEADERS. Wendell Willkie's candidacy was ended by the primaries of 1944. Thomas E. Dewey, entering most of the available primaries in 1948, lost to Stassen in Wisconsin and Nebraska, then defeated him in Oregon and was able to enter the convention as the favorite. In 1956, Adlai Stevenson was reluctant at first to do extensive primary campaigning, but after losing in New Hampshire and Minnesota, he recognized that he could not win at the convention without evidence of some success in the primaries. With changed tactics and intensified campaigning he gained the victories in Oregon, Florida, and California that did much to win him the nomination.

The record suggests that any titular leader who wishes to run for the Presidency should make himself available in any primaries where his presence on the ticket is strongly desired, either by the local party organization or by factions capable of putting up an effective slate. Reluctance is very likely to be interpreted as an admission of weakness.

OTHER WILLING CANDIDATES. Candidates who seek the active cooperation of the state organizations usually negotiate carefully to assure a welcome before entering a primary, stay out of contests with favorite sons, and avoid other contests unless the chances of victory are reasonably good. The Florida, New Hampshire, and Oregon systems present special problems for a candidate of this kind, since a name can be entered without the candidate's consent. In 1960 the Kennedy forces avoided engagement in Florida, on condition that the Johnson forces would do likewise. In New Hampshire, Kennedy won unopposed, while in Oregon he defeated favorite son Wayne Morse.

For willing candidates who are prepared to enter any and all primaries, with or without the cooperation of the state party organizations concerned, these three systems are as useful as any others. Stassen and Kefauver each came to national attention as presidential timber largely because of their striking victories in some of the primaries. In the end, both began to suffer defeats, but they had meanwhile forced the party organizations and the other candidates to take the primaries more seriously.

OTHER POTENTIAL CANDIDATES. The Florida, New Hampshire, and Oregon primaries are also exceptional in the extent to which they can be used to promote a reluctant candidate when the situation is appropriate. If the candidacy requires either a draft or a substantial showing of popular support to make it actual—as that of General Eisenhower in 1952 before his decision to return from Paris—Florida and New Hampshire permit a slate of favoring delegates to organize and perhaps be elected without any action whatever by the candidate, and the Oregon law has a similar effect through different mechanisms. The potential candidate is not harassed by this use of his name, because the supporters are expressing their views, not his.

A somewhat different situation was presented by Dewey's candidacy in the early months of 1944. Dewey was a potential candidate of high availability, but could well have had his own reasons for preferring not to run until four years later. Partial slates were nevertheless organized for him in New Hampshire and Wisconsin;

Dewey withdrew his name from the preference poll in each state, but his supporters persisted in running for delegate seats. The two delegates pledged to him in New Hampshire were elected, and most of the Dewey slate was elected in Wisconsin. A few weeks later Dewey announced his active candidacy.

PARTY ORGANIZATIONS

The national conventions of both parties had to adjust their rules in 1912 and 1916 to accommodate to primary laws. For the Democrats, the weakening of the unit rule was an important result, but in general the primaries seem not to have deprived either national party organization of important functions. The convention retains its vitality as the nominating authority and as the base where coalitions are organized to work for victory in the election.

The party organizations in the states, however, have felt the impact. If it is true that deprivation of function leads to atrophy, the primaries that have transferred the election and instructing of delegates away from the state party organizations have presumably tended to weaken those organizations. The actual extent of transfer has been variable. An uncomplicated primary election of district delegates, as in New York, may do little to prevent the effective nomination of the delegates by a strong organization where it exists. Where there is no strong organization, a primary system like that of New York or the District of Columbia will do little to promote one, on behalf of either a candidate or the party.

Wherever would-be delegates can be identified with a candidate on the primary ballot, a state organization faces the threat of invasion by a Stassen or a Kefauver, with a party-splitting fight as the minimum consequence. If an actual invasion is successful, control of delegate selection is lost for the time being unless terms have been made in advance for a compromise. The whole affair may leave the organization seriously weakened, at a time when strength is needed for the oncoming national election campaign. Organizations can claim with some justice that the primary systems which give maximum popular control may tend to weaken either party and are therefore not desirable in states with strong two-party competition. The argument is largely irrelevant, however, concerning states dominated by one party or those where state-wide organization is weak—many of which, in fact, have never introduced a presidential primary system.

Which Primaries Are Effective?

Each of the existing primary systems has some features that can be called self-defeating, but there appears to be a rather broad range of effectiveness within which what is lost from one point of view may be gained from another. Within this range, the total effects of the various systems involve so many imponderables that an exact assessment of net comparative advantage is not easy to make.

INEFFECTIVE SYSTEMS AND PROVISIONS

Any of the systems that are built on preference polls separated from delegate election may be gravely hampered in performing their intended functions, because they are fundamentally incapable of assuring that the elected delegates will be in sympathy with the mandate provided through the preference poll. The poll also distracts the attention of voters from the process of delegate election—and it is the delegates who will vote in the convention, with or without heeding mandates.

The West Virginia system is one of those just referred to, and the West Virginia experience in 1960 was no exception to these conclusions. The delegates were elected without much regard to the contest between Kennedy and Humphrey for the preference vote, and, as previously noted, only 15 of the state's 25 votes were given to Kennedy at the convention, despite his striking victory in the preference vote. That vote found its importance almost entirely outside the state and through its effect on sentiment elsewhere. Perhaps this demonstrates that any preference vote in a sharply focused contest may take on national importance under present conditions, but the conditions that made the issue important in West Virginia in 1960 were so nearly unique that it would seem impossible for them to be repeated very often.

The relative success of the Oregon system over a long period of years, in terms of the respect delegates have shown for its mandates, seems to be due to the somewhat unusual political traditions of the state. But the state's own purposes would probably be served better by the New Hampshire or Florida type of primary, which is about what Oregon would have if it were to abolish its preference poll while retaining its other provisions for delegate election.

Among the delegate election systems, those of Category Four, permitting would-be delegates to run only under the name of a candidate who gives consent, are inherently ineffective, because the purpose of the primary is often frustrated by the unwillingness of potential leading candidates to enter it. The voters may thus be unable to give to the delegates anything but an invalid mandate, simply because the system requires a specific mandate. The prohibition of Category Four systems against running on a "no-preference" basis is especially unrealistic when slates must be organized in January or February of the presidential year, before important future candidates have announced their intentions. The tradition of favorite son and stand-in candidacies is thereby fostered. The attempt to compel would-be delegates to declare a preference at a time when they have not had a fair chance to form one, or when they can be refused permission to specify their preference by the candidate himself, has been a failure and merits repeal.

EFFECTIVE SYSTEMS AND PROVISIONS

The systems of Categories One, Two, and Three all appear to be basically effective—if stripped of the preference polls that clutter them in some cases. All of them avoid to a commendable degree the serious hazards of confusing the voters, offering one-sided choices, or producing mandates that are invalid.

The systems of Category Two, where delegates may identify their preferred candidate on the ballot—if they wish and are able to obtain consent—avoid the difficulties of the California system because delegates can also run on a "no-preference" basis. The requirement of candidate consent does not necessarily keep voters from having a realistic choice in critical years, and it gives the party organizations some control over slate-making and betters the relationships with out-of-state candidates who seriously consider campaigning in the state.

The Category One systems—as in New York—for the direct election of delegates unidentified with a candidate are of value in still a different way. In the course of the election, the relationship of each delegate to a defined constituency of party voters has been made clear; among the many consequences of this is the fact that no unit rule can bind the state delegation. The system makes no statutory attempt to provide express mandates of any kind; if the voter does not like the way his implied mandates are carried out at the convention, he can always vote for the candidate of the other party in the November election. This option has sometimes been used with devastating effect by voters in a number of the Category One states.

For developing valid popular mandates and making them effective, the most successful systems are those of Category Three, as practiced in New Hampshire and Florida, where delegates can identify their candidate preferences on the ballot without obtaining consent.

In several respects, the Florida statute is the most advanced of the existing presidential primary laws. The voters are given the possibility of an informing campaign in the state, followed by a meaningful choice on a short ballot. The candidates are given a mechanism which places a maximum of responsibility upon their supporters in the state. The would-be delegates must work within an organized framework that rules out individuals running as mavericks; the resulting relationships to each other and to their candidates are superior for campaigning purposes—and if they win they go to the convention as an experienced and well-knit team. The state government is given a type of election to administer that is almost immune to frivolous candidacies, yet readily open to genuine candidates and with an uncluttered ballot and a vote easy to count—a type of election that should do credit to any state.

11

Other Systems
for Mandating Delegates

■

In more than two thirds of the states, national convention delegates are elected in party bodies of one sort or another. About 55 per cent of the delegates of 1952 and 57 per cent of those of 1960 came out of this older method of selection and instruction, many features of which have survived from the earliest days of party function. The most common pattern has its base in the local *ad hoc* meeting of party voters to choose representatives who will attend the next higher-level meeting, but the systems vary so much in specific procedure that classification is difficult.

The party bodies finally responsible for the choice of convention delegates differ widely. All, however, are representative institutions within the state parties, and all base their political legitimacy on some connection with the rank and file. In effect, they claim to produce delegations that represent the mass of party adherents in the state. The method by which they obtain this popular sanction is therefore an essential factor to an understanding of the systems. The classification below (based on the 1952 David, Moos, and Goldman survey and updated for known changes since then) moves from the most formal to the least formal of these methods.

CLASS 1: Party bodies derived from primary elections.
(a) State party committee members elected in primaries: Louisiana, Georgia, Arkansas (Democratic only); New York, Pennsylvania (delegates at large only).
(b) State and district convention delegates elected in primaries: Delaware, Maryland, Indiana.
(c) State and district convention delegates chosen by local bodies elected in primaries: Michigan, Rhode Island, North Dakota, Wyoming, Arizona, Montana; Illinois (delegates at large only).

CLASS 2: State and district party conventions derived partly from primaries and partly from *ad hoc* meetings: Idaho, Kansas, Washington.

CLASS 3: State and district party conventions derived from *ad hoc* meetings.
(a) Delegates elected directly in *ad hoc* meetings: Maine, Vermont, Connecticut; Virginia, Kentucky, Tennessee; Georgia, Alabama, Arkansas, Louisiana (Republican only).
(b) Delegates chosen by county conventions derived from local *ad hoc* meetings: North Carolina, South Carolina, Mississippi, Oklahoma, Texas, Minnesota, Iowa, Missouri, Colorado, Utah, Nevada, New Mexico.

The party organization procedures that select delegates do not always provide mandates as explicit as those in some primary systems. Nevertheless, the act of selection, however performed, always has mandating implications, and when it occurs in a party meeting can easily be accompanied by advice or instruction that may become highly specific.

Party Processes for Mandating

The range of mandating possibilities was first illustrated in the preparations for the Democratic national convention of 1844, when former President Van Buren was seeking his third nomination. The instructing formulas varied from state to state (as they still do). The Democratic caucus of the Massachusetts legislature actually placed Van Buren in nomination, "subject to the decision of the democratic national convention to be holden in Baltimore in May next." Eight state conventions and several district conventions simply instructed their delegates to vote for him. Vermont delegates were told to "use all honorable means" to procure his nomination, Pennsylvania delegates to "use all their influence," Alabama delegates to "use every practical effort." Connecticut refrained from direct instruction but expressed "decided preference" for Van Buren. Arkansas "recommended" him. Calhoun was Georgia's favorite and the delegates were so instructed, but the Georgia convention also resolved:

> . . . whatever may be the prepossessions of the members of the democratic party of this state in favor of any one of the distinguished . . . names . . . connected with the contemplated nomination, they will as a party sustain and support the nominees of said convention.

North Carolina gave no instructions except a pledge to support the outcome; several states sent entirely uninstructed delegations. But Tennessee, avowing no preference for the Presidency, strongly recommended for the Vice Presidency its favorite son, Polk—who in the end became the presidential nominee and President.

CONFLICTING MANDATES

The practice of electing a representative through one procedure and instructing him through another has few rivals as a source of confusion. In certain situations, the party process systems are as open to such confusion as some of the primary systems. Conflicting mandates may arise in a state convention, for example, when delegates openly committed to one presidential candidate have been selected—and then are instructed by resolution to vote for a different candidate.

In the Democratic party, when delegates are not elected in primaries, district caucuses are usually held in advance of the state conventions to agree informally on the choice of district delegates. They often also undertake to instruct, but the mandate, which at this level is likely to correspond closely with delegate preference, later may be overridden in the state convention, either by resolutions of instruction or by adoption of a unit rule.

In the Republican party, national rules have long favored the election of district delegates in district party conventions. In about a dozen states, mainly southern, these are usually held separately from the state convention—in both time and place; such meetings may instruct and are not subject to being overridden by the state convention. But in other states, Republican practice may resemble Democratic; a case of overriding occurred in Indiana in 1952, when the state convention passed a resolution instructing the entire delegation for Taft. Two delegates who had been selected by their district conventions as known Eisenhower supporters refused to recognize the authority of the state convention—and afterward obtained assurance from national convention officers that they would be allowed to vote as they saw fit.

MANDATES OF NONCOMMITMENT

A mandate of noncommitment deliberately postpones decision, either because the basis for decision does not yet seem adequate or because there is a desire to enhance the effect of a decision when it comes, i.e., to be in a position to make a good trade. Governor John S. Fine's followers in the Pennsylvania Republican delegation of 1952 deliberately assumed an uncommitted posture to strengthen their position at the convention. The New Jersey Democratic delegation of 1952, unpledged, uninstructed, and unbossed for the first time in twenty years, decided in May to take no stand on candidates at that time; at a meeting in June it adopted a resolution committing its members not to make public any preference until they met again in Chicago five weeks later.

Noncommitment may sometimes be the consequence of stalemate among competing factions. At other times it may reflect indecision because the preferred candidate seems to be unavailable; the Indiana Democrats in 1952, for instance, went to Chicago "uninstructed," but were for Stevenson "when the time came." And when several candidates are attractive but none is overwhelmingly so, the desire to avoid getting on the wrong band wagon is a powerful incentive to delay.

Conflicting pressures on the timing of decision are frequently apparent. The enthusiastic followers of a preferred candidate, seeking to take their state party organization into camp, plump strongly for early commitment. And for the party organization there is the tempting prospect of easy access to the White House if it commits itself early to a candidate who wins both nomination and election. By waiting, a delegation may be able to get a good price for a negotiated commitment at a strategic moment, yet if the band wagon starts to roll early there will be scrambling for a place on it.

A commitment strategy that waits too long and misses the band wagon is one of the nightmares of all politicians. Only the possibility of trading on the candidate's need for support in the general election is left—and such delayed support never produces the intimate access to the seats of power than can be built by helping in the early stages of a successful campaign, as Jim Farley's regard for those who were "For Roosevelt Before Chicago" taught.

MANDATES ON NON-NOMINATING ISSUES

Although the main business of the convention is the choice of candidates, instruction on other issues occasionally becomes important, and may be given through a resolution by the state body, or as part of a formal state platform. In both conventions of 1896, for example, free silver, bimetallism, and "16 to 1" were the rallying cries, and most of the delegates arrived with mandates on these issues, often by specific resolutions in state party conventions. For the 1948 Democratic convention most of the southern delegations had specific instructions to oppose the civil rights policies advocated by President Truman, and some were prepared for a bolt, if necessary, to make their opposition felt. The northern delegations had no specific instructions from any source on how far to go in dealing with southern revolt. Relatively clear in their support of the President on the issues, they fumbled the problem of maintaining party discipline.

Seating Contests

When two competing delegations from the same state appear at a national convention and demand seating, the contest usually reflects a serious disorder in the party and mandating processes of the state. Accusations of irregular procedure are almost invariably made by both competitors.

The Democratic national convention of 1832 inaugurated the practice of appointing one delegate from each state to a committee that would report a list of all delegates. The 1835 committee, faced with two "setts" of delegates from Pennsylvania, reported both without recommendation; after debate, both were seated, with voting rights divided between them. The 1840 committee was "vested with power to ascertain who were entitled to seats in this convention, and also to report their names." In 1848, faced with the contesting delegations of Barnburners and Hunkers from New York, the committee refused to open discussion of the contest "until each . . . shall pledge themselves to abide the decision of said Convention, and agree to support, by all honorable means, the nominees of this convention." The Barnburners insisted on unconditional admission or none; the Hunkers accepted the pledge. After floor debate, the convention voted, 126 to 124, to seat both delegations, a decision not acceptable to either. The Hunkers remained but did not vote; the Barnburners withdrew and later took part in a separate convention that nominated Martin Van Buren.

When the newly established Democratic national committee issued the call for the convention of 1852, over 700 delegates appeared to fill the authorized 296 seats. The committee was accordingly authorized to specify in 1856 the number of seats to which each state

was entitled and to "secure the same to the delegates
elect." This began the practice of having the national
committee make up the temporary roll; as the committee members explained in 1856, they

> . . . regarded all papers which on their face bear
> prima facie evidence of the regular election of the per-
> son presenting them, as entitling those persons to seats
> in this hall. They considered it their duty to issue
> tickets to all delegates who presented themselves with
> such prima facie evidence of election by the people.

The potentialities of controlling a convention by means
of seating contests became apparent at the two Democratic conventions of 1860. At the Charleston convention, in April, contesting delegations appeared from
both New York and Illinois; in each case the national
committee made a choice and seated only one on the
temporary roll of the convention. The credentials committee upheld the decision, and the convention con-
curred. But after the walkout later of many other delegations, the convention broke up. A new meeting was
called in Baltimore, where again seating contests began,
centered around the nomination of Stephen A. Douglas. The southern anti-Douglas delegations left, and
Douglas was finally nominated by the delegates remaining.

Republican seating contests were linked from the
first with the problems of apportionment and rotten
borough representation. In 1860, in opposing the seating of delegates from several slave states, David Wilmot of Pennsylvania voiced arguments that became
familiar in succeeding conventions:

> This is not a mass convention, in which a mere nu-
> mercial majority of all who choose to attend control
> the result, but this is a Convention of delegates repre-

senting a constituency, and having constituents at home to represent. Now sir, can it be possible that those gentlemen who come here from states in which there is no organized party, or from states in which they cannot maintain an organized party—is it possible that they are to come here and by their votes control the action of the Convention? I can see nothing better calculated to demoralize a party, and to break it up, than just such a proceeding.

Despite Wilmot, the delegates were seated.

The basis was thus laid for what was to be known as the Republican "steamroller"; Mark Hanna is credited with the dubious honor of bringing it to its highest point at the convention of 1896 in support of McKinley's candidacy. In hearings preceding the convention, more than 150 seats were contested; the national committee awarded 32 seats to anti-McKinley or uncommitted delegates and 78 to delegates favoring McKinley. Later the credentials committee settled other cases in favor of McKinley. On the convention floor the remaining opposition was flattened by a vote on a procedural issue, and on the first nominating ballot, McKinley was an easy victor. Similar tactics in later years brought on the party split of 1912.

RECENT SEATING CONTESTS

In both parties since 1928, and in the Republican party for a longer period, most of the contests have been a by-product of local factions in southern politics. Campaign managers of national candidates no doubt made some efforts to manipulate the contests, but none of the settlements had significant influence on the nominations from 1916 through 1948. In 1952 the situation was more complicated for each party.

Flagrant steamrolling occurred in local Republican meetings in Louisiana and Texas, where clear majorities of Eisenhower supporters were repeatedly over-ridden by tactics that favored Taft. In Georgia, where rival Republican parties had existed for several years, the one previously recognized by the national committee was dominated by Taft supporters, the other by Eisenhower supporters; when this contest reached the national committee, it voted to seat the Taft delegates. The Louisiana contest resulted in most of the Taft delegates being seated by the national committee; the Texas delegates were split in accordance with a formula suggested by Senator Taft.

The convention's first test vote came on the so-called "Fair Play" amendment, suggested by the "manifesto" of the Republican governors' conference at Houston, to restrict the voting rights of delegates if they had been seated by less than a two thirds vote in the national committee. The Taft forces lost the test vote by 658 to 548. The credentials committee then supported the national committee on the Georgia and Texas delegates, but the Taft forces conceded in the Louisiana contest and later lost Georgia and conceded Texas after debate in full convention. In effect, the nomination had also been lost on the first test vote.

The Democrats' controversy in 1952 concerned the so-called loyalty oath and questioned the seating of several southern delegations. Eventually all of them were given full seating rights—but not before it was clear that their willingness to bolt was nearly equaled by the willingness of other party elements to see them go. The basic question in the conflict was the extent to which it was proper or expedient for the national party to enforce majority rule when factions disagreed—as the 1952 battlers had already been doing since 1944. The question led to the work of the Mitchell committee, which between 1952 and 1956 strove to define the minimum obligations to the national party that should be assumed by the delegations and the state parties that send them. As a result, restricted credentials were much less in evidence at the 1956 and 1960 conventions.

PROBLEMS OF LEGITIMACY

No delegation elected in a primary has been the subject of a seating contest of any significance since 1912. Even delegations elected in open primaries that were apparently raided by members of the other party have been seated without comment on the questionable nature of their credentials; apparently the losers have been unwilling to face the political unpopularity that would result at home should they raise a question that would reflect on the cherished primary system. That no such contest has recently been pressed testifies to the public belief in the legitimacy of primary elections.

Among delegations chosen by party bodies, seating contests have been extremely rare in strongly two-party states. Obviously, the pressures of competition make it necessary to safeguard the public reputation of each party even when internal conflict is deep and bitter; codes of appropriate political behavior are better observed, and, even when they are not, the victims hesitate to bring the issues to public attention by creating a seating contest. In either convention the contests originating in the one-party South have rarely involved Virginia, North Carolina, Kentucky, or Tennessee—in all of which the Republican party has had a certain strength and continuity.

Because seating contests have frequently been exploited to favor candidate interests, to hope for a reform of national party practice in settling contests has often been considered wildly impractical. Yet the fact is that the parties have already reformed their own behavior to a considerable degree in handling contests, and would probably find it possible to go even farther in devising other procedural changes. In the main, however, the most effective reforms will come through building truly competitive state systems, in which each party in a state is sufficiently in accord with national sentiment in its own party to accept majority rule at the conventions, and sufficiently strong and cohesive to deal with its own factional problems at home. This is a problem for both national parties that goes far beyond the immediate questions involved in the seating contests.

The Mandates Compared

The party processes built on *ad hoc* meetings plainly embody the theory that party voters should be given an opportunity to impose a relevant mandate at an appropriate time and place. But the mandate given in party meetings—unlike the mandate given in a statewide primary election—may become blurred as it moves up through the hierarchy of meetings and representation. The semipublic meeting can readily become a very private meeting, held at an inappropriate time and place. The presiding party official, having his own vested interests, may be prejudiced in the decisions he must make. The defined terms for party voters in attendance, while probably no more variable than the terms written into public law for the primaries, are open to question both in what they say and how interpreted. Procedures for taking and recording the votes can readily become faulty. And the infirmities of each level may be inherited and increased by successive levels.

Nevertheless, impartial observers who studied many such meetings in 1952 were impressed in general with the respectability of the procedures in most of the states visited. If mandates were inadequate, voter apathy was judged to be more responsible than any other single factor.

The party process and the primary perhaps differ most in the timing possible to each. In the party systems the selection and mandating of delegates remain largely open until almost the final moment of choice; thus changes in voter opinion can be more flexibly taken into account—especially on whether to instruct formally and to what extent. No assumption is made about how soon the party voter will make up his mind, whereas the primary systems must assume that by the date of the primary the voter can make an informed choice among candidates for delegate and sometimes candidates for President.

ADEQUACY OF THE MANDATE

Some discretion to deal with contingencies must always be left to the delegate if the process of representation is to have real meaning. If the instructing constituency is not willing to leave room for this essential discretion, an invalid mandate often results. This is the hazard in the type of presidential primary which invariably requires delegates to pledge themselves to a named candidate long before the filing deadline. Even after candidates have filed, an early ballot cannot possibly place before the party voter all of the principal choices that may be considered months later by the conventions. In 1952, perhaps the only Democratic primaries that produced valid mandates were those like New York's, which gave the delegates discretion, without commitment to a specific candidate.

A party process that commits delegates to a specific candidate at the time of their election runs less risk of an invalid mandate than a primary does, because it is free to look over the entire field of possible candidates. At the same time, a state party convention or committee made up of organization "regulars" may instruct delegates according to preferences that differ widely from those of the party voters. Senator Robert A. Taft was much more popular among organization workers, for example, than among the rank and file of Republican voters.

Party regulars are typically more conservative than the voters; for obvious reasons, the candidate who will work harmoniously with the organization is favored, the independent disliked. On the other hand, the organizations are usually intent on finding and nominating candidates who can win. Much can be forgiven any candidate who looks like a winner, if he will at least refrain from openly attacking the organization. In close elections the state organizations, even when hostile to the national organization, are under pressure to support the candidate who will be most preferred by the voters of their own party, and who can pull votes from the other party and the independents.

An adequate mandate is particularly difficult to create when the possible candidates are not well known to the voters; for example, voters throughout the country would rarely be in a position to know which of a party's several promising governors might be most deserving of consideration for the next presidential nomination. In solving this kind of problem, the party process systems can usually do a better job than those primary systems that require delegates to become committed.

POSSIBLE IMPROVEMENTS

It seems unlikely that party processes, however changed, could ever bring masses of voters into action in the presidential nominating contests. But some of the systems have already shown that they can avoid the invalid mandates that result when organization bias is allowed to remain too long undisturbed by infusions of a justified insurgency. In many states, for instance, the party bodies responded with alacrity to the wave of voter insurgency indicated by the "new Republicans" of 1952. Relatively modest amounts of public pressure might help to make the systems in other states more responsive to the popular will.

Voters can be brought into closer touch with the party organization if the *ad hoc* meetings are more consistently scheduled and located. Further, if all such meetings could be held statewide on the same date, say late in the spring of the presidential year, the attention thus focused on them would encourage attendance and discourage malpractice. The states which have attained political order by using primaries instead of *ad hoc* meetings in the lower levels of party organization have paid too high a price. A readoption of the meetings, but with uniform scheduling late in the spring, might enlist the interest of more party voters in the nominating campaigns and in the general election campaign. Even if the voters coming out totaled a number no higher than for the precinct primaries—and it could hardly be lower—the meetings are much more likely than the primaries to make recruits for further party activity.

In the primary systems nearly every procedure has been formalized by public law. The possibilities of malpractice are thereby reduced—but effectiveness is also reduced by the unavoidable rigidity. The informality of the party processes leaves room for malpractice, but may be their greatest strength because it also leaves room for open contention and flexible adaptation.

The improvement needed goes beyond matters of procedure. Using the processes with skill and wisdom is related first of all to the health of the party system as a whole. Procedural reform is of course a worthy first step in dealing with situations that are clearly unhealthy, but much more basic is an examination of the ideals and objectives with which political activity is undertaken, and the energy and readiness with which great public causes are pursued. These are questions that cannot be avoided in dealing with the problem of nominations for the highest political office in the United States.

12

The Delegates

■

The nominating process as a whole is often attacked in terms that question the character of the delegates as individuals. An objective evaluation of the convention process has therefore an obligation to seek information about this group that constitutes the working, vocal link between the public and the operations of the conventions.

First of all, are the delegates, in general, reputable people who could be expected to make their decisions on reputable grounds?

Second, to what extent are they a representative group? Do they properly represent their party constituencies or only the party organization? And do they reflect accurately the differences between the Democratic and Republican electorates of their states?

Third, to what extent are they competent to perform with efficiency the functions for which they are assembled: the nominating function, the platform-drafting function, the campaign-rally function, the governing-body function?

Fourth—looking with some skepticism at the relevance of the other questions—just how important are the delegates in the nominating process? Does it really matter whether a delegate is reputable or representative or competent?

This chapter attempts to provide information that will answer some of the questions, although direct answers are not easily come by. The information has been gathered from several sources: two mail questionnaire studies of 1948 convention delegates, one by Charles L. Braucher, the other by Daniel W. Tuttle; the 1952 David, Moos, and Goldman study; personal observation of the 1956 and 1960 conventions by the authors of this present book; the historical and biographical records of the participants in earlier conventions.

Age

The age distributions of the delegates to the conventions of 1948, the only year for which such information is available, are shown in the diagram below, which is based on the two questionnaire studies. All age groups from 30 to 75 were substantially represented, with a scattering of delegates below 30 and above 75. The

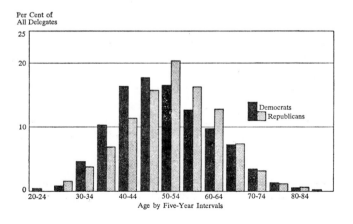

average age of the Democrats was 50, of the Republicans 52. In most age groups below 50, there were proportionately more Democratic delegates than Republican; from 50 to 70, the reverse was true. The general contours of the diagram suggest that in 1948 the Democrats were somewhat more successful than the Republicans in bringing in new blood.

Women Delegates

Before women's suffrage had been generally achieved, a few states with advanced views sent women delegates to the national party conventions. With the coming of the Nineteenth Amendment in 1920, the Democratic national committee expanded to include as many women as men, one from each state, and in 1924 the same step was taken by the Republicans, but no equivalent rule was applied generally in making up the delegations.

In 1952, Democratic delegations included 203 women as regular delegates, 322 as alternates; Republican delegations included 129 and 260 respectively. The following tabulation of the per cent of women delegates in 1952, according to regions, shows noteworthy differences in the regional averages.

	Per Cent of Women Delegates, 1952	
Region	Democratic	Republican
Northeast	7.8%	10.9%
Middle West	12.8	8.6
South	10.3	7.4
West	21.6	16.5
Non-State Areas	17.6	9.5
National Average	12.5	10.5

Half of the members of the 1952 Florida Democratic delegation were women, as required by Florida state

law for delegations elected in a primary. Of all delegations at the 1952 conventions, six Democratic and eight
Republican contained no women, despite provisions in
the convention rules of each party for a platform committee composed of one man and one woman from
each state delegation. Women were more likely to be
admitted to delegations from states where their party
was loosely organized or easily susceptible to insurgency. However, they were also fairly well represented
in delegations coming out of well-knit party situations,
if the controlling leadership was not in the hands of
male politicians of the older generation.

At both 1952 conventions the only notable difference
between the sexes in their voting was related to the
amount of recognition that should be accorded women
in politics. For instance, the Republican women delegates made common cause against the proposal to
enlarge the national committee by adding state chairmen from the states carried by the party—a move that
would upset the existing sex balance on the committee.
The proposal carried nonetheless.

Negro Delegates

In 1952, Negro delegates held about 2.6 per cent of
the voting strength in the Republican convention, about
1.5 per cent in the Democratic convention. The only
southern Democratic delegation admitting Negroes was
Kentucky's; outside the South each party seems to have
selected about the same number of Negro delegates and
alternates, most of them from districts with large Negro
populations. Very few were delegates at large.

The 1952 patterns suggested that both parties and
several of the candidates were showing increasing interest in the Negro vote. Several northern Negroes were
active in responsible posts at the various candidate

headquarters and at the two national committee headquarters. The two Negro members of the Eighty-second Congress were delegates at the Democratic convention —William L. Dawson representing the Chicago first district, Adam Clayton Powell, Jr., of the New York twenty-second (Harlem) district, as a delegate at large —and each had convention committee and headquarters posts.

Most of the Negroes at the Democratic convention were well integrated into their respective delegations. A racial bloc as such did not emerge; no Negro caucus was held, the nearest thing to it being a purely social gathering on Sunday—to which Senator Richard Russell of Georgia, who was in the running for the presidential nomination, sent a ham and a turkey.

Strains within the parties were revealed by oddities of convention behavior. For the Republicans the blessings of Heaven were invoked by no less than two Negro ministers, and seconding speeches by Negroes were arranged for both the Taft and Eisenhower nominations. Such arrangements were lacking in the Democratic convention, yet a civil rights plank that would retain the Negro vote or at least avoid affronting it was a major objective pursued by the party managers with some success under great difficulties.

At both conventions, Negro voters were under represented, as far as the arithmetic of proportions goes. But even token representation can have an importance in certain situations; the addition of even one Negro to a previously all-white delegation may profoundly change its behavior on civil rights.

Religious and Ethnic Group Representation

Protestants made up the largest percentage of delegates for each 1948 convention—63.8 per cent of the

Democratic, 87.1 per cent of the Republican; by de-
nominations, more Republicans than Democrats were
members of those usually associated with relatively
higher social and economic status. This was in accord
with known differences in the social and economic com-
positions of the party followings in 1948. The Catholic
percentage was 27.5 at the Democratic convention, 6.1
at the Republican; the Jewish, 2.1 and 0.7. It can be
inferred from the figures that Italian, Polish, and other
ethnic groups predominantly of the Catholic faith were
represented mainly at the Democratic convention.

In any year, most of the existing religious and ethnic
groups are usually represented to some degree in both
party conventions, but there is much variation from
state to state. In a competitive two-party state such as
Massachusetts, where minorities are conspicuous in
political activity, the delegations of both parties are
likely to show a balanced ticket. Where one party is
dominant, its delegations rarely include much minority
group representation.

Education

The educational status of the delegates of 1948 is
indicated by the tabulation opposite, based on an average of results from the Braucher and Tuttle studies.
These figures suggest that delegates are an exceptionally
well-educated group, even allowing for possible upward bias in the figures because of the greater tendency
of educated persons to respond to questionnaires. Over
one third had received one or more years of postgraduate education—in most cases probably in law schools,
in view of the high proportion who were lawyers. The
differences between the parties were remarkably small.

In looking at the 20 per cent who had not attended
college, it should be remembered that nearly 40 per

Education Reported	Democratic Delegates	Republican Delegates
College and Postgraduate Training	34.3%	34.0%
Complete College Only	21.9	24.5
Attended College Without Finishing	21.8	23.1
	78.0	81.6
Completed High School Only	11.4	11.3
Attended High School Without Finishing	5.3	3.9
	16.7	15.2
Elementary Schooling Only	5.3	3.2

cent of the delegates of 1948 were then 55 years of age or older—which means that they would have completed their formal education before the 1920's and the great expansion of secondary and higher education that followed World War I. By 1960, the conventions were undoubtedly composed almost exclusively of persons who had finished high school and who had gone on to obtain college training.

Income Levels

The 1948 conventions of both parties were drawn to a large extent from the upper-income levels of the population. For each convention, the heaviest concentration was around the $10,000 level—which in terms of fifteen years later would mean an economic and social status associated with at least a $15,000 level or higher. The figures on the next page show the distribution by income levels of respondents to the Tuttle questionnaire.

The differences shown here between the delegates of each party are not sufficiently great to give clear expression to the average differences in income levels between the parties in the electorate. Voter surveys

Reported Annual Income	Democratic Delegates	Republican Delegates
$50,000 or more	4.0%	9.4%
25,000-49,999	8.1	11.3
10,000-24,999	37.7	31.3
5,000- 9,999	29.0	31.7
3,500- 4,999	11.9	10.0
Under 3,500	9.3	6.3

made in 1948 indicated that income groups under $3,000 were voting Democratic two to one, those above $5,000, Republican two to one. The break-even point between the parties was apparently around $4,000 at that time.

Precise income-level information is not available for either 1952 or 1956, but in 1952 there was apparently some widening in the difference of average income between Republican and Democratic delegations outside the South. In New Jersey, for example, most of the 1952 Democratic delegates were in the $5,000 to $10,000 bracket; three fourths of the Republicans were in the over-$10,000 group. In the South, average incomes probably continued to be higher in the Democratic delegations, but persons of ample means were found in the delegations of both parties. The Kentucky Republican delegation, for example, was reputed to include at least four millionaires, while the Arkansas Democratic delegation was referred to as having "only two." Delegations of both parties from Texas, Oklahoma, and Louisiana were studded with names of wealthy individuals.

The privilege of taking part in a convention is an expensive one. When $100-a-plate fund-raising dinners are held in a state during the preconvention campaign, it is assumed that delegates will attend. In a few states it is still the custom to require large contributions to party treasuries as a condition for being a delegate. The delegate usually pays any personal expenses involved in his selection, his transportation expenses to the convention city and living expenses while there, and he contributes if necessary toward maintaining his delegation's convention headquarters.

Arrangements are sometimes made to assist delegates with their travel expenses. In 1952, North Dakota provided by law for reimbursing such expenses from public funds up to a flat rate of $200, with the result that personal ability to pay was not as important in delegate selection there as elsewhere. The Republican party headquarters in Wisconsin continued a custom of offering each delegate $100 toward his expenses. In the California Kefauver delegation the chairman and his alternate were "provided funds by the treasurer of the northern California Kefauver campaign committee."

Whether delegate expenses could properly be paid out of candidate campaign funds was a sensitive issue throughout the preconvention campaigns of 1952. The Taft organization charged that the Eisenhower headquarters was paying travel expenses for delegates who wished to visit the General in New York, Abilene, or Denver before the convention opened. A later furore rose over the charge that the Kefauver California delegation had been offered free tickets to Chicago by Senator Robert Kerr if they would switch votes to Kerr after the first ballot. Both charges were vigorously denied and never proved.

Information on the extent to which delegates receive financial assistance is always difficult to obtain. An observer who lives in a western state commented as follows in 1952:

> I am convinced it is an area where delegates can be picked up. Some delegates would refuse any help on

their expenses—others do not find the obligation
galling. But I could not say who receives and who
doesn't. When I check politicians on the point they
give a knowing look and proceed to the next question.
If I were a candidate or his manager and had the
money and few scruples, I should certainly investigate
this area thoroughly before accepting the thesis that
all delegates want to pay their own way and remain
independent.

Other 1952 observers did obtain many positive statements from reliable sources that members of specific
state delegations were all paying their own expenses.
Even a cynic may conclude that, under the suspicious
scrutiny with which delegates and candidates were con-
fronting each other in 1952, the delegates who compromised themselves by accepting assistance cannot
have been very numerous.

A more important point is that the high cost of being
a delegate favors the selection of the well-to-do. In
1952, only persons with very substantial means were
able to serve as delegates from Hawaii or Puerto Rico,
for example. But travel expense was a problem in
making up Democratic delegations in states as close to
the convention as Michigan and Wisconsin, where there
was an unusually strong desire to include working-class
representatives in the delegations.

Occupations and Connections with Interest Groups

The occupations of the delegates are of interest both
for what they reveal directly and for what they suggest
concerning relations with the economic-interest groups
of political importance that were discussed in Chapter
6. Table 14 shows the occupations of the 1948 dele-

TABLE 14. OCCUPATIONAL DISTRIBUTION OF THE
1948 NATIONAL CONVENTION DELEGATES

(in per cent)

Occupations	Democratic Delegates	Republican Delegates
Public Officials	5.3%	2.8%
Lawyers and Judges	35.4	36.0
Publishers and Editors	3.8	3.6
	44.5	42.4
Other Professional Occupations		
Physicians	2.3	1.7
Engineers	1.2	0.6
Educators	3.1	2.1
Others Not Classified	5.0	7.9
	11.6	12.3
Business Occupations		
Bankers	1.9	2.8
Contractors	1.6	0.2
Manufacturers-Owners	6.6	10.2
Merchants and Dealers	6.2	3.8
Real Estate and Insurance	7.1	8.8
	23.4	25.8
Farmers and Ranchers	6.6	7.5
Labor Union Representatives	2.1	0.2
Homemakers	5.3	4.1
Retired Persons	0.5	1.1
All Others	6.0	6.6
	100.0	100.0

gates, according to the Tuttle questionnaire. Both the similarities and the differences were relatively characteristic also of the picture in 1952 and 1956. The two categories that reflect important interparty differences are those of public officials and labor union representatives.

The occupational connections need also to be interpreted against the background of the delegates' party activities and offices. Four fifths of the 1948 respondents in both parties had regularly attended state and county party organization meetings. Three fifths either were or had been state party officers. The typical 1952 delegate devoted much of his time and energy to politics as an engrossing side line, and frequently contributed money while also doing party work. Occupations in which an interest in politics might be occupationally helpful were liberally represented; occupations in which an active interest in partisan politics is frowned upon were under represented.

The question of when politics ceases to be an avocation and becomes a vocation is not easily answered. A party chairmanship is likely to become a strenuous full-time activity during any campaign period. Incumbents of such posts come to be considered party professionals, even when they draw no direct pay. Indirect remuneration is highly variable; it may include access to useful information, an improvement in occupational prospects and money-making opportunities, and the substantial rewards of political power and prestige. State chairmen are likely to be provided with paid staff and other facilities, but most of the 3,000 county chairmen in each party provide their own facilities. However, in recent years an increasing number of state and county chairmen have been paid salaries from funds raised for party activities.

Public and Party Officials as Delegates

The conventions have always brought together a cross section of current and past officialdom from all levels of government and from all elements of the party hierarchies. Over several recent decades, an increasing proportion of this group has been of high rank and distinction, and the increase seems to be continuing. In 1952 the number of high-ranking officials serving as delegates was 492; in 1956, it was 628, which included 219 state and national party officials.

GOVERNORS

Thirty-two state governors were members of delegations in 1952, thirty-four in 1956 and forty-five in 1960; most of them served as delegation chairmen. Being a delegate is far from equally convenient for all governors, however. Those engaged in difficult re-election campaigns are presumably in the poorest position to serve, yet in 1952, of the twenty-two running actively for re-election, thirteen were delegates. In certain situations, service at the convention can be used to help the campaigns at home. In 1952, Governor Allan Shivers of Texas was among those running for re-election. He faced a contest in a primary election to be held on Saturday of the week of the Democratic convention. This coincidence may not have been entirely unrelated to his much-televised behavior and tactics at Chicago. He won renomination.

SENATORS

Of the ninety-six United States senators in 1956, fifty-nine were delegates, ten of them as delegation chairmen; in 1960, sixty-four of the hundred senators served as delegates. The century-long tendency toward increasing participation in the conventions is as apparent for senators as it is for governors, but the senators started sooner. Republican senators, however, have lagged behind the Democratic senators and also behind the Republican governors.

The senators most likely to be found as delegates are those from the competitive two-party states, especially those that have one senator of each party. State and national politics are usually most closely related in these states; it can be supposed that their senators therefore find it both desirable and necessary to take an active part in the conventions. In recent years most of the senators of the southern one-party states have gone to the Democratic conventions as delegates, presumably because they are needed to help defend the minority positions on critical issues in which the southern delegations have increasingly found themselves.

A senator can attend the convention without serving as a delegate or alternate, usually receiving many privileges as a distinguished guest—a position preferred by many in times past, especially when divisive issues were certain to come to a vote. But delegate status seems now to be much more required as a condition of attendance, even when senators might prefer otherwise.

HOUSE MEMBERS

Members of the House of Representatives have not served on convention delegations proportionately as often as senators; traditionally, they have been less oriented to national politics and less capable of securing prestige recognition from their state party organizations. But since 1948 there has been a marked change in the number of House members who have served as delegates or alternates, as the following tabulation shows:

Year	Democrat	Republican
1948	32	20
1952	56	18
1956	80	39
1960	136	32

The representatives (if any) of the minority party in a state dominated by one party are usually sent as delegates; those of the majority party often are not. The

House members who belong to a minority group of any kind seem to become delegates more often than others —seven women members went to the conventions in 1956, for instance, and the Negro congressmen serve as delegates more often than most congressmen.

The old criticism of congressmen as delegates—on the grounds that the conventions were supposed to remove the nominating function from Congress and restore it to the people—is usually no longer heard. In any case, under present apportionment rules, even if all House members were delegates, they would rarely hold as much as one quarter of the voting strength in either convention. The few present-day objections to House service on delegations stem mainly from situations in local politics. The general absence of congressmen from the New Jersey delegation in 1952, for example, was said to reflect "a conviction that a candidate's name should appear only once on the ballot, that party honors should be spread over as wide a field as possible, and that valuable prestige patronage should not be wasted."

The increase from 1948 to 1960 in House representation at the conventions shows that in general congressional delegates are more favored than frowned upon. Perhaps an increasing number of state party leaders decided that it was helpful to have at least one House member in their delegations as long as the party leader in the House was likely to be the convention chairman. And perhaps the congressional leaders quietly suggested to their fellow members that it would be helpful if more of them were on the floor at the conventions.

Experience and Leadership

About 40 per cent of the delegates in each convention of 1952 had served on an earlier delegation at least once. As might be expected, many of these were also the more distinguished members of delegations; continuous service in three conventions or more was several times as frequent among the delegates listed in *Who's Who in America* as among other delegates. In general, the leadership resources of the conventions depend on this combination of experience and distinction.

An institution as complicated as the modern party convention would hardly be able to function, much less complete its work in four or five days, if it did not have an enormous accumulation of convention experience within its ranks. For the newcomer, the scene is one of utmost confusion. Yet an immense amount of purposeful business is being conducted with great rapidity and effectiveness. That the results of all this activity fall quickly into place is largely due to the skill and experience with which the old hands go about their business.

The Evolution and Recent Status of Delegate Characteristics

The information that has been presented here is not directly conclusive on any of the questions of reputability, representativeness, and competence with which the chapter began, yet it does form a pattern that seems to refute much of the derogatory comment directed at the delegates. The facts suggest that the majority of recent delegates were well qualified to deal with the problems of their parties, and that they were about as reputable a group as could reasonably be expected in any large political assembly in this imperfect world.

If this is true, was it always true? Has there been a sharp break with the past at some point, or a gradual improvement, or not even that?

Looking back over the sequence of American political history, there seems to be no one point of decisive change. There have been, however, four striking developments, all since 1900: the presidential primaries for the election of delegates in some states, first important in 1912; the reform of Republican apportionment rules after 1912, which reduced the representation of the rotten-borough districts of the South; the ratification of the woman suffrage amendment in 1920, followed by greatly increased inclusion of women in the conventions; and the Hatch Acts of 1939 and 1940, which prohibit many state and federal executives from serving as delegates.

Even more important, however, may be a host of more intangible factors. Among these are the virtual disappearance of the state bosses of the Boss Platt type; civil service reform and more enforcement of standards of honesty in the awarding of government contracts; organized labor's interest in direct political action; the increasing public-service activities of middle-class and upper-class voters in the organizations of both parties; the shift of political power from the party officials, whether bosses or not, to elected officials, such as governors and senators, with a direct responsibility to the public; and finally, the rising standards of education and social responsibility throughout the country.

Of the broad outlines of the change there is no doubt. Since 1948 the delegates have been measurably better educated, less boss-ridden, better adjusted to the requirements of an open political system, and generally more trustworthy in all respects than the delegates of 1900. The American political system still leaves much to be desired, but it is much more reputable than formerly; to a large extent this is mirrored in the composition of the delegate groups.

As for representativeness—delegates who were boss-ridden, ill-educated, and preoccupied with the hope of political spoils were not proper representatives of any normal constituency. To the extent that present-day delegates are more reputable, they are also more representative. Yet many of them, in being white males of mature age, usually with a college education, a business or professional occupation, and a higher-than-average income, are not typical of their constituents.

There is every reason to believe, however, that this is the kind of representative that most constituents wish to have; certainly it is the kind they usually elect whenever a choice is presented—apparently because they want a representative who can take care of their interests better than they themselves could hope to do.

Two further questions should be asked about recent conventions. Was there adequate representation of minorities? Were majority groups too often represented by professional politicians?

Minorities who recognize themselves as such are intent upon being represented by a quota of delegates from their own ranks proportionate to their numbers. If this is the test, most of the identifiable minorities have definitely been under represented in the recent conventions of both parties.

The question about professional politicians goes to the heart of a major problem of any party system. The attitudes of men who make politics either a vocation or a major avocation inevitably differ in many ways from the attitudes of the electorate, yet someone must do the party work—and it is the workers who are most likely to turn up as delegates. The many organization regulars in recent delegations, even when they said and did what their constituencies desired, were probably not the kind of delegates that the constituencies would have most preferred.

What, finally, of delegate competence to deal with the four functions of conventions? On the whole, the delegates appeared well qualified to deal with the nominations. For the platform, the essential problem is the manning of the resolutions committee; here the Democrats appeared to be better situated than the Republicans in view of the greater number of Democratic senators and House members serving as delegates and thus available for assignment to the committee.

On the campaign-rally function, the delegates of both conventions have usually done a reasonably good job. The unity of the respective parties is signified, when it actually exists, and sentiment is usually rallied for all of the concurrent campaigns that occur in the presidential years.

For the governing-body function, most of the delegates seem to have been ill prepared, but the failures have typically been much more due to failures in leadership than to the actual voting of the delegates on issues laid before them. The problem of organizing and integrating the party leadership is involved here—one of the vital problems both parties face.

13

The Delegations

∎

Although the individual delegate is the essential building block in the convention voting structure, the actual working unit for most purposes is the state delegation as a whole. In the process of its selection, by whatever method, a whole series of express or implied commitments has accumulated in regard to candidates, issues, and its relationship to state and national party organizations. The first step in identifying itself as a unit to deal with these matters is the organization meeting.

Traditionally, it was assumed that each delegation would hold its organizing meeting in its hotel after arrival in the convention city, but the delegations of recent years tend to organize in their home states. If delegations fail to organize early, and thus delay the designation of the members who will serve on convention committees, the advance committee work that is characteristic of modern conventions is impeded. Republican national rules have long required each delegation to choose its members for the credentials and resolutions committees "immediately" after its own selection. In 1959 the Democratic party provided that the delegations for 1960 should select members for the major committees at least fourteen days before the convention opened.

A delegation customarily reaches the convention city on the day before the opening Monday. It is free to make its own decisions on nearly all delegation activities; convention rules only require that members be seated together in the convention hall and that there be a chairman to act as spokesman. A delegation meeting is usually held soon after arrival. In 1952, because both conventions faced the unusual possibility that roll call votes might occur even before the conventions were fully organized, the first meeting was important for almost every delegation. The delegates were coming to grips, sometimes for the first time, with the issues on which they might be required to take an immediate stand on the following day. Debate was earnest and prolonged.

The frequency of subsequent meetings depends on a variety of matters—the traditions of each state party, the unfolding business of the convention, and, especially in recent years, delegation size. In 1952 the survey of that year's experience discovered that a delegation of average size—twenty-four to sixty members including alternates—usually met daily or oftener to keep abreast of events and develop its strategy. Small delegations often found formal meetings unnecessary. Large delegations, such as those of New York, Pennsylvania, Ohio, and Illinois, tended to leave matters to their inner groups of leaders; the large California delegations in both conventions were exceptions in holding frequent caucuses.

Many of the 1952 meetings were closed to outsiders, except for a few favored guests. In the others that were open to observation, parliamentary rules on the whole were used. Any delegate could have his say, although the leaders usually suggested the decisions in the end. Rank-and-file delegates were obviously heavily dependent upon the leaders for information bearing on tactical decisions, and this tended to limit the character of the debate.

It happens that there is more information of this kind about the two conventions of 1952 than for any national party convention held previously or since. In 1952, teams of political scientists reported on the history of each state delegation, from the pre-conditions surrounding its selection to its voting behavior at the convention it attended. The results were published in the 52 state and territorial chapters of the five-volume study *Presidential Nominating Politics in 1952,* edited by David, Moos, and Goldman. The present chapter draws mainly on the data of that study, supplemented by the observations of the authors at the conventions of 1956 and 1960. Because of those observations, it can be said with some assurance that the case studies of 1952 are still highly indicative of the range of state delegation behavior as it has recently occurred and as it remains in prospect for the near future.

Delegation Leadership

CHAIRMEN

About 80 per cent of the delegation chairmen of 1952 and 1956 were incumbents of some public or party office, with public officials outnumbering the party officials in the Democratic party but not in the Republican. Governors, when present as delegates, served as chairmen over 80 per cent of the time in the four conventions studied. In the absence of a governor, the state's ranking senator was frequently the choice.

A delegation chairman occupies a strategic position. The *ad hoc* nature of most convention arrangements, the short time span, and the characteristic confusion, all tend to place responsibility on him, and presumably also give him a considerable measure of power. It is he who reports the vote of the delegation, and he often has some discretion about the report, although always subject to challenge through a demand that the delegation be polled. In a cohesive and disciplined delegation, his powers may approach those of the traditional political boss; in a splintered delegation, he is at least an important communication center.

Yet the chairmen have been in some respects the unknown men of the conventions. Neither party had ever recorded the list of chairmen in its official proceedings until 1956, when the practice was adopted at the suggestion of the American Political Science Association. Chairmen seldom undertake to meet as an organized group, but if they would do so, the result might provide an extremely useful executive committee for the conventions.

THE INNER CIRCLE

The chairman and other officers of the delegation are not always effective leaders. In rare instances a delegation is a mere collection of individuals going their several ways. Occasionally there are two or more factions, each with its own leader. Even when a delegation is unified, its real leadership is sometimes not physically present at the convention; the Arkansas Democratic delegation of 1952, for instance, awaited word on its decisions from the governor back home.

Most commonly, however, delegations seem to contain some sort of an inner circle that supplements the leadership of a strong chairman or takes the initiative in mobilizing when the chairman is weak. Various inner circle practices were observed at the 1952 conventions, of which the following seemed to be the most consistent.

1. When a delegation contained a strong group of public and party officials, they usually selected the chairman and constituted themselves an inner circle around him.

2. National committee members, because of their strategic position as convention officers with special privileges, could provide relatively effective leadership when they served on delegations and especially when elected chairmen.

3. When a delegation was strongly backing a favorite son the inner circle was usually made up of his main supporters in the delegation.

4. In large delegations, the leaders were usually found among the delegates at large rather than the district delegates.

5. Some delegations were composed largely of "leaders"; some others had very few or none.

6. Large delegations tended to subdivide into several groups along territorial or factional lines, and each of the groups might have its own leadership.

7. Opposing voting commitments sometimes divided a delegation into rigidly separate groups that might or might not be able to work together on other matters.

8. In tightly knit delegations lifted intact from the political organization of the state party, all members knew in advance their position in the scheme of things. Many other delegations had to find their internal leadership, if any, after they had been formed. Delegations that lacked leadership groups were usually those coming out of state party situations that involved disorganization, instability, or successful insurgency.

Decision-Making and Candidate Support

The major subjects for delegation decision are comparatively few—consisting essentially of the position to be taken on candidates, on platform issues, and on the seating and rules problems that often involve the relationship of the state and national party organizations. There are also the questions of delegation role and tactics, which can lead to still other questions or back to the major issues.

This interlocking aspect of every matter that must be resolved by a delegation is of course most marked for the decision that is paramount—its position on candidate support. This is never a single decision, but a compound of all the indecisions, deliberations, stresses, and influences to which the delegation has been subject as a working unit during and since its selection. Even when it has been and remains firmly committed to a candidate, the progressive phases of the process demand new tactical decisions and reinforcement of old ones.*

* In the unabridged 1960 edition of this book, one important aspect of delegation decision-making discussed was the extent to which a delegation agreed within itself on candidate support in a contest situation. A statistical concept was developed by the authors, termed "the average index of candidate agreement," by means of which the contested conventions from 1896 to 1956—twelve for the Democrats and nine for the Republicans —were analyzed. It was found that the division in voting in the convention was more usually *between* delegations than *within* them—in other words, that each delegation tended to take on an identity as an organized group, and even when its vote was split, a more lopsided majority was usually given one candidate or the other than was the case in the convention as a whole. However, the long-term tendencies of each party in this regard showed a decline in delegation unity which might be interpreted as pointing to a new national convention voting pattern in which split voting within delegations may become much more common than formerly. For the full analytical discussion of this concept, with accompanying statistical tables, see Chapter 15 of the original book.

The story of 1952 for both conventions is especially well adapted to illustrate the complexity of the nominating decision.*

THE DEMOCRATIC NOMINATION

The range of early commitment among the fifty-four Democratic delegations of 1952 included seven in which the majority was firmly bound to a leading candidate (Kefauver and Russell); six in which the majority preferred a leading candidate (Stevenson, Kefauver, Russell, and others); nine committed to a non-leading candidate (President Truman, Averell Harriman, and five favorite sons); and thirty-two undecided or preferences unknown (including a very small scattering for Stevenson).

Adlai Stevenson had few delegates, having refused to enter any primaries or to campaign. By the opening of the convention Harriman had announced and had acquired the nearly solid support of the previously un-

---

* An account of how the voting decisions evolved in the critical delegations at Los Angeles in 1960 can be found in T. H. White's *The Making of the President, 1960* (Pocket Books edition, 1961), pp. 189-201. This differed both from the diffuse situation in the Democratic convention of 1952 and the highly bi-polarized situation in the Republican convention of 1956; but in all three conventions, the decisive margin of the winning vote was found among individual delegates and in state delegations where there were prolonged periods of indecision while an agonizing choice was being faced. In the 1960 case, White's account is particularly good in its reporting of the effects of Stevenson's indecision on the delegations and delegation leaders that were most friendly to him.

A briefer account can be found in Paul T. David, ed., *The Presidential Election and Transition 1960-1961* (1961), pp. 9-14.

Specific and somewhat detailed accounts of the action in the Pennsylvania, Illinois, and California delegations at Los Angeles, written by political scientists assigned to act as observers, can be found in Paul Tillett, ed., *Inside Politics: The National Conventions, 1960* (1962), Chaps. 17, 21, and 22.

committed New York delegation. The tally two days before the convention was as follows, according to the Associated Press:

Stevenson	41½
Kefauver	257½
Russell	161½
Harriman	112½
Others	277
Uncommitted, in Dispute, or Unknown	380
	1,230

During the intensive debate in the first few days of the convention, sentiment for Stevenson gathered rapidly in the previously uncommitted delegations, and on the first ballot he polled 273 votes. Russell polled 268 votes on the first ballot and was still polling 261½ on the third. Kefauver reached a maximum of 362½ votes on the second ballot and was holding 279½ at the end of the third ballot after losing the others to Stevenson. Most of the strength previously committed to Harriman and the other lesser candidates switched to Stevenson on the third ballot, giving him a near majority which was then made complete.

How did the delegations that voted for Stevenson reach their decision? The probability is that he was an acceptable second or third choice for almost all the delegations, except those making up the hard-core support for Kefauver and Russell. Many of the middle-of-the-road delegations had always been willing to take Stevenson as their first choice, if assured that he was available and would campaign actively.

The changes in top-leadership attitudes had influence along the way. President Truman was an important factor after Vice President Barkley withdrew, but the swing was well along before that. The leadership of the

liberal-labor bloc at a certain point concluded that neither Kefauver nor Harriman could be nominated;
Stevenson became the only satisfactory remaining
choice. Harriman himself had been aware before the
balloting began that he might find it desirable to con-
cede early, for the New York leaders were finding it
difficult to hold the delegation for him. Leaders of the
uncommitted delegations kept assessing top-leadership
attitudes, rank-and-file sentiment, and their own per-
ceptions of the candidates—and drifted steadily toward
Stevenson. Individual delegates by the hundreds made
their own assessments. The result was a gathering consensus that showed little evidence of dictation or overwhelming influence from any single power center.

THE REPUBLICAN NOMINATION

The 1952 Republican pattern of delegation commitment preceding the convention differed remarkably
from the Democratic. Among the fifty-three delegations,
thirty-eight had firm or preferring commitments to
one or the other of the two leading candidates, Taft and
Eisenhower. For thirteen of these, the commitment extended uniformly to the entire delegation; for most of
the others, the majorities were lopsided. Three delegations were committed to favorite sons: Warren of California, Stassen of Minnesota, and McKeldin of Maryland.

By opening day, ninety-six delegate seats were involved in seating contests. When the convention acted
on these, the distribution of the 96 votes changed as
follows: before the contest, twenty-one temporarily
seated delegates for Eisenhower, seventy-two for Taft,
three undecided; after the contest, sixty-four for Eisenhower, twenty-seven for Taft, one for another candidate,
four undecided. This was obviously a blow to Taft,
but he was still leading in total committed delegate

strength, with 485 votes to Eisenhower's 470 (604 votes needed to nominate).

The balance of power in the conflict thus rested mainly with the uncommitted and favorite son delegations. The chairmen of the two largest uncommitted delegations—Pennsylvania and Michigan—withheld commitment until final delegation caucuses before the balloting, urging their delegates to do likewise. Each delegation met with each candidate and deliberated at length. Eventually both delegations gave most of their votes to Eisenhower.

McKeldin released his Maryland delegates on the first day of the convention, when invited to place Eisenhower's name in nomination. Several of Stassen's Minnesota delegates developed an early preference for Eisenhower, and the entire delegation soon was increasingly anxious to join the Eisenhower band wagon. On the morning of the balloting Stassen released several who wished to move at once and authorized the others to shift at the end of the first ballot if Eisenhower should receive as many as 580 votes. The California delegation, pursuing a strategy that depended on a convention stalemate, stayed solidly with Warren until the end. The final shift of the Minnesota delegation at the end of the first ballot completed the Eisenhower majority of 614 to Taft's 500.

* * *

In both conventions, frequent polls were taken of the delegations—on the initiative of members and in no way binding. The delegates simply wished to know where other delegates stood, but the results of each poll necessarily influenced the delegates still undecided.

Of the delegates who arrived at the convention with no definite mandate, how many were in a position to act independently and in good faith as representatives of their constituencies? How many were subject to undue influence?

Various known possibilities existed in 1952 for what might be considered undue influence. The Arkansas and Georgia Democratic delegations were almost completely controlled by their respective governors, but there were indications that the governors might be acting mainly as channels for popular mandates. Governor Dewey of New York was reported on several occasions as engaging in tactics that some delegates found oppressive. County leaders from metropolitan areas seemed highly influential in a number of delegations.

There were no reported "deals" involving whole delegations at either convention. This could possibly be related to the highmindedness of the candidates, and certainly, in the Democratic case, to the fact that the two-thirds rule, which throughout its history was a basic element in generating deals, no longer existed.

Voting Behavior as End Product

When a vote is taken, the individual delegate has an inescapable personal responsibility. This is true even under the unit rule, since the vote must be counted within the delegation before the rule can be applied. The votes that precede the nominating vote probably allow the individual his greatest freedom of judgment, but if the nomination is at all in doubt, the vote on it is the act in which each individual delegate most fully justifies his existence as a member of the convention.

Convention voting behavior has not been previously subjected to the kind of research and analysis that has been attempted, for example, for presidential and congressional elections. The fact that convention delegations differ in their voting behavior is recorded in a century and a quarter of roll call history. But voting behavior is only the end product of many factors of difference, each one of which may involve both a consciously planned decision and an unplanned motivation that may never reach the level of conscious perception. Convention voting behavior is essentially a summation of these factors as mirrored in the decisions of the individual delegates.

VOTING MOTIVATIONS

If the final nominating votes of 1952 are examined at the point where the outcome became visible and assured—the critical moment when the transfer of a few votes would complete a majority—the small number of delegates who had departed from their earliest commitment to a leading candidate is striking. The decisive votes came from the delegates formerly committed to a minor candidate, and even more from those who were uncommitted.

The delegates who stayed to the end with the principal losers—Kefauver, Russell, Taft, Warren, and Barkley—take on special interest. Why did they stay after the probability of defeat had become all too apparent?

Most of these die-hards were evidently more interested in defending a cause to which they had become attached than in finding a place on the winning side. They had assimilated a set of dogmas and had acquired the characteristics of the "true believer." The California delegates pledged to Kefauver, many of whom were party dissidents to start with, undoubtedly brought the most hostile attitudes to the convention as an institution. Believing that they represented the "voice of the people" and that the nomination was in danger of being "stolen" by the "party bosses," several of them developed something akin to a persecution complex. Their minds were unprepared to take part effectively in a convention that regarded itself as having an entirely free field of choice and full responsibility for naming the candidates.

On the other hand, the high-status individuals who made up the noteworthy Ohio Republican delegation were politically sophisticated, strongly cohesive as a group, and highly efficient. Each delegate had an assignment which he reportedly carried out on a day-and-night schedule up to the final vote. Every detail had been arranged with meticulous care for a supreme effort. All of this reflected in part the traditional Ohio wisdom about convention operations—but it also reflected the fanatical and long-frustrated devotion to Senator Taft and his cause.

The California delegates who stayed with their favorite son, Governor Warren, were pursuing a planned strategy that was effective in also holding the Warren delegates from Wisconsin and attracting a Rhode Island delegate. Whether this strategy was fully rational is a good question, but the delegation had little to lose by waiting through one ballot, and it had a certain pride in maintaining the dignity and status of its candidate. In the case of the die-hard Barkley delegates from Kentucky, emotion took over; state pride and loyalty to their favorite son after a public rebuff seemed to be mainly responsible for their staying power.

In both conventions the delegates from those states where it is traditional for a delegate to be selected on his own merits or for his party loyalty, rather than because of his association with some national candidate, usually avoided commitment at the time of selection and thereafter often maintained freedom of action. Sometimes they had announced a decision before leaving home, but more often not. Lacking the emotional involvement of a commitment, they seemed better able to judge the merits and prospects of the candidates as they came down the home stretch. But the position of these delegates was most complex. From the time of selection to the time of final decision they were subjected to an intensive cross fire of pressures—sometimes so heavy and so much from one direction as to resemble coercion. Through all of this, they faced making an eventual choice that would involve both a final clarification of their personal preferences and a final estimate of constituency and party organization reaction.

Voting as the Final Test of Representativeness

Representation involves much more than the issues of mandating. What the constituent presumably wants is a delegate with satisfactory characteristics who expresses satisfactory views and votes in a satisfactory way. The delegate becomes fully representative to the extent that he meets all three tests and is able to engage in "expressive acts," as when taking part in floor debate, and in "acts of power," as when voting.

To gauge the expressive acts of the delegates, one would need to look mainly at what goes on in delegation meetings, to which public access is unfortunately seldom available. When important debate occurs directly on the floor of the conventions, however, a few delegates become conspicuous for their expressive acts, sometimes with important consequences in terms of their standing with their constituencies.

Few delegates were able to take part directly in the emotion-laden debates of the 1952 conventions without affecting their own political futures. Governor Gordon Browning of Tennessee did much to bring on his re-election defeat when he supported the Moody resolution in the Democratic convention and later cast the entire vote of the Tennessee delegation against the seating of Virginia. Orville L. Freeman of Minnesota, at the time a candidate for governor but young and politically unknown outside his state, became conspicuous at the Democratic convention for the courage with which he repeatedly challenged the rulings of Chairman Sam Rayburn when better-known leaders were unprepared to act. He lost the race for governor that year, but was successful in the elections of 1954, 1956, and 1958.

Voting is the final test of the representativeness of the delegates. For the 1952 conventions a considerable amount of information on this point is available. When the debate began on the Republicans' "Fair Play" resolution and the Democrats' "loyalty pledge," public opinion was unformed and the delegates largely uninformed. But public and delegates alike learned something from the informal discussions, credentials hearings, and formal debate that preceded the votes. Were the delegates representing their party constituencies accurately when they voted?

Militant and committed supporters of Taft or of Eisenhower followed a clear line of candidate interests, in line also with their mandates. The delegates who were undecided between Taft and Eisenhower almost all voted for the Fair Play amendment, undoubtedly believing that they were making a long overdue reform of which their constituencies would approve.

The loyalty pledge and Virginia seating votes in the Democratic convention involved issues that were by-products of acute factional conflict; the factional militants on each side had no trouble in deciding how to vote, and were probably representative of constituencies of the same stripe. The moderates had more difficulty, and so did their constituencies, in following the argument; the desire for party harmony that eventually led a majority of the delegates—including 132 who changed their votes—to vote for the seating of Virginia was evident also among interested members of the electorate.

On the nominating votes, evidence for the appraisal of representativeness is available from the public opinion polls and the presidential primaries. Eisenhower was leading Taft by an average of 44 to 35 per cent among Republican voters on the last of several Gallup Polls before the convention. Among independent voters, his lead was estimated at 50 to 18 per cent on July 1; the independents had no direct claim to representation, but their views had to be considered by any delegate whose mandate was to seek a winner.

The returns in the presidential primaries are more difficult to interpret but reflect a special kind of reality not to be found in public opinion polls: the votes of registered voters who were prepared to go to the polls and vote a Republican primary ballot. The general primary pattern suggested that Eisenhower was the preferred choice of a majority of the normally Republican voters in most eastern, western, and southern states, while Taft was the preference in several middle-western states. If this is so, the vote by which Eisenhower was nominated—614 to 500 for Taft—was remarkably representative.

The contest for the Democratic nomination was eventually conducted mainly among Kefauver, Russell, and Stevenson, but others were prominent before the convention. In Gallup Polls of Democratic voters prior to the Democratic national convention of 1952, comparative percentage standings were reported as follows:

> June 8, Kefauver, 45 per cent; Barkley, 17; Stevenson, 10; Russell, 10; Harriman, 5; Others and Undecided, 13.
>
> July 13, Kefauver, 45 per cent; Barkley, 18; Stevenson, 12; Russell, 10; Harriman, 5; Others and Undecided, 10.

Kefauver had entered almost all of the available presidential primaries. In the four cases where he had an active opponent of presidential candidate stature, he defeated Truman in New Hampshire and Kerr in Nebraska, and was defeated by Russell in Florida and by Harriman in the District of Columbia. What preconvention fame Stevenson had was largely due to indications that he would be the choice of the party leaders if he consented to run. His welcoming speech at the opening of the convention, widely seen and heard on television, made a strong impression on Democrats throughout the country as well as on the delegates, and as the convention proceeded he became increasingly prominent as the most likely nominee. Soon after the convention a poll of voters who considered themselves Democrats reported that 55 per cent were pleased by the nomination. As the election proved, Stevenson was clearly weaker than Eisenhower in terms of rank-and-file support within his own party, but he was probably the strongest candidate available to the Democrats when the nominating decision was made.

Successful representation involves giving effect not only to genuine mandates when they exist, but also to the unexpressed desires of the constituents in a way that they will later approve. In some ways the Stevenson nomination was a triumph for the convention as a representative institution, since he was seemingly the one choice most generally acceptable throughout the party's national constituency. The choice would probably not have been available to a national primary at the time needed. Unlike a primary election with frozen alternatives, the nominating convention can enlarge its field of choice to include new alternatives when necessary; the 1952 experience was a striking illustration of this capability.

14

Voting Power
and Strategy:
The Road to Consensus

■

The formal action by which a candidate is nominated
for President of the United States is the most impressive,
deliberate, and carefully safeguarded act of each convention. All the other activities and functions are only
prelude to or consequences of this central action—the
nominating vote. It is in this final application of votes in
support of the winner that the effective uses of power
are most concretely displayed. Preliminary events and
votes also involve power and attempts to use it strategically, but these must all be assessed in terms of
their relation to the grand climax of the nominating
ballots.

Voting Procedures

Two methods of voting are used predominantly in the
full convention: "Aye" and "No" voice votes, for which

the chairman rules the result, and roll call votes, for which the roll of delegations is called in alphabetical order of the states, with each chairman reporting his delegation's vote. All roll call votes are recorded verbatim, and the records appear in full in the official report of convention proceedings. In both parties the rules have provided almost from the beginning that nominations shall be made by roll call vote, but any other business may be settled by voice vote unless there is objection.

In recent years, as the conventions grew larger and more cumbersome and delays in procedure correspondingly more irksome, the number of roll call votes taken on non-nominating issues has declined sharply. A voice vote can be taken with ease and speed; unanimity is customary, since most of the motions so put to a vote usually involve routine convention business or formal approval of actions which have been agreed upon elsewhere. However, business that is not only important but often highly controversial is sometimes also decided by a voice vote, with no objection being made to its use.

In the Democratic convention of 1936, the two thirds rule, which had been a source of conflict for a century, was rescinded by a mere voice vote. In 1952 the Taft forces, recognizing defeat, moved to settle the Texas seating contest by a voice vote—after a debate that occupies eighteen pages in the printed record.

VOICE VOTES VS. ROLL CALLS

A demand for a roll call can always be made, and in the past the privilege was used—and abused—to such an extent that both parties developed rules that somewhat limited the practice. The limitation has helped to expedite the work of the conventions and has also prevented some of the obstructionist tactics of warring factions to which the demand for a roll call so easily lent itself. But when the voting division on an important matter is closer than two to one, a voice vote becomes exceedingly questionable as a method of reaching a just decision in a meeting as massive and noise-ridden as the modern convention.

There are many possible sources of error in calling close voice votes, of which the discretion held by the permanent chairman is probably the principal one. If at any time he feels that a more precise procedure is needed, it is his prerogative to ascertain whether there is demand for a roll call. Recent chairmen have usually ruled on voice vote results without hesitation, asking for a roll call, even when the vote is very close, only on demand—if then.

Since a roll call is taken by alphabetical order, states early in the order are always faced with committing themselves before much evidence of the voting trend has appeared. If they wish, they may pass and be called again at the end of the roll. Any delegation may also change its vote at the end of the roll up to the time the final tally is announced. A member of a delegation is permitted to challenge the vote reported by his chairman, in which case the delegation is polled. All of these privileges add to the inherent slowness of the roll call procedure.

Voting by roll call is the most accurate procedure available to the conventions, and as used seems in general to be reasonably accurate. However, discrepancies have frequently been found in the tallies taken by different tally clerks, and the published proceedings as stenographically recorded frequently contain internal inconsistencies. In recent years the parties have used electrical scoreboards, on which a cumulative record of the roll call could be displayed as it was being taken.

Apparently neither party has made any recent effort to find an alternative to the voice vote that would provide a greater degree of accuracy without going all the way to a roll call. But the current procedure has not adequately protected the institutional integrity of the conventions; the validity of a voice vote is never assured when an important issue is being hard fought and the division of voting is close. Until some decisively improved substitute is found for voice voting, the roll call should be more widely used—and even for undramatic questions when an accurate tally is essential.

COMMITTEE VOTES

The recent and continuing increase in the amount of work transacted prior to the convention in the national committee and both before and during the session in the credentials, rules, and resolutions committees has helped to expedite action in the full convention. But the fact that each state has equal committee representation—two members on the national committee, and either one or two on the others—makes a serious difficulty: the states with a majority in convention voting can be outvoted in committee. The result can be overturned when it reaches the full convention—but only at the cost of much trouble and delay.

No form of weighted voting has so far been adopted for any of the convention committees, partly because the method has certain drawbacks, but action of some sort is clearly needed. A simple and readily feasible alternative to weighted voting would be a proportionate increase of committee representation for the larger states. One proposal discussed would give each state one member in each committee for every twelve votes that it has in the convention, while leaving to every state a minimum of one or two members, as the case may be. The committees would then be substantially more representative, and the large states could assign committee seats to delegates from major regions, many of which have distinctive political identities.

Nominating Votes as Measures of Effective Power

The most obvious source of power in nominating a President is bigness: the large California delegation, for instance, is a prize for any candidate. But in anything as complex as the nominating process, where relative power is dependent on so many shifting factors which in combination are difficult to control, *effective use* of power is also a most important source. If the elements that had made a delegation—or, over time, a state, or a region—effective or ineffective in convention action could be distinguished, they might add considerably to an understanding of the nominating process. And the result of such understanding might be an increase in the efficiency of the conventions as instruments for producing nominations that most nearly represent the desires of the party electorates.

The first step is to discover where and how effectiveness or ineffectiveness had been displayed. The simplest gauge is the extent of the contribution made by a delegation, in proportion to its allotted voting strength, to the eventual winning candidate at the critical point in the nominating vote. The information on which the gauge can be used is fortunately available in the roll call records of the nominating vote since the beginning of the convention system. The Republican party has never dispensed with the calling of the roll on a presidential nomination in its entire history; the Democratic party has done so only in 1888, 1916, and 1936—all occasions when an incumbent first-term President was being renominated by acclamation.

As an aid to the study and understanding of the data, three interrelating methods of measuring effective uses of power were developed by the authors of this book as tools to be applied to the contested conventions since 1896:

1. The percentage of total convention voting strength held by each delegation.
2. The percentage of the total critical vote for the winner contributed by each delegation.
3. A winner-support ratio, consisting of the ratio of the percentage of contribution to the percentage of voting strength.*

The three measures can be readily illustrated; the record of New York will serve the purpose. In the Democratic convention of 1952, New York held 94 of the 1,230 convention votes. On the third and critical ballot, it gave 86½ votes to Adlai E. Stevenson, who received a total of 613 votes before vote shifting began. From these figures, by simple arithmetic, New York had 7.6 per cent of the convention voting strength; it contributed 14.1 per cent of the winning critical vote; and its winner-support ratio was 1.85, or 14.1 divided by 7.6. A delegation that divides its votes precisely the same way as the whole convention has a winner-support ratio of 1.00; one that is unanimously backing a loser at the time of the critical vote has a ratio of 0.00.

Regional Patterns of Effectiveness

Almost every convention shows some minor shifting in regional voting strength. The West, with its rapid growth in population, has steadily increased its proportionate voting strength at the expense of the other

* The reader is referred to the unabridged 1960 edition of this book (Chapter 16) for a fuller discussion of these statistical concepts and for tabular illustration of their application to the contested conventions from 1896 to 1956.

regions, especially the Middle West. From 1896 to 1908 western voting strength was around 9 per cent; the steady increase brought it to nearly 17 per cent in 1956 in both conventions. The West has benefited disproportionately from the bonus voting systems of both parties, as the South has also done in the Democratic party. In the Republican party the voting strength of the South was reduced in the reforms of 1916, and southern voting strength is still somewhat smaller in Republican conventions than in Democratic.

CONTRIBUTIONS TO WINNING VOTES

The regional fluctuations in contribution to the winner in the contested conventions show various noteworthy features. Some votes were much more sectional than others, and especially so in Democratic conventions. The alignments register the principal sectional disputes of the time. Bryan, the westerner most prominent in the East-West dispute over free silver, was opposed in the Northeast, supported in the South and West. Truman and (in 1952) Stevenson, both concerned in the North-South dispute over civil rights, were opposed in the South and supported in the Northeast.

Six Democratic nominations since 1896 received more than 40 per cent of their support from a single region—Bryan (South) in 1896, Parker (South) in 1904, Wilson (Middle West) in 1912, Smith (Northeast) in 1928, Stevenson (Northeast) in 1952, and Kennedy (Northeast) in 1960.

In the contested Republican conventions, regional differences were less strongly marked. McKinley in 1896 was pushed by the Middle West as a favorite son. In 1912 the rotten borough delegates from the South supported William Howard Taft, the incumbent President, with over 40 per cent of his total vote. Hoover, Willkie, Dewey, and Eisenhower were favorites of the

Northeast; Eisenhower in 1952 drew over 50 per cent of his support from the Northeast, the only candidate of the whole period in either party to do so from a single region.

WINNER-SUPPORT RATIOS

The percentage of the winning vote given by a region does not satisfactorily indicate the sentiments of its delegations unless judged in proportion to relative voting strength. Changing patterns of regional effectiveness in supporting winners at the conventions are evident in the figures for both parties.

In the Democratic case, the Northeast has fluctuated widely, with low winner-support scores in 1896, 1924, and 1932—being especially affected in 1932 by the sharp contest between Smith and Roosevelt from New York.

The Middle West has had the most consistent record as a region, seldom dropping to a winner-support ratio below 1.00 and never very far below.

The South was more successful in supporting winners in earlier years than later. It led the way to John W. Davis in 1924 and to Franklin D. Roosevelt in 1932, but has ranked low in every convention since that year.

The West swung erratically in the earlier years but has backed winners most of the time since 1928. California's choice of Kefauver in the 1952 primary, however, pulled down the western record for that year.

The non-state areas generally have thrown their limited strength to the winners, except in 1904, 1912, and 1940. Their behavior in 1940 was especially surprising, since they were opposing the renomination of an incumbent President.

In the contested Republican conventions of 1896-1952, the Northeast moved from low-average success in winner support to relative dominance. Only in 1916 of the earlier years, when Hughes was nominated, was its ratio above 1.00. In 1940, 1948, and 1952, however, the Northeast was very high—the only one of the regions above 1.00.

The Middle West has failed to back a winner strongly in any contested Republican convention since McKinley in 1896. Particularly in the more recent conventions, has it been notably low.

For the South, high ratios usually occurred when a Republican occupied the White House, but also occurred in 1896, when Mark Hanna's well-executed pre-convention campaign proved fruitful, and in 1920 when the ratio was especially high for Harding.

The West, with the exception of 1920 when Hiram Johnson, a loser, held the California delegation, was relatively high through 1928, but has since been below average. The western pattern in recent years has been heavily weighted by the big California delegation, which has frequently been tied to an unsuccessful favorite son.

The non-state areas followed somewhat the same pattern as the South, which in some ways they resembled in the Republican party. In recent years, however, they have behaved more erratically.

Big States vs. Small in Winner Support

The mathematical equations of power indicate that a presidential nomination is unlikely to be seriously contested unless some of the big state delegations are opposed to each other on the issue. A group of small delegations might provide a substitute for one or two large ones in putting up a candidate when sectional bonds are unusually strong, but this has not happened often. Usually, each of the major candidates is supported by several delegations of large and average size. When this occurs, do the small delegations leap into the struggle like the large ones? Or do they quickly find the band wagon and support the winning candidate?

During the period since 1896, in each party the delegations of the large states held about one third of the total convention voting strength, as did the delegations from the middle-sized states; the delegations from the small states and the non-state areas together held the other third. Grouping the delegations by size with their winner-support ratios shows that no group has had a monopoly of winner support. Some curious differences appear, however, when the patterns of group differences by size are compared for the two parties.

Usually the small states and non-state areas had the highest average winner-support ratios, while the large states as a group had the lowest. These regularities were clearest for the Republican groups during the earlier years when the Republican party was strongly dominant—1896 to 1924; next so for the Democratic groups during the more recent period when the Democratic party was moderately dominant and for the Republicans during the same period of their party's moderate weakness; and least of all for the Democrats during the years 1896 to 1924 when their party was very weak.

Average differences in winner support very similar to those between the big states and small states can also be found within each party when the states are classified in terms of their party alignment. At Democratic conventions of 1928-1956, the delegations from the most strongly Democratic states were the ones that averaged lowest in winner support on nominating votes (ratio 0.85) while the delegations from the weakest Democratic states ranked highest (ratio 1.19). Conversely, in the Republican party during its period of dominance from 1896 to 1924, the delegations from the most solidly Republican states averaged lowest in winner support (ratio 0.76) while the delegations from the weakest Republican states (mainly southern) ranked highest (ratio 1.37), being exceeded on the average only by the delegations from the non-state areas (ratio 1.49).

This suggests that the centers of power that are at work during the nominating process become more effective and more highly organized during the periods when a party frequently wins possession of the White House. When there is a band wagon that is likely to go somewhere, the weaker units of the system are usually the quickest to climb aboard.

The mechanisms through which these influences work can be identified to some extent. In the party in power, delegations from small states, non-state areas, and areas of party weakness are probably more amenable to pressure from the incumbent administration when it is seeking to influence the forthcoming nomination. The party organizations and the party voters in small states and in states where the party is weak may be more easily swayed by active preconvention campaigns when victory is in the air. Federal patronage may be relatively much more important to the party in some states than in others, thus intensifying their desire to hop on the band wagon before the critical vote if the party has a hope of winning the election.

The Idiosyncrasies of the States

State delegations are usually either high or low in winner support, seldom providing merely average support; this is the consequence of the tendency of members of a delegation to agree on candidates. Further, successive delegations from a state often tend to support winners (or losers) at successive conventions. This may continue for as long as a generation.

New York's Democratic delegations were among the

few exceptions; in six contested conventions New York support was given mainly to a winner on three occasions and mainly to a loser on the other three. Between 1928 and 1956 there were only nine such exceptional states on the Democratic side and only five on the Republican.

The large and the middle states with the highest winner-support scores and those with the lowest, for the period 1928-1956, were as follows:

Democratic		Republican	
Michigan	1.47	New York	1.72
Pennsylvania	1.35	New Jersey	1.53
Iowa	1.27	Massachusetts	1.51
Minnesota	1.26	Missouri	1.25
Illinois	1.24	Pennsylvania	1.20
New Jersey	1.22		
		California	0.43
Georgia	0.46	Illinois	0.42
Virginia	0.11	Ohio	0.32
Texas	0.00	Wisconsin	0.19

A continuing tendency to support losers at consecutive conventions could not easily occur except in a state where factions are persistently dissident in relation to the national party. This is shown by the identity of the states that have ranged near the bottom since 1928 in supporting winners. Factionalism of this scale and duration, moreover, has involved deeply entrenched sectional or economic forces and a durable leadership that could provide and develop definite, though unsuccessful, candidates for the presidential nominations.

The extent to which the position of the major states can change in the course of a generation is illustrated with special clarity by the record of the states that have ranked in recent years as the top seven in population. The winner-support ratios of the seven states for the two periods were as follows:

State	Democratic		Republican	
	1896-1924	1928-1956	1896-1924	1928-1956
New York	0.72	0.95	0.97	1.72
Ohio	1.15	0.88	1.14	0.32
Pennsylvania	1.11	1.35	0.13	1.20
Illinois	1.08	1.24	0.35	0.42
California	0.62	0.93	0.84	0.43
Texas	1.09	0.00	1.35	0.91
Michigan	1.29	1.47	1.35	0.78

The changing positions reflected in the figures should provide warnings about prediction for the future. It cannot safely be assumed that the states most effective in presidential nominating politics during the last thirty years will be equally so in the next thirty. New York has seemingly benefited in recent years from the increasing nationalization of politics, communication, and economic life. Its position may also be especially strong because of its central location in the eastern metropolitan complex—the geographic area from Boston to Washington, D. C., in which a population of more than 25 million is now aggregated.

The alternative power centers in Ohio, Illinois, Texas, and California have fared poorly in each party when they attempted to stand alone. If they could unite in either party against the leadership of the Northeast, they might succeed in dominating one party or the other. But without such a coalition it is difficult to see what any of these states would have to gain by continuing a policy of dissidence in either party for another generation.

High winner-support ratios may signify either skill in finding the band wagon or successful leadership in directing where the band wagon is to go, just as the converse may signify either bad guessing or stubborn adherence to a losing cause. The big state delegations are clearly more likely to be influenced by the presence or absence of a favorite son of some stature, but, even aside from this factor, they seem more compelled than the smaller delegations to exercise the prerogatives of leadership or of responsible choice.

The big states probably tend to become committed somewhat earlier than the others; once committed, they often stay with their choice, even when the result is defeat. Smaller states can probably avoid commitment to a loser with less difficulty, and therefore find it easier to shift to the winner on or before the critical ballot. But even among the small states there are some that have backed losers in one party or the other for all or most of a generation.

Even when conditions appear to be similar, every state is to some extent unique and has its own patterns of behavior within each of the national parties. Where those patterns are both persistent and important for the effectiveness of state action, they merit examination on a state-by-state basis; such examination, however, goes far beyond the possibilities of the present chapter or the present book. Various bases have been suggested here for effectiveness or non-effectiveness in voting; beyond these, there are the marked idiosyncrasies of the individual states, some of which stem from peculiarities in the state primary election systems, as discussed in earlier chapters. Mainly, the analysis serves to identify the areas where power has been shown, and under what conditions. When the direct story of each convention is examined, the specific techniques by which power is applied, all with the final nominating vote as the goal, can be more fully seen.

Voting Strategies

The basic voting procedures of the conventions give contending factions many opportunities for strategy. Issues can be developed and dramatized, especially when the voting is by roll call. The early votes that deal ostensibly with non-nominating matters can be used to test sentiment, to measure the strength of opposing groups, and to demonstrate and limit the practical alternatives.

As noted earlier, the Democrats' two thirds rule and the conflict over its application were a recurring focus of strategy for a century. The seating rules and the contests they generate have lent themselves frequently to strategy in test votes—most recently in 1952 when they provided the test vote, engineered by the Eisenhower managers, that signaled the probable defeat of Senator Taft. In each step that leads up to the beginning of the actual nominating procedure, there are further opportunities for strategy, of which the order of business is itself one. And when the level of tension is high, procedural issues may be raised even after the convention has begun the actual balloting, although such occasions have been rare.

The fact that the vice-presidential nomination has invariably followed the presidential has limited its use for strategy, and limited as well the kind of attention given the choice. In recent years, suggestions that the candidates for both offices might be nominated together as a ticket or that the vice-presidential nomination might be made first have received some consideration. A change in procedure would probably have the effect of establishing a visible group of separate candidates for the vice-presidential nomination, who might then ally themselves in one way or another with the various presi-

dential candidates. A vote on the vice-presidential nomination, if taken first, would have the close attention of
the delegates and the country and, when the presidential
nomination is being contested, might provide the most
important test vote leading up to the final balloting.

The Strategy of Non-Nominating Roll Call Votes

The most obvious reason for taking a roll call vote
is to reach a decision that will be in accord with the
will of the majority where views are closely divided.
Thus it could be expected that most non-nominating
roll call votes would be settled by rather close margins,
and a voice vote should suffice when the division is
heavily in one direction. That more than one third of
the non-nominating roll calls taken since 1864 in both
parties have been settled by majorities of 65 per cent
or more is a clear indication of their use for strategic
purposes.

Majorities already assured of their strength have
sometimes obtained roll call votes to smoke out the
minority, possibly for later punitive action. Minorities
have often sought roll calls that they knew they could
not win, but also knowing that the issue seemed calculated to split the majority or otherwise embarrass it.
Occasionally roll calls are used as a tactic for delay.
Their use for any purpose has been rare in the conventions that moved easily toward a first-ballot choice,
most common in the conventions involved in close contests. In the latter case, however, they have sometimes
been avoided by tacit consent, because no candidate
yet was in a position to demonstrate strength.

When the critical votes of the conventions from 1832
to 1956 were studied in relationship to the prenominat-

ing roll call votes, it was found that the critical nominating vote was significantly parallel to at least one earlier roll call vote on some subject in about three quarters of the contested conventions. It was also discovered that the early voting behavior of the delegations that were eventually high for the winner was frequently quite different from that of the delegations that eventually proved to be low for winner. The votes were therefore examined separately for each of these groups as well as for the convention as a whole. In the usual case, but with interesting exceptions, the delegations that opposed each other on the nomination were opposed in about the same degree on a related earlier vote.*

The 1948 Democratic convention provided a clear example in the vote on the resolution to amend the platform on civil rights, moved by ex-Governor Dan Moody of Texas. The delegations high for Truman voted 97.5 per cent for him on the nomination and 98.7 per cent against the Moody resolution. The delegations low for Truman voted 95.6 per cent against him on the nomination and 100 per cent for the Moody resolution. The anti-Truman delegations thus were solid on the platform issue and only slightly less so against his nomination.

For each of three groups of conventions—those with a first-ballot winner, those with a front-runner who went on to win the nomination, and those in which the eventual winner was weak on the first ballot—the average relationships between selected roll call votes and the critical nominating ballot for the winner have been computed. In each party the highest indexes of relationship are found for the conventions that began with a strong front-runner who required more than one ballot

* Again, the reader is referred to the unabridged edition of this book, where the full discussion and tabular material of this comparative analysis will be found in Chapter 17.

to win; the next highest for the conventions with first-ballot winners; and the lowest for those in which the eventual winner was weak on the first ballot.

In contested conventions that move quickly to a first-ballot winner, the leading candidate is usually so near to nomination when the convention opens that the result seems inevitable. He has little need to seek a test vote to prove his strength, but opposition groups may insist on an early record vote—for home consumption, for publicity purposes, to demonstrate that their strength though limited is real, or just because they are angry. In such cases the opposition to the winner is often more nearly solid than is the support of his followers, many of whom may be simply riding the band wagon; thus it comes about that the index of relationship is higher for the opposition delegations than for those supporting the winner.

In conventions with a strong front-runner whose victory is not yet assured, an early vote on an issue that can demonstrate convention control is likely to be sought either by the front-runner or by a coalition of the forces trying to stop him. Because such a vote is so clearly a test of strength, the relationship between it and the subsequent nominating vote is likely to be very tight, and the patterns of voting in general are much more consistent than those found in other types of convention.

In conventions that begin with fragmentation of strength and great uncertainty about the eventual winner, there is less tendency to force issues to provide test votes. Nevertheless, roll call voting may occur with some frequency simply because of the amount of confusion and internal conflict. The results usually have a visible relationship to the nominating vote, but typically not a close one.

THE ART OF THE STRATEGIST

The convention history of the two parties on the strategic use of prenominating votes is told by these indexes of relationship. Many of the specific instances have become part of the lore of American history. Convention strategists are always prepared to take credit for test votes that advanced the fortunes of their candidates, but in many cases the probability is that an early vote, being known to be important to one or more of the candidates, merely brought out an expression of a voting preference already in existence.

However, this assumption does not cover all cases. There is no doubt that sometimes the strategists were practicing their highest art, which is to arrange a vote on which the uncommitted delegates, or even delegates committed to another candidate, will find themselves compelled to vote in a direction favorable to a particular candidate—thus committing themselves by that much to his fortunes.

The early votes in the Republican convention of 1952 seem to have served this purpose perfectly: the delegates who were uncommitted as between Taft and Eisenhower mostly voted for the proposals put forward by the Eisenhower managers. At the Democratic convention of 1912 the heart of Bryan's strategy was a series of actions that had the effect of splitting the support of Champ Clark. Woodrow Wilson's support was mainly from the progressive wing of the party, whereas Clark entered the convention with considerable support from both progressives and conservatives. By forcing divisive issues, Bryan compelled the Clark progressives to vote against the interest of their own candidate. Eventually they abandoned him.

Reaching Consensus

The number of ballots required to complete a presidential nomination is related to the amount and kind of division with which a convention opens. It seemed likely that the division would be in turn related to the type of leadership being confirmed, rejected, or selected by the convention. Therefore, the basic nominating categories of leadership confirmation and succession (as identified in Chapter 7) were examined, with the expectation that each might have its own special pattern of convention voting.

CONFIRMING EXISTING LEADERSHIP OR INHERITANCE

In seventeen of the sixty-five major-party nominations from 1832 to 1960, the conventions confirmed an existing leadership by renominating an incumbent President; eight of the cases were Democratic, nine Republican. Titular leaders were renominated by the Democrats four times, by the Republicans once, producing a total of twenty-two cases of leadership confirmation. The voting pattern suggests that in many of the cases a high degree of consensus had been achieved before the convention even met.

All of these nominations were made by a single convention ballot, except for the Dewey nomination in 1948, which required three ballots. In only five cases was there any other other candidate who polled as much as 10 per cent. In twelve conventions, no prior roll call vote was taken on any subject, and in the others, such a vote was usually related only slightly, if at all, to the nomination.

Twice in the Democratic party, three times in the Republican, and twice in Republican predecessor parties

—seven cases in all—a nomination has recognized and confirmed an inheritance of leadership, or has recognized a leader already so outstanding that the nomination was his as a matter of course. The voting pattern was identical with that confirming an existing leadership. All were one-ballot nominations; in four conventions, including the 1960 Republican, there was no prenominating roll call vote on any subject.

ACCEPTING INNER GROUP SELECTION

Six Democratic nominations and four Republican were classified in Chapter 7 as instances of inner group selection. Five of these required only a single ballot, but in most of the ten cases one or two minority candidates each polled at least 10 per cent. In five of the Democratic conventions prior roll call votes were taken, usually several and rather sharply divided. In the four Republican conventions, there was a prior roll call vote only in 1916.

The voting pattern suggests that some degree of consensus had been worked out before the convention met, but that the decision was usually one requiring negotiation, opportunity for dissent, and final adjustment at the convention.

FINDING A COMPROMISE CHOICE

In the four Democratic and three Republican nominations that were classified as representing compromise at the end of a factional struggle, long balloting was the rule, and the number of minor candidates polling at least 10 per cent at one point or another was four, five, or six. Without exception, divided votes on other issues preceded the nominating vote, some of them closely contested.

The most recent cases were those of Harding and

Davis in 1920 and 1924; all the other five are distant by at least three quarters of a century. Most of the conditions conducive to a compromise choice have disappeared in recent years, among them the two thirds rule. The tactic of awaiting or even promoting a deadlock was formerly encouraged by the absence of reliable information about attitudes and intentions; under modern conditions, with so much information systematically collected and published, the opportunity for deadlock has been reduced.

DECIDING A FACTIONAL STRUGGLE

Of the nine Democratic nominations and ten Whig and Republican classified as factional victories, only three—Dewey's in 1944, McKinley's in 1896 and Kennedy's in 1960—had outcomes that were generally anticipated in advance of the convention. Tilden in 1876 and Roosevelt in 1932 were front-runners in popular support, but they faced stiff opposition and at least a possibility that they could be blocked under the two thirds rule. In the fourteen other cases a hard fight was anticipated, and in some of them a candidate who placed second, third, or fourth in the early balloting came from behind to win—Bryan, Wilson, and Cox among the Democrats, and Lincoln, Benjamin Harrison, and Willkie among the Republicans.

Four of the Democratic nominations (all under the two thirds rule) required extremely lengthy balloting; for the Whig and Republican nominations, this was true only for Winfield Scott, the last of the Whig nominees. There were several roll call divisions before the nominating balloting began in all of the Democratic conventions in this category except that of 1960, and usually in the Republican. On many of the roll calls the conventions were sharply divided into nearly equal groups, with the victors having majorities barely over 50 per cent.*

* * *

The long-balloting conventions seem to be mostly of the past. The probability is that the outcome of most nominating contests in the future will be generally anticipated before the conventions meet. Even if the lines are closely drawn between candidates of nearly equal strength, the issue is still likely to be settled with a minimum number of ballots. Both the long-term trends in convention balloting and action in recent conventions support that conclusion.

Despite the heat of the Taft-Eisenhower contest in 1952 and the closeness of the division among the delegates, the issue was decided in a single nominating ballot, as was the Kennedy nomination in 1960. In the Democratic convention of 1952 a reluctant candidate was brought to the point of nomination in three ballots, all taken during one day. In both parties the preconvention campaigns, ably abetted by the party leaders and the mass media, had settled much of the convention business before the convention even met.

Split Conventions

Any convention is split when it has two or more actively competing candidates, but the basic split may be concerned either with the candidates as personalities or with something deeper that merely finds expression through them. The nature of any basic split is highly relevant to the kind and amount of conflict that will occur.

* The reader who would like to consult the tables which provided the materials for this section will find them in Chapter 17 of the unabridged 1960 edition.

A bifactional pattern has persisted in the Republican party throughout most of its history. Many of its candidates had been previously identified as factional leaders, but Republicans (and Whigs before them) have been more willing than Democrats to resolve conflict by taking a candidate from outside regular politics. Democratic factional patterns have been more complex and less clearly linked to candidate interests; they include long-term strain between urban and rural adherents, persistent sectionalism involving the South, and occasional struggles about some temporary issue of immediate importance.

In conventions where one candidate is strong enough at the start to be assured of the nomination, any opposition that puts up a fight is likely to represent a continuing factionalism, but it may have difficulty in finding any strong personality as a center for its interests. This was true in 1928 of the opposition to Al Smith's nomination and to Herbert Hoover's.

Conversely, in conventions where the situation is so splintered that three or four contenders seem almost equally strong at the beginning, the problem frequently is to find a cleavage line that will identify a majority. In the Democratic convention of 1896, the silver issue served the purpose. An early procedural vote made clear the division and showed the strength of the silverites. Thereafter, the silver group dominated the convention and the only question was which of their number would be nominated.

At the Republican convention of 1920 there was no pronounced ideological split. The three strongest candidates—Wood, Lowden, and Johnson—had each disqualified himself in some way during the preconvention campaign, and each was unacceptable to most of the delegates other than his own supporters. The convention majority wanted a "regular" Republican who was popular and broadly unobjectionable. It found him in Harding.

The most difficult conventions are those in which two strong candidates are each in a position to veto the nomination of the other. The heat of the battle will often bring the candidates to extremist positions, and the partisans of each may develop a strong distrust for his opponent, so that neither can become a second choice. The choice must in the end then be made by the center groups who are uncommitted—yet these groups may have come to distrust both candidates. This is the classic situation for the choice of a compromise candidate—which was avoided by the Republicans in 1952 mainly because only Taft was a genuine factional leader. Eisenhower had done relatively little to arouse factional hostilities, had made no personal attack on Taft, had demonstrated his popular appeal, and could thus receive the votes of the uncommitted delegates.

The Processes of Alliance

The motives that have been most frequently drawn upon for alliance and support can be classified as follows:

1. Presence and absence of shared goals
    a. Issues
    b. Group affinities
    c. Party regularity
2. Attractions and repulsions of candidate personality
3. Bargaining considerations
4. Sanctions
    a. Prospects for reward
    b. Dangers of reprisal

In any alliance move, bargaining considerations of one sort or another are usually present. Bribery and other corrupt bargaining have often been charged but seldom proved. "Deals" presumably take place more often in the form of "You support my man for this, and I will back yours for that." Exchanges of support may also involve transfers of campaign funds and the assumption of campaign deficits; there is a shadowland in this area that needs to be opened up to public inspection.

All of the processes of alliance have long been known in terms of the lore of the conventions as they existed during the nineteenth century and well into the twentieth. Some aspects of the situation have changed, with the changes in nominating campaigns. Popular mandates have become more definite, and information concerning them is much more widely available; this clearly affects the extent to which the choice of nominee is left to the conventions and the kinds of alliance that can be made. The classic situations thus may occur less frequently and sometimes not at all. But when two front-runners are closely matched or the situation somehow spreads out into a contest between three or four candidates of nearly equal strength, the outcome will certainly remain in doubt and the processes of alliance within the convention will be important.

The Limits of Convention Action

It is well to recall that the opportunities for strategy and maneuver that are open in practice to any party convention are limited by the situation within which it meets. Sometimes there is no apparent opportunity to change what has already become preordained.

Even when major decisions remain to be made by the convention, it is free to act only in a relative sense. Issues have already been drawn. Candidates and their supporters have waged their campaigns openly or covertly. The stage has been set for certain possible coalitions, and other coalitions have been made improbable if not impossible. The emotional pitch has been established. The pieces for the game are all there —what remains is how skillfully the players will use them. As in the end game in chess, the available strategies are restricted by the pieces, their value, and their position when the players take their seats.

Many who participate in conventions see them mainly as recurring bouts in the internal struggles of the parties, but the decrease in roll call votes suggests that the processes once most useful for factional display are beginning to atrophy. In any event, a convention is predominantly a strategic crossroad in the more comprehensive nominating and party processes.

To the extent that the conventions do have power, their capabilities for damaging their respective parties may be greater than for repairing and rebuilding them. Any convention has the power to degrade its party image even in victory, or to lessen its popular appeal and make victory impossible for the time being; on the other hand, when the party has already been severely damaged by the preconvention campaigns, the convention has only limited capacity to heal the breach. But hope springs eternal, and the conventions, like other aggregations of humanity, can always hope to transcend their own usual limitations. Sometimes they even seem to succeed.

15

Convention Action and Election Results

Inevitably, the choice between candidates is also a choice between strategies for the pursuit of goals that include winning the election if possible; winning in a way that will commit the party in one direction rather than another; holding together the coalition that the party represents; enlarging the party's following in the electorate, especially when this is essential to win.

Working politicians usually begin their calculations for strategy by reviewing the voting statistics of the previous election; in doing so they are concerned not only with national totals but also with the distribution of the vote by states and the record of the interest groups that may again take a hand in the outcome. When potential candidates are discussed, their prospective effect on the status of the party vote as last recorded is a major factor in the reckoning.

The prospective influence of convention action on the election result is clearly central to the decision on the candidate, but the basis for anticipating the relationship is frequently cloudy indeed. Past experience, which must form the basis for expectations, is so infinitely complex that few can attempt to understand more than some very small portion of it. Insofar as research can assist, it must seek out those portions of historical experience that may best lend themselves to a clarification of expectations.

Fluctuations in Growth in the Party Vote

From 1832 to 1892 the popular vote in presidential elections increased by an average of 16.5 per cent from one presidential election to another. From 1896 to 1960 the average was 11.3 per cent, despite the influence of women's suffrage in 1920 and later years. The growth has not occurred evenly from year to year, but has come in spurts, sometimes as the result of extraneous factors, but frequently in circumstances in which the nominees may have been a critical element. The figures for election years since 1896 are shown in Table 15 on page 294.

Repeat engagements by the same opponents seem to retard growth in the vote. In 1900, Bryan and McKinley were running against each other for the second time, and the total vote increase was almost nil. The second engagement between Stevenson and Eisenhower in 1956 led to virtually no increase in the total vote.

The Presidents who won a second term usually increased the vote of their own party substantially, but at a lesser rate than in the first election. Wilson was exceptional for the large increase in his second race, after achieving no increase in his first. Spectacular falloffs in the party vote were associated with the failures of Taft and Hoover to win second terms.

Renominated titular leaders of defeated parties have tended to repeat their previous vote but not to increase

TABLE 15. LONG-TERM GROWTH IN THE POPULAR
AND PARTY VOTE FOR PRESIDENT, 1896-1960[a]

Year	Ratio of Popular Vote to That Cast in Last Previous Election[b]			Percentage of Popular Vote Polled[c]	
	Total	Democratic	Republican	Democratic	Republican
1896	1.15	1.15	1.37*	45.9	51.1
1900	1.00	1.00	1.02*	45.5	51.7
1904	0.97	0.80	1.06*	37.6	56.4
1908	1.10	1.26	1.01*	43.1	51.6
1912	1.01	0.98*	0.45	41.9	23.2
1916	1.23	1.45*	2.45	49.3	46.1
1920	1.44	1.00	1.89*	34.1	60.3
1924	1.09	0.92	0.97*	28.8	54.0
1928	1.27	1.79	1.36*	40.8	58.1
1932	1.08	1.52*	0.74	57.4	39.7
1936	1.15	1.20*	1.06	60.2	36.5
1940	1.09	0.98*	1.34	53.9	44.7
1944	0.96	0.92*	0.99	51.7	45.9
1948	1.02	0.97*	1.00	49.4	45.0
1952	1.26	1.13	1.54*	44.4	55.0
1956	1.01	0.94	1.05*	41.5	57.4
1960	1.11	1.32*	0.96	49.7	49.5

[a] Sources: Election returns for 1896-1932, inclusive, from Edgar E. Robinson, *The Presidential Vote, 1896-1932* (1934); 1936-1960, inclusive, from Bureau of the Census, *Statistical Abstracts, 1936-1960*.
[b] Winner indicated by asterisk (*).
[c] The aggregate figures for parties other than the two major exceeded a range of 0.6 to 6.0% only in 1912 (34.9%) and 1924 (17.2%).

it. The popular vote for Bryan was highest on his first try, almost the same on his second and third. In 1948, Dewey failed to increase the vote he had polled in 1944, a war-time year, which in turn was smaller than Willkie's vote in 1940. Stevenson's vote in 1956 fell off 6 per cent from his vote in 1952.

One of the clearest findings is the rarity of the occasions on which either party has been able to grow by taking votes, net, directly from the other. There are always a few floating voters who move from one party to the other, but large net transfers usually occur only when there is an actual decline in the vote of one party. Such declines have been associated with increases of 1 per cent or more in the vote of the other party in only seven cases since 1832, one of which was the election of 1932—the most outstanding case in modern times in which large blocs of voters transferred directly from one political party to the other. The Republican vote declined 26 per cent while the Democratic vote increased by 52 per cent.

Since the average growth in the popular vote from one election to another was around 11 per cent for the period 1896-1960, either party can grow by a corresponding amount without being dependent on taking votes from the other party, assuming the turnout rates do not change. But the whole look of the figures suggests that substantial upswings in the total popular vote usually reflect an induction of new voters into the system and a change in turnout rates that is much more favorable to one party than the other. When the prospective winning party seems likely to achieve a great increase in turnout, even the losing party may achieve some increase—as the Democrats demonstrated with their 13 per cent increase in 1952.

Convention Action and State Voter Turnout

The irregularity of growth of the national vote throughout the years is even more noticeable when the records of individual states are examined. For the period 1896-1956 the total popular vote dropped from one presidential election to the next in an average of nearly one state in four on each occasion. Irregularity is also conspicuous for each party's vote in the individual states: the Democratic vote registered declines in 42 per cent of the cases, the Republican in 36 per cent.

FACTORS AFFECTING VOTE-SWING RELATIONSHIPS

To what extent is this fluctuation related to the choice of candidate and the success or failure of each state delegation in securing the candidate it preferred at the conventions? A perfect relationship could not be expected, since a great many other factors, such as weight of public opinion, degrees of party loyalty, actions of opposition party voters, intervene. Such factors in general resist precise measurement, but a close study shows that some of them operate with frequency and important effect in connection with the vote fluctuation pattern. Those most often found have therefore been used as elements in an outline of relationships between voting at the conventions and the subsequent swings in party vote in the respective states.

Although the factors operate in different ways and with different relative weight under varying conditions, they can be classified under one of three general types of situation, according to the relationships toward which they tend to lead: positive relationships where the party vote in the state moves in the same direction as the state delegation's action at the convention, whether in *support of* or *in opposition to* a candidate; random relationships, resulting from the obscuring or flattening effect of the factors; negative relationships, resulting from the reversal effect of the factors.

1. *Factors Leading to Positive Relationship.* A positive relationship between convention voting and vote swing in the states is most likely to occur when the

issues and the personalities of the candidates are clear to both the delegates and the voters. When issues are sharply drawn and candidates are well known both as individuals and as identified with important issues, the mandates given to delegates can be more definite and delegate action can be clearly appraised by their constituents. The delegate who does not obey a genuine mandate from a majority of his constituents can expect an adverse reaction at the polls. The following situations are among those likely to result in clear mandates, sharp decisions, and strong voter response.

A high level of public awareness on a major national issue.

A high level of geographic orientation on an issue.

A widely known candidate, whose reputation is based upon his political activity and whose stand on issues is clear.

A sharply fought preconvention campaign, which has intensified loyalties and sharpened enmities.

Clear identification of a candidate with political, social, or economic groups that can become apparent in the geography of voter alignment.

2. *Factors Leading to Random Effects.* Ambiguity tends to reduce positive relationship. When no major issue divides the nation, or when a candidate has little identification with the issues that are currently most dividing, delegates have no way of knowing how their constituents will respond and may expect a response of apathy. When a candidate is little known to the general public, its opinion of him must be formed by his actions after nomination. A candidate from outside the political world is usually chosen for the vote-getting qualities he is presumed to have—but those qualities have had little previous testing and can only be estimated. The follow-

ing situations are among those likely to produce random effects and an absence of relationship, either positive or negative.

Low level of conflict over issues and between prospective candidates, or compromise selection after deadlock of leading candidates.

Lack of a clear *political image* of the nominee. Preconvention campaigns in which delegates are selected by party organizations and without much publicity or commitment.

A band-wagon effect, when one candidate is so far out in front that his nomination seems inevitable, thus encouraging delegates to join the coalition early and without regard to whether their constituents would approve.

A heavy cross-over vote by the voters of one party for the candidate of the other, often as a protest against their own party's candidate.

3. *Factors Leading to Negative Relationship.* In at least three situations a negative—or reversed—relationship between convention voting and the swings in party vote can be anticipated.

The first occurs when there is a profound change in the political situation between convention and election —a change with which the candidate becomes identified in a way that tends to reverse his field of support in the electorate. (The qualification is important; in its absence, change between convention and election would have merely random effects.)

The second occurs when the candidate's election campaign position on issues proves to be quite different from what was assumed to be his position when he was nominated—in fact, he is discovered to be definitely in opposition to major goals of the nominating coalition.

The third occurs when party leaders from areas where the party is relatively strong deliberately unite to nominate a candidate best suited, in their judgment, to appeal most where the party is weak. In extreme cases this may be a strategy of desperation in a party situation of great weakness, but when it results in lifting the party's national vote substantially it can be viewed as a response made to a national mandate by delegates who are prepared to give the national situation more weight than the immediate views of their own constituents.

*   *   *

The statistical record of elections in the past reveals a wide range from high positive to equally high negative reaction of the party voters to the actions of their delegates in the conventions. When it is analyzed, some of the direction and degree of the total relationship is seen.*

The tools of measurement used in analyzing the records included the following: for voting at the conventions, the winner-support ratio developed in Chapter 14; for vote swing in the states, the simple ratio between the party's total popular vote in one presidential election and that in the preceding election. By means of these ratios, it was possible to arrive at a four-way classification for each contested convention year in each party, assigning the states to groups as follows:

HH, High for winner at convention, high upswing in party vote.

* The previous outline of hypotheses was tested by the authors against the actual experience in an array of tables based on the statistical record of convention action and election results for the 1896-1956 period. This statistical analysis may be consulted in Chapter 18 of the unabridged edition of this book.

HL, High for winner at convention, low upswing in party vote.

LH, Low for winner at convention, high upswing in party vote.

LL, Low for winner at convention, low upswing in party vote.

The HH and LL categories both provide examples of positive relationship, since there is consistency in the two kinds of movement, while the HL and LH categories both provide examples of negative relationship.

When the historical record of the personalities and forces involved in each convention year is examined in relation to the information provided by these groupings, further clues emerge that may lead to a better understanding of the total process. In the two sections that follow, the historical experience of the parties is interpreted in the light of the statistical record.

THE DEMOCRATIC EXPERIENCE

When the Democratic experience was examined for winner-support and vote-swing relationship, the most extraordinary showing was the record of the results of Al Smith's nomination in 1928. Often considered one of the most badly defeated candidates of modern times, Smith has occasionally been given some grudging recognition for pulling up the party's percentage of the popular vote in the 1928 election to 41 per cent—from the disastrous 29 per cent at which Davis left it in 1924. But the present analysis revealed that his 79 per cent increase from 1924 to 1928 in the national Democratic party vote was and still is an all-time high for a Democratic convention nominee. In the states that were high for Smith at the convention the average increase in Democratic vote was 127 per cent; in those that were low at the convention it was 16 per cent. In states high for him at the convention and also high in vote swing—56 per cent of the electoral college—his increase in the party vote was 2½ times (HH ratio 2.53); in the states that correlated low (LL), with 29 per cent of the electoral college, the party vote stayed level with a vote-swing ratio of 1.03. The Hoover nomination of the same year also produced a dramatic increase in the Republican vote, largely as a response to Smith's nomination; the two combined produced the highest rate of increase in popular vote between 1876 and 1956, with the sole exception of 1920, the year when national women's suffrage arrived.

The Smith case thus emerges as the leading example of what a sharply defined nominating decision can do to the party vote. When nominated, Al Smith was one of the best-known political figures in the country. His whole reputation, moreover, was based on his record in politics, and his always clear issue positions on the Ku Klux Klan, prohibition, and the rights of a Roman Catholic to run for office. He was a symbol of the desire of the urban masses for political recognition— and thereby his 1928 vote contributed to the later development of the Democratic party by enlarging its working class following in Massachusetts, New York, New Jersey, Pennsylvania, and Michigan; in ten of the states where the Progressives had been strongest in 1924 he more than doubled the Democratic vote, and in Wisconsin, Minnesota, and North Dakota, the increase was sevenfold.

The nomination also illustrates almost all of the factors previously identified as leading to positive relationship between convention voting and vote swing. True, in 1928 there was no sharply fought preconvention campaign, but the party struggles of 1920 and 1924 had already served the purpose so far as Smith's candidacy was concerned. The relationship was not perfect, however; three states in which the vote swing was high had voted *against* Smith at the convention: Ohio, Florida, and Nebraska. In six other states that had voted *for* Smith at the convention, the vote swing was rated low: New Mexico, Kentucky, Delaware, West Virginia, Arkansas, and New Hampshire. The last two nevertheless increased their Democratic popular vote over 40 per cent.

Opinions can differ on whether or not the Smith nomination was a good thing for the Democratic party, but it is difficult to argue that any other possible candidate could have increased the party vote so much in 1928, especially in states where the party was so much in need of an increase if it was again to become competitive. The contrast is especially striking against the record of his two immediate predecessors, Cox and Davis.

The Kennedy case of 1960 invites comparison with that of Al Smith in 1928, but these were candidates with quite different factors. For Smith, there was a high level of public awareness on a major national issue: his position on the Ku Klux Klan in 1924 was certainly well remembered. Kennedy had kept a moderate position. As governor of New York, Smith's political image was sharp and clear; Kennedy's position in the Senate was not well understood by the public, and he lacked a clear political image.

Both of these candidates were out in front, though Smith was in a better band-wagon situation. But Kennedy was in a position of receiving a heavy cross-over vote from the opponent party, and this affected the correlation considerably.

In the states that were high for Kennedy at the convention, the average increase in Democratic vote was 36 per cent, against 26 per cent in the states that were low for Kennedy at the convention. The case was thus one of positive relationship, but not nearly so sharply structured as that of 1928. Twelve of the states that were high for Kennedy at the convention, including Pennsylvania and Michigan, were low in vote swing (HL), while ten that were low in convention vote, including California, New Jersey, and Texas, were high in vote swing (LH)—thus raising questions in each case about the reasons for these inverse relationships between delegation voting and constituency sentiment. The presence of Lyndon Johnson on the ticket was presumably one of the major factors that reduced the correlation between Kennedy's nominating vote and the election returns, but Kennedy's own reputation as a moderate on most issues may have had some influence. Kennedy shared his religion with Al Smith, but his candidacy differed in many other respects.

Four other Democratic nominations—those of 1896, 1904, 1932, and 1948—were clearly followed by positive relationshp and noteworthy effects in vote swing. The Truman case in 1948 was the clearest of all in displaying the resistance of a minority at the convention, backed strongly by the minority's constituents in the election.

Three cases displayed in various ways the factors leading to random effects: Davis in 1924, a compromise choice after one of the most extreme instances of convention deadlock; Bryan in 1908, a third-time nominee, a first-ballot winner on a lopsided vote, a beneficiary of organizational type preconvention campaigns and band-wagon movements, and opposed mainly by factional adversaries whose voter support was limited; and Stevenson in 1956, whose chief opponent had conceded before the convention met, and who, like Bryan in 1908, was the beneficiary of a preconvention campaign conducted primarily through organizational channels, with large elements of bandwagon vote in his first-ballot victory.

Highly significant negative relationships were found in three nominations—1912, 1940, and 1952. In 1912, the final nominating coalition, achieved with great difficulty, was a strange mixture. In the election Wilson ran somewhat better in the states that had voted against him at the convention than in those that had voted for him—a negative relationship that is in general accounted for by the fact that Wilson was bracketed in the public mind somewhere between the progressive Roosevelt and the conservative Taft. In 1952, Stevenson ran 16 per cent better in the states that voted against him at the convention than in those that voted for him—one of the clearest cases of negative relationship between convention voting and party vote swing.

In one sense it was a classic example of selection by the party leaders—without reference to established popularity with the general public—of a candidate who was expected to run reasonably well in areas opposed to his nomination and in which the party had suffered a previous bolt. But the leadership of the draft-Stevenson movement, and much of his actual convention support, came from liberal and labor leaders who wanted a candidate who could run well in their own states, and would be sufficiently acceptable to the party leaders to have some chance of nomination.

Stevenson ran fairly well in the northeastern areas where much of his convention support had centered; he ran even better in California and in the southern states, all of which except Arkansas had voted against his nomination. In the middle west states he fell below his national average in most of those that had supported his nomination at the convention, with random results in those that had opposed it. In nearly all rural areas he proved rather consistently not to be an attractive candidate, despite the band-wagon support he had received from a number of rural states at the convention.

For the party leaders who were trying to bridge the gap between the party's urban and industrial elements, on the one hand, and its southern strength, on the other, while holding the party vote elsewhere, the results of the nomination confirmed the wisdom of their choice. In view of the sharp cleavages to be bridged in the aftermath of the 1948 bolt, the maneuver probably would not have been possible except with a candidate such as Stevenson whose issue positions were both moderate and little known at the time.

THE REPUBLICAN EXPERIENCE

The Republican experience offers fewer cases of contested nominations for study than the Democratic, and still fewer in which relatively high degrees of positive relationship are found between convention voting and vote swing. The leading case was that of 1912, in which the convention was sharply divided; in the party split that followed, Taft brought out 50 per cent of the previous party vote of 1908 in the states that had supported him at the convention, 41 per cent in those that had not—a clear case of positive relationship between convention and election voting.

The Harding nomination in 1920 produced random effects, on the basis of the proportions of electoral college strength held by the states in four relationship categories. In the election the party vote more than doubled in the states that supported him at the convention, against an 82 per cent increase in the others—a positive relationship—but the percentages of vote swing were heavily affected by a few states in which many women were voting for the first time in a national election. For most states the nomination was clearly one of random relationships—or even negative. The Progressives had returned to the Republican fold in 1916, but were still touchy, and a compromise candidate was needed who could satisfy the majority coalition without again repelling the erstwhile bolters. Harding met the tests, and, despite his somewhat colorless appeal, he produced one of the party's greatest victories.

Three nominations—those of 1916, 1940, and 1952 —were followed by vote swings showing a highly significant negative relationship. The Hughes case in 1916 was a prime example of motivations that can be powerful in a year following a disastrous party bolt: the search was for a candidate who would at least be acceptable to the bolters—even if he was not the first choice of anybody. Hughes had been aloof from the struggle as a Supreme Court justice. He was not popular with the erstwhile Progressives at the convention, but he ran 16 per cent better in the states that had opposed his nomination, including the former bolting states, and came near defeating the incumbent Wilson, thus suggesting that the strategy was well justified even if not wholly successful.

Eisenhower had the almost solid support of the Northeast at the 1952 convention, yet pulled up the Republican vote in that area less than elsewhere. In the Middle West, where much of the convention opposition had centered, there was a mixture of random results and positive relationship on the low side, with many states in the LL category. In the West, where convention opposition was equally strong, Eisenhower ran well and the relationship was thus mainly negative. In the South he pulled up the Republican vote from under 2 million to nearly 5 million, yet most of the southern delegations had opposed his nomination.

In the country as a whole, Eisenhower ran better by about 3 per cent in the states that voted against him at the convention than in those that voted for him—a difference so small that it suggests random effects. But the negative aspects of the relationship are indicated especially by the influential leaders who searched out and later gave long and unremitting support to a candidate whose characteristics presumably could heal breaches in the party and also pull out masses of new voters. Eisenhower was a success in part because in many of the areas of Taft organization strength he was able to run even better than in the areas where his own convention support had been mobilized.

*   *   *

The party with a minority following, especially when it is also the party out of power, cannot hope to win by nominating a candidate in its own image—one who will meet with favor only among its previous following; if it insists constantly on such a choice, it can justly be accused of trying to commit political suicide. But any political party with a will to live usually has some men among its leadership who have an eye for finding additional voter support without losing what the party already has, who take a national view of their party's problems, and who are disposed to search out candidates who can broaden the party's popular appeal in states and regions where it has lost ground.

The nominations of Willkie in 1940 and of Eisenhower and Stevenson in 1952—all cases of noteworthy negative relationships between convention and election voting—illustrate in some degree the efforts of leaders of this kind. The recent tendencies toward this type of nomination have undoubtedly been helped along, and such leadership has been strengthened, by the public opinion polls. It is quite possible that neither Willkie nor Eisenhower could have been nominated without the indications provided by the polls that each could broaden the party's popular base. Stevenson was not the choice of the polls in 1952, but his nomination was facilitated by the extent to which the polls had demonstrated that the alternative Democratic candidates were unlikely either to defeat Eisenhower or to hold together the party's following.

The polls have also increased the leverage of the independent voter in the entire nominating process, both because they provide indications of independent voter sentiment that would not be available otherwise and because they tend to concentrate the attention of the delegates and the party leadership on national voting trends, as distinguished from the trends of individual states and regions. When a delegate is presented with a relatively authoritative measure of the national electorate's sentiment, he can more easily—and more profitably, in the end, for the party—disregard divergent sentiment at home.

All of this very probably relates to the noticeable decline in sectionalism that has been going on for many reasons, and it may well have helped the decline along. For the conventions of the 1832-1892 period, the vote-swing relationships have not yet been investigated, but it could be supposed that positive relationships between convention action and voter response in the states would have occurred in that era of highly sectional politics much more often than they have recently. If the supposition is correct, the considerable number of recent negative relationships found in our inquiry on a state-by-state basis can be regarded as major evidence of the increasing nationalization of American politics.

Nominating Conflict and Election Victories

In studying the sixty-five major-party presidential nominations classified earlier in a series of nominating patterns, it became apparent that some patterns were more frequently associated with electoral success than others. Table 16 indicates the proportion of success for

TABLE 16. PROPORTION OF PRESIDENTIAL NOMINATIONS
RESULTING IN ELECTORAL SUCCESS[a]

Type of Nomination	Party In Power		Party Out of Power	
	1832-1892	1896-1960	1832-1892	1896-1960
A. Confirmation	3/6	9/11	1/1	0/4
B. Inheritance	1/2	2/3	0/1	0/1
C. Inner Group Selection	1/2	0/0	1/5	0/3
D. Compromise in Stalemate	2/2	0/0	2/3	1/2
E. Factional Victory	1/4	0/3	4/5	5/7
Total	8/16	11/17	8/15	6/17

[a] In each cell of the table, the denominator is the total number of nominations and the numerator is the number of nominees who won in the ensuing general election.

each pattern, in terms of the party out of power and the party in power. For example, of the six in-party nominations between 1832 and 1892 that confirmed an incumbent President in the party leadership, three led to victory at the polls. The proportion of these cases resulting in electoral success was thus 3/6. The similar proportion for the most recent sixty-year period is 9/11. It is thus apparent that the renomination of an incumbent President has been both more frequent than formerly and more frequently successful. On the other hand, renomination of out-party titular leaders has become more frequent without so far becoming more successful; Grover Cleveland's third nomination is still the only successful instance of its kind.

Nominations reflecting inheritance were more successful for the in-party than the out-party. Nominations producing inner group selections and compromise nominees had a mixed record; they served the in-party reasonably well before 1892, but none were made by an in-party between 1896 and 1960. Inner group selections did poorly for the out-party in both periods, with three losers in three tries in the more recent period.

Nominations reflecting factional victory in the party in power have rarely led to success in the following election. But in the out-party, factional victory has led to election victory in most of the instances in which conflict occurred over the nomination.

Each of the relationships expressed by a fraction in the table has meaning in its historical context, but, from the statistician's point of view, the numbers are too small in most of the cells to be significant. Further results can be obtained, however, by collapsing the table into a smaller number of cells. Types A, B, and C—confirmation, inheritance, and inner group selection —have enough in common as low-conflict patterns to justify combining them. There is also obvious merit in considering the items without regard to when they occurred. Thus the table is brought down to six cells with the following proportions of wins as the result.

Type of Nomination	In-Party	Out-Party
ABC. Low-Conflict Patterns	16/24	2/15
D. Compromise in Stalemate	2/2	3/5
E. Factional Victory	1/7	9/12

The Type D cases of compromise in stalemate are seen here to be ambiguous in indicating the proportion of wins or losses. They are therefore discarded when reassembling the tabulation according to winning and losing situations, as shown below.

Winning situations
Low conflict in the in-party (ABC)	16/24	67%
High conflict in the out-party (E)	9/12	75%
Total	24/34	71%

Losing situations
High conflict in the in-party (E)	1/7	14%
Low conflict in the out-party (ABC)	2/15	13%
Total	3/22	14%

This statistical statement can be translated into a set of four propositions as follows:

1. When harmony attends the nominating process for the in-party, its chances of winning the election are good.

2. When conflict leading to factional victory attends the nominating process for the in-party, its chances of winning the election are poor.

3. When harmony attends the nominating process for the out-party, its chances of winning the election are poor.

4. When conflict leading to factional victory attends the nominating process for the out-party, its chances of winning the election are good.

RESULTS WHEN NOMINATING PATTERNS ARE PAIRED

Each major-party nomination, with the exception of that made by the Democrats in 1836, was one of a pair. If the nominating patterns are considered in the combinations provided by these pairs, a second set of propositions can be derived.

1. When harmony attends the nominating process in both major parties, the in-party nominee almost invariably defeats the out-party nominee.

2. When vigorous conflict attends the nominating process in both parties, the out-party nominee usually defeats the in-party nominee.

3. When the in-party nominating process is harmonious but the out-party nomination involves vigorous conflict, the out-party nominee has more than an even chance to win.

4. When the in-party nominating process involves conflict but the out-party nominating process is harmonious, a conjuncture that is extremely rare, no generalization can be made concerning the probable outcome.

The opposing pair combinations from which these propositions were drawn are listed by categories in Table 17, in which the contrasting in-party and out-party positions are strikingly apparent. In twelve pairings of low-conflict nominees (A, B, or C) at the top of the table, the in-party lost only in 1892. The in-party won in 1856 with a Type E nominee—the only win in seven such tries listed at the bottom of the table. The out-party won only in 1884 and 1892 with a low-conflict nominee, out of fifteen tries, but its record of success with factional victory nominees was spectacular —nine wins in twelve tries.

The propositions would seem to have some predictive value during periods when the national party system is operating in what has been considered normal fashion and as long as relevant factors in the system itself remain unchanged. The rare exceptions to the first two propositions listed above have occurred mainly

TABLE 17. NOMINATING PATTERNS
AND ELECTORAL SUCCESS[a]

Year	Party in Power, Party and Nominee	Party Out of Power, Party and Nominee	Opposed Nominating Types[b]		Ratio of In-Party Vote to Out-Party Vote[c]
1936	(D) F. D. Roosevelt	(R) Landon	A/C	S/S	1.65
1904	(R) T. Roosevelt	(D) Parker	A/C	S/S	1.50
1928	(R) Hoover	(D) Smith	B/B	S/S	1.42
1956	(R) Eisenhower	(D) Stevenson	A/A	S/S	1.38
1832	(D) Jackson	(NR) Clay	A/B	S/S	1.30
1872	(R) Grant	(D) Greeley	A/C	S/S	1.27
1864	(R) Lincoln	(D) McClellan	A/C	S/S	1.22
1908	(R) Taft	(D) Bryan	B/A	S/S	1.20
1900	(R) McKinley	(D) Bryan	A/A	S/S	1.14
1948	(D) Truman	(R) Dewey	A/A	S/M	1.10
1916	(D) Wilson	(R) Hughes	A/C	S/M	1.07
1892	(R) B. Harrison	(D) Cleveland	A/A	S/S	0.93*
1924	(R) Coolidge	(D) Davis	A/D	S/M	1.87
1868	(R) Grant	(D) Seymour	C/D	S/M	1.11
1844	(W) Clay	(D) Polk	B/D	S/M	0.97*
1940	(D) F. D. Roosevelt	(R) Willkie	A/E	S/M	1.20
1944	(D) F. D. Roosevelt	(R) Dewey	A/E	S/S	1.13
1888	(D) Cleveland	(R) B. Harrison	A/E	S/M	1.02*
1960	(R) Nixon	(D) Kennedy	A/E	S/S	1.00*
1848	(D) Cass	(W) Taylor	C/E	M/M	0.90*
1840	(D) Van Buren	(W) W. H. Harrison	A/E	S/M	0.88*
1932	(R) Hoover	(D) F. D. Roosevelt	A/E	S/M	0.69*
1912	(R) Taft	(D) Wilson	A/E	S/M	0.55*
1880	(R) Garfield	(D) Hancock	D/C	M/M	1.01
1876	(R) Hayes	(D) Tilden	D/E	M/M	0.94[d]
1856	(D) Buchanan	(R) Frémont	E/C	M/M	1.37
1884	(R) Blaine	(D) Cleveland	E/C	M/M	0.99*
1852	(W) Scott	(D) Pierce	E/D	M/M	0.87*
1920	(D) Cox	(R) Harding	E/D	M/M	0.57*
1896	(D) Bryan	(R) McKinley	E/E	M/S	0.90*
1952	(D) Stevenson	(R) Eisenhower	E/E	M/S	0.81*
1860	(D) Douglas	(R) Lincoln	E/E	M/M	0.74*

[a] For the years 1832 and 1840-1960; includes all cases in which both major parties nominated their candidates in national conventions.
[b] The first pair of symbols indicates the categories of the respective nominees on the basis of the classification developed in Chapter 7; the second pair of symbols indicates whether each nominee was a single- or multi-ballot choice of his convention. In each pair the in-party nominee appears first.
[c] Out-party win is indicated by asterisk (*).
[d] The vote was contested in several states, and Hayes won by an electoral majority of one when all contests were decided in his favor.

under conditions that were quite exceptional in the history of the party system.

The two sets of propositions discussed involve a situation that is all too familiar—one in which the statistical evidences of relationship are relatively clear but the problems of causation remain obscure.

DO THE RELATIONSHIPS INDICATE CAUSATION?

Does the in-party win because of harmony? Lose because of conflict? If either answer seems obviously yes, why does harmony in the out-party indicate defeat— and conflict lead (sometimes) to victory? Is conflict over the out-party nomination actually a cause of victory? Or is it merely a response, not necessarily helpful, to a situation in which victory is possible?

The in-party and the out-party occupy situations so different that the sources of harmony and of conflict are also distinctly different. Harmony over the succession in the in-party is essentially the product of organizational activity in a situation of strength. Potential competitors are deterred by the strong position of the party's leader and also by the difficulties in securing backing for a bid that smacks of insurgency.

Out-party harmony is typically the product of a situation of weakness in which victory seems impossible or unlikely. There may be few strong candidates from whom to choose, especially if the party has lost most of the elections for governor and senator in pivotal states. Several of the few potentially strong candidates may prefer to wait for a more promising occasion.

Conflict situations are the converse of the situations just described. For the in-party, conflict is typically the product of disorganization in a situation of relative weakness, when the incumbent leader is unwilling or unable to achieve a united choice of a successor. The prospects of victory are usually also limited, so that the disciplinary methods available to the leadership are weak. At the same time, defeat, if it is anticipated, is usually considered a temporary condition during which party control will remain important. Thus the nomination remains valuable and will be actively contested if the situation is open enough to permit a contest.

In the out-party, conflict is associated with the expectation of victory in situations where organization discipline is weak and open factional contests are the rule. The hope of victory usually stems from a series of party successes in electing governors and senators—who provide the crop of potentially strong candidates for the presidential nomination. Typically no central leadership is strong enough to outrank the rising candidates or to prevent them from competing in the forums of national attention. Glamour accumulates for those who excel in this type of competition, and they have eventually provided the winners in the classic cases of party overturn.

In-party harmony probably does have a causal relationship to party victory, even in a situation in which victory is likely. Organization discipline is usually considered a necessity, since effectiveness in the conduct of the government is impossible without it, and conflict over the in-party nomination can rarely occur without seeming to discredit the party's governmental record—as it did so conspicuously in the Republican case in 1912.

Out-party conflict also probably has a causal relationship to victory, within limits. Conflict as such is not discreditable in the out-party, since no single leader is usually acknowledged as entitled to supremacy. If the contestants do not discredit each other too severely, an open competition is one of the best means of attracting public attention and displaying the qualities of the candidates. But there is food for thought in the fact that while the party in power was able to win only eight of the sixteen elections between 1832 and 1892, it won eleven of the seventeen between 1896 and

1960. The in-party has obviously gained strength by greater unity, but it does not seem likely that the out-party could win similar advantages by becoming more intensely divided.

An out-party probably does little to help its own position when many candidates with minimal prospects enter the field, or when several of the most able leaders devote themselves to coalition efforts to stop a front-runner by discrediting him. An out-party may also be self-defeating when it requires so vigorous a contest before a titular leader can secure renomination; the sharp conflicts that were required of Dewey in 1948 and Stevenson in 1956 did their parties no good.

In the Democratic Advisory Council, the Democratic party experimented between 1956 and 1960 with a device for strengthening the collective leadership of the presidential wing of the party out of power. Whether such a device might ultimately reduce the intensity of conflict over out-party nominations remains to be seen. It can be regarded, however, as a part of a general change, in which a more circumspect attitude toward the more undesirable forms of conflict may be developing in both parties whether in power or not.

Mechanisms of Long-Term Change

The nominations merit attention as a central mechanism through which the parties can influence their own longer-term futures. This influence is of course most apparent when a convention decision splits a party so completely that its defeat is catastrophic. But every convention nomination, with its differential effects among the states, has some influence on the long-term drift in party composition.

Since 1860, party bolting has been happily free of the threat of civil war, but it remains as the most potentially dramatic consequence of a nominating decision. The major bolting episodes since 1900 have been relatively short lived, but each left its mark on the parties; eventually the party bolters were reabsorbed, but not always into the party they had left. Many of the bolting Republicans of 1912 and 1924 moved into the Democratic party of 1932 and later years. Many of the bolting Dixiecrats of 1948 evidently voted for Eisenhower in 1952; in 1956 they either stayed home, voted third-party, or voted Republican. Their future moves, as the most dissident element in either national party, remain uncertain.

The elections of 1928, 1932, and 1936 were unique as a progression of events that changed the party system. In 1928, even though its nominee lost, the Democratic party was restored to competitive status by a great enlargement of its following in critical areas. In 1932, by virtue of the economic adversity that had overtaken the Republican party and the country, the Democratic electorate was enlarged by another 50 per cent. In 1936 these gains were consolidated by another 20 per cent increase—the response to the first term of the Roosevelt administration. The Smith nomination was critical in 1928; the Roosevelt performance in office was critical in 1936. The three successive elections rebuilt the Democratic party.

In the longer perspectives of a century or more, these three elections can be seen as the basic shift that brought the American party system into accord with the requirements of a modern economic order. Economic issues that cut across all sections of the population were recognized as controlling in a time of general economic adversity. The Democratic party became truly national in its orientation, as it had not been for most of a century. The Republican party was placed on notice that it would probably have to become truly national in order to become again effectively competitive. In successive pairs of candidates since then, the parties have offered the voters a meaningful choice: Roosevelt and Willkie; Roosevelt and Dewey; Truman and Dewey; Stevenson and Eisenhower; Kennedy and Nixon. The clarity of the choice has varied from election to election, but at no time has it returned to the ambiguity of a decision between Calvin Coolidge and John W. Davis.

In most of the large industrial states—and in many of the smaller ones—the realignment in the national party electorates has been accompanied by a party realignment along parallel lines within the electorate of the state. Changing party patterns have also occurred in those southern states that are being subjected to industrialization and the movement into metropolitan areas. Recently this process has been obscured by the sharp effects of the desegregation decisions of the Supreme Court, but these effects too are showing signs of passing into history.

The results of the realignment are apparent at the conventions. The delegates of both parties are oriented to the great American middle class and to the central concerns of the whole national electorate, but in each party they are still aware that they represent a party that has its own distinctive identity—one that must be preserved, renewed, and further developed, if it is to be politically successful. Their search is for the candidate, in each case, who can best express that identity while mounting the broadest possible appeal to the voters who will come out only if they like the candidate.

This is a formula that has much to recommend it. In terms of the practicalities of the moment, the preservation, renewal, and further development of the identity of the Democratic party may involve some shrinkage in its total party following, particularly in the South, if it is to become sufficiently homogeneous to be able to live with itself. The Republican party's problem is equally or even more difficult. Somehow it must recover from the divided personality of the days when it was a dominant party, and learn to live with a situation in which it must become more effective if it is to be competitive. This in turn seems to involve the problem of how to become a modern political party that is both conservative and vital—a problem not necessarily beyond solution.

16

The Nominating Process and the Future of the Party System

■

The nominating contests at the conventions and the elections that follow provide regular opportunities for decisive change in the ordering of political affairs. It is very possible that the decisions at the conventions are more critical than those left to the general election; certainly, if a systematic general theory of political change in the United States is ever constructed, it must give a central place to the nominating process.

Each successive convention helps to shape the future evolution of the party institution. It affects also the extent to which the party can bring cohesion and clear purpose to the work of government—or the extent to which it will retreat from this task, leaving a governmental vacuum to be filled by other mechanisms of some more obscure and less definable sort.

The conventions were created to cope specifically with the presidential and vice-presidential nominations and to remove the early dominance of Congress in this process. They have unavoidably become a central political mechanism with a potential for power far beyond anything their original sponsors dreamed. For each of their decisions they have an inescapable responsibility; questions for the future, concerning what can and should be done about both the nominating process and the party system, thus become largely synonymous with what can be done by the parties in convention assembled.

The Central Position of the Nominating Process

The principal and most clearly defined function of the presidential nominating process in each party is to identify the candidate who is entitled to be designated the party's nominee—with all this entails in the conferring of legitimacy, securing a place on the ballot, and assuring the loyalty and the votes of the party faithful. A much less clearly defined function, but an important one and seemingly in process of becoming recognized, is to designate the candidate also as the chief party leader. The ambiguity of this second function results from the dependence of effective leadership on victory in the election.

At the beginning of the convention system, Andrew Jackson let no one doubt that he was his party's leader. But for many decades after 1840 the nominating act was merely the designation of a candidate for the ensuing election—a candidate to be discarded if he lost and to be disregarded as much as possible in party matters even if he won. Recently it has become settled custom that winning the Presidency entitles the incumbent to recognition as the chief leader of his party —in the government, in the party organization, and in the electorate. The defeated candidate, however, has no secure entitlements. He is generally known as the titular leader of his party, but the extent to which the label has meaning remains obscure.

Whatever the eventual fate of the candidate, the nomination—the last hurdle but one on the course that leads to the highest position open to an American citizen—is still a sufficient glory in itself to exercise a profound effect upon all political arrangements. The nominating process occupies its central position in the party system chiefly because it exerts a substantial influence on the behavior of all actors throughout the system, an influence much greater than they are able to exercise on it. Although the relationship is not exclusively one-way, it is primarily so. For this reason, certain basic questions about the legitimacy and effectiveness of the relationship are justified.

CANDIDATE COMPETENCE

Is the nominating process capable of selecting the most able candidates available in the two parties for a final choice by the electorate? Or, if not the most able, candidates who are at least fully competent to meet the responsibilities of the office? The question comes close to the issues of national and world survival, and is no more capable of a conclusive answer than most such questions. But it does suggest the importance of elements that may either move the process toward or push it away from the selection of competent candidates.

One such element is the choice that must be made between short-run and long-run considerations that compete for recognition. The choice is posed most vividly in the traditionally contrasted bases for candidate selection: ability to win the election—or ability to lead and operate the government. Obviously some thought has usually been given to both sets of considerations and to others as well, but there have been times in American history when the contrast has been starkly put. The Whig party hastened its own end by its penchant for selecting vice-presidential candidates without regard for whether they could provide party or governmental leadership if called upon to do so.

Only a system that seeks a balanced pattern of electoral and governmental success in its choice of top leaders could be said to have achieved the degree of maturity that is compatible with survival. The American political system has not yet reached full maturity in this respect, but there have been many recent indications that the balance of the short-run and long-run considerations has changed for the better. If it has so changed, three of the several factors for change discussed earlier in the book may be given most of the credit.

One is the increasing influence throughout the nominating process of responsible elective officials of high rank, as distinguished from party bosses who can hold political power without becoming directly accountable for the conduct of government. The second factor is the recent tendency of public-spirited and intelligent citizens to join the party process in various states to an extent that did not exist when bossism was more rampant. This may be partly responsible for what seems to be a growing disposition in the whole electorate to judge candidates by qualities that are required for competence in office, and not merely by those conducive to proficiency in campaigning.

The third is an apparent tendency for elective office to be more attractive and more accessible to the members of each oncoming generation who are marked for success and have the widest field of choice in deciding on their careers. The remarkably numerous able young candidates for the elective offices of inter-

mediate rank who have come over the horizon in recent years suggest that a public-service type of motivation may be spreading; if so, it would be one of the
most hopeful signs for the future.

POPULAR CONTROL

Although the convention system was established in
part as a revolt against the undemocratic aspects of
nominations by the congressional caucuses, popular
control continued for many years to be indirect, to say
the least. To the extent that it existed, it was necessarily
based on the most meager information about many of
the candidates before their nomination. Clearly there
has been a great increase since 1900 in popular participation—brought about by the spread of the mass
media, the presidential primaries in certain states, the
public opinion polls, and the responses of the candidates to these and other factors. The candidates have
developed new attitudes on the extent to which it is
appropriate and essential to appeal to the popular will,
along with new attitudes on the kind and amount of
campaigning that are legitimate in doing so.

Much of the struggle that used to occur in the conventions has been shifted to the preconvention period,
and with the great modern access to information about
delegate commitments and intentions, most of the losers
in recent times have probably known that they were
beaten before the convention opened. Generally they
were too deeply committed to withdraw, but their
power to make "deals" before admitting defeat was
greatly reduced.

When public opinion is clearly developed in support of a majority choice, popular control now seems
almost complete within either party. And even when a
clear popular mandate is lacking, in practice there has
been a considerable shift away from the traditional

situations of convention stalemate in which a compromise candidate can or must be selected. The 1952 contests in both conventions and the Democratic contests of 1956 and 1960 were quickly resolved through clearly defined voting victories. The development and reporting of widespread public sentiment within the parties had much to do with this.

The values associated with popular control of the political system are deeply imbedded in the ethic of democracy but, by itself, popular control provides no complete answer to the problems of discovering the basis of a truly national consensus and of finding a leadership adequate to develop it. The dangers of the times demand a consensus that is not only broadly based, but also adapted to the requirements of national and world survival. Political leaders are clearly needed who will not merely follow their followers, but will assume the burdens of political education and grasp the nettle firmly when moral leadership is the country's greatest need.

These are the capacities of wisdom, yet men of wisdom also recognize their own limitations and may thus hesitate to volunteer for the rough-and-tumble of political life. Unless they have already been brought into political office at lower levels, they are unlikely to enter the race for the highest elective offices. When they do not volunteer, they may have to be drafted; and if the system fails to bring such men into positions where they can be recognized, the system itself may need to be changed.

CLARIFICATION OF PARTY ROLES

In choosing a candidate, a political party is also deciding its future, which depends mainly on its continuing success in developing the position it proposes to occupy in relationship to the needs of the times. This is a far more complicated problem than the writing of formal platform statements. Essentially it involves the clarification and adaptation of the party role.

By comparison with other types of organizations, political parties are relatively plastic, but each party is limited at any one time by its inherited character. The task of party leadership is to find a road to success through the prejudices of the past, the expediencies of the moment, and the demands of the future—a task especially beset by perils when a former top leadership is declining and a new top leadership has not yet come to full authority. It is a special characteristic of American political parties that large portions of their total life history are devoted to passing through such interregnums.

Many voices then speak on the future party role. They speak with unequal authority, and no one voice is likely to be decisive. The process goes on until some of the alternative concepts of the role begin to crystallize and candidates for the nomination begin to align themselves with one concept or another.

The act of choosing a candidate generally produces an immediate clarification for the time being of the party's future role: the candidate stands before the public as the most concrete expression of the direction in which the party has decided to move. As he campaigns, he continues to clarify the party position, mainly by expounding the party conception of the national position. This is his most important function in the period between convention and election.

Only in the event of victory can the wisdom of the party choice be fully tested. After the election a defeated candidate is committed at best to a holding operation in which he seeks to maintain his definition of the party role; the other leaders of the defeated party resume their accustomed activities, and the party awaits another opportunity for decisive action.

To the candidate who wins comes the great reward of consolidating the concept of the party role that he represents. As President of the United States, he has an unmatched opportunity to organize and direct his party as a basis for governmental power. When he performs with skill, the party learns how to make its greatest contribution to the national consensus. It also revitalizes itself for the future.

Problems of Preparation

The cycle of the nominating process was traced through at some length in the previous section in order to underline the importance of some of the essential characteristics of the choice at the convention. The competing aspirants for nomination differ not only in representing alternative concepts of the party role, but also in their capacity to bring any concept to success. The greatest hazard in going outside the normal channels of recruitment to find a candidate lies here. There are times when only the inspired amateur will do, but it would be strange indeed if competence for the highest public and party leadership could ordinarily be developed without the extensive training that only a previous political career can provide.

Most proposals to reform the presidential nominating process start with the assumption that there will always be an ample supply of well-qualified candidates. But, since the most unplanned part of the American political system is that which controls career advancement in the direction of the Presidency, the problem of supply starts with the question of who is willing to enter politics and why. Although the gifted amateur may now

and then be called into politics at a high level, most of
the candidates for high elective office have previously
held office at some lower level and have several times
been through the testing experiences of a political campaign. The recruitment problems presented by many of
the state primary election systems become most acute
at these lower levels.

THE PROBLEMS OF THE PRIMARIES

The problems presented by primary elections were
summarized as follows in 1951 by a committee of the
National Municipal League, the most respected civic reform organization in the country:

> The present direct primary systems have often pro-
> duced disorderly scrambles for office by self-seekers
> and have not, as a rule, resulted in the nomination
> of qualified and civic-minded citizens who should be
> attracted to public life. They have not provided voters
> with effective choices between suitable candidates,
> which is essential if the democratic process is to have
> its true meaning. Unless good candidates are nomi-
> nated, good candidates cannot be elected to public
> office. Reform of the primary system is needed to
> bring about healthy, vigorous party life, to provide
> more effective party leadership, to attract abler candi-
> dates to run for public office and to enable the rank
> and file of voters to hold the party leadership to an
> effective responsibility.

The committee advocated, as a principal reform, a reversal of the long-held belief that party organizations
should not interfere in the selection of primary candidates, and insisted that the organizations had a positive
duty to seek and recruit suitable candidates, who should
then be given a preferred place on the primary ballot.
Fortunately, despite many legal obstacles, more re-

sponsibility has been taken in recent years by some of the party organizations. And in several states, new forms of local party clubs, joined together in state assemblies and based on an explicit, dues-paying membership, have provided channels through which widely scattered bands of activists with a concern for public policy can play a continuous role in party affairs. Such groups can encourage able young people to run for offices on the lower rungs of the political ladder, and help them climb to higher levels of leadership as rapidly as they are ready.

THE TRAINING OF SENATORS AND GOVERNORS

The candidates for President and Vice President are drawn most typically from among the senators or governors who have held office during the previous ten years; the talent available at any one time reflects mainly the political practices and the career inflow of the previous thirty years. If senators and governors are to continue highly available, as seems likely, it is important to improve the potentialities of each. Each office has its own characteristic limitations as a preparation for the Presidency.

Senators often suffer from a lack of executive experience, from specialization in legislative work, from a habit of mind in which time is rarely of the essence, and from an over-identification with the *rights* of the legislative branch of the government. These traits are accentuated by long years of habituation in Congress; and they suggest that members of the Senate who seek presidential nomination must win the prize during their early years in the Senate or not at all. Those who have ranked high on the scale of availability in recent years have been relatively junior men, usually in their first or second terms. They have displayed many of the personality characteristics that are so glamorous in the rising young governors of the hard-fought, competitive, two-party states.

The governors suffer most of all from a lack of association with the issues of national policy, especially in the areas of defense and foreign relations. They are restricted by the tradition that a governor should stay close to the job in his own state; they have limited access to the centers of national and international news attention, and, in many states, are hampered by peculiarities of the term of office.

However, governors of New York have been conspicuously available for the presidential nomination, partly because the form of government allows the governor to be master in his own house, and to control his own schedule sufficiently to find time for policy issues and for extended absences from the state when necessary. The term of office, four years staggered against the presidential term without limitation on number of terms, is ideally adapted to campaigning for the Presidency. There are built-in potentialities for access to the mass media, and the size and complexity of the state justifies the governor in taking an active interest in practically every national issue. Matching those opportunities is difficult, but the other large states could do more than they have done to assist the presidential possibilities among their chief executives. The same could be said of another dozen states that are sufficiently large and complex to develop the abilities of any executive.

The annual governors' conference is deserving of more attention and development. The party caucuses that inevitably occur at the conferences could be recognized more openly as legitimate additions to the institutional apparatus of the national parties; for example, the national committees might undertake to provide appropriate assistance to the caucuses of each party.

The time has come to abandon the amiable pretense
that occasions when all governors of both parties are
present are "nonpolitical." *

OTHER SOURCES OF NOMINEES

The Vice Presidency has evolved in recent years
into a collection of duties and roles that are usefully
preparatory for the Presidency. The development seems
likely to persist, if the parties continue to nominate
vice-presidential candidates who are reasonably compatible with their ticket leader and have similar qualities of availability.

The Cabinet could be a natural source of well-pre-
pared candidates for the nominations of the party in
power. Modern Presidents clearly need political lieutenants, and the need might be met more fully if there
were a greater disposition to appoint former governors
to Cabinet office. Meanwhile, the functions of Cabinet
members as political leaders need further development
for many reasons.

The out-party titular leadership also has further possibilities as a road to the White House; its many special
problems will be discussed later in this chapter.

* * *

Toward the end of the last century James Bryce
summed up his view of the channels of advancement

* In the interval since this recommendation was first published
in 1960, the Republican governors have moved steadily in the
direction suggested, as indicated by news reports from the annual governors' conferences. In 1963 the Republicans created a
Republican Governors Association at the Miami Beach meeting
of all the governors, July 21-24. The new Association held a
separate meeting in Denver on September 15, 1963, at which
they completed their formal organization and adopted a widely
publicized statement on tax policy. Thus the Republican governors have begun to perform, for their party, the function performed by the Democratic Advisory Council from 1957 to 1960
while the Democratic party was out of power.

to the American Presidency in an essay that has often been quoted (Chapter 8 of *The American Commonwealth,* "Why Great Men Are Not Chosen Presidents"). Since then the system has become more successful in producing Bryce's ideal type: "men of education, of administrative experience, of a certain largeness of view and dignity of character." But the system is still characteristic of the American federal union in looking mainly, not to those who have had preparatory training in the national government in the highest administrative posts short of the Presidency, but rather to those who have held the office that is the counterpart of the Presidency in the most important states of the union, or those who have served in the Senate without having necessarily obtained substantial executive experience.

However, the door has never been closed to any source of talent, and there is much about this system that is altogether desirable. In any event, its basic characteristics are not likely to change soon. They provide a broad field for choice; for this very reason it would be well to improve the quality of preparatory opportunities across a broad front.

Problems of Popular Control

Although the recent increase in popular participation in the nominating process has been highly apparent and has affected the process deeply in many ways, the actual effect of the intervention has stopped far short of control. And many of the advocates of popular control, including some of the most accomplished students of political institutions, have been reluctant to contemplate its further extension, because too frequently the existing measures seem gravely defective. If the influence of the presidential primaries, for instance, were to be extended, their more serious deficiencies would need to be cured and other goals be kept in balance. Popular control can be useful in a political system, but so also are such other virtues as stability, competence, foresight, and a gifted leadership.

PROPOSALS FOR A
NATIONAL PRESIDENTIAL PRIMARY

The varied proposals for a national presidential primary that have been before Congress almost continuously since 1912 have had as their general objective a national election held throughout the country on the same day, at which the presidential candidates of the two major parties would be selected through the direct action of the voters. According to the Gallup Poll, such a proposal has had majority support among the electorate for a long time; at times it has also had substantial support in Congress.

The basic vice of all such proposals, in our opinion, is their failure to recognize that the essential characteristics of the nominating process differ in many important respects from those of an election choice between major-party nominees. As this book has endeavored to demonstrate, the most critical aspects of the nominating process arise from the fact that the alternatives of choice must be discovered as a part of the process. The choices must somehow be reduced to a manageable number, and in open nominating situations, even after a considerable amount of clarification, the availables usually still include several actual and potential candidates of varying status, each of whom is part of an extremely complex structure of first-, second-, and third-choice preferences in the minds of those who must make the final choice. Seldom are the genuine availables as few as two.

A primary election is an especially poor instrument for choice when the alternative candidates number three or more, as they do so often in open nominating situations at the national level. No one would want a merely plurality winner, one who had not even achieved a majority in the vote, as candidate for President. Yet a run-off system with two primaries of the kind provided in some state systems would bring to the national level the kind of hazard reflected in the Wisconsin presidential primary of 1948. On that occasion, Governor Thomas E. Dewey, as the man in the middle, ran third in a field of three candidates, the others being Governor Harold E. Stassen and General Douglas MacArthur. In all probability, Dewey could have defeated each of the others in a two-way test. But on the run-off system, an outcome like that of Wisconsin in a national primary would have eliminated him.*

For this and other reasons, if a choice among all the noteworthy alternatives were to be submitted to a primary election in which all party voters could take part, there could be no assurance that the most generally preferred candidate would be chosen—unless a pre-primary convention had been held to narrow the field by convincing some of the candidates that their prospects were hopeless, while rallying party support for the candidate or candidates most favored by the convention. And inherent in almost any conceivable

---

* The problems involved in creating a suitable election system to handle choices among three or more have been clarified considerably through recent research, without finding any satisfactory solution for the problems. The result is to leave the theoretical case for a national primary even weaker than it was before. See the articles by Paul T. David, "Reforming the Presidential Nominating Process," *Law and Contemporary Problems,* Vol. 27 (Spring 1962), pp. 159-177, and "Experimental Approaches to Vote-Counting Theory in Nominating Choice," *American Political Science Review,* Vol. 56 (September 1962), pp. 673-676.

See also the discussion of this problem in the last section of Chapter 3, above, including the footnote on the British experience of 1963.

kind of primary is the risk that the most attractive candidate may not even be on the ballot, and the further risk that the turnout of voters may be too low to insure representation of actual party sentiment about the candidates who do happen to be on the ballot.

The campaign fund requirements would be prodigious, automatically restricting candidacy because so few individuals could find the immense backing necessary. Every candidate would need a strong organization to fight with him from one end of the country to the other, and the lines of factional division within each party would sharpen as a consequence; the disruptive effect would seriously weaken the position of both parties in the election and leave even the winner poorly equipped for the tasks of government.

ACTION BY THE STATES

The presidential primaries are the most obvious current form of popular control of the nominating process. The disorder of the system is largely the result of the varied and sometimes conflicting actions taken by states in trying to reach or preserve the original objective of popular control. The provision of primaries by additional states is frequently advocated, but at the moment there is more need to clarify the objectives of the systems that exist by amending their statutes with measures that will more effectively attain them.

The points that were made in Chapter 10 can again be emphasized in summary here. All presidential preference polls that are merely advisory or are separated from the election of delegates should be eliminated because of the gratuitous confusion that they introduce. All systems requiring would-be delegates both to name a preferred candidate on the ballot and to obtain his consent before doing so should be repealed because they restrict voters to an inadequate set of alternatives, foster favorite son and dummy candidates, and lead frequently to invalid mandates.

If primaries are desired that give a high degree of direct popular control yet avoid the prevalent technical deficiencies, the Florida model is available. Its system usually puts before the voters the most attractive available candidates, is compatible with the operation of a draft, will probably cut down any favorite son who is not a genuine favorite, and seems unlikely to produce a seriously invalid mandate very often. Its installation requires a minimum of change in customary election procedures, while protecting and extending the characteristics of the national conventions as representative institutions. If it were possible to install this type of primary in as many as six or eight widely distributed states, the presidential nominating system as a whole would be moved much farther toward relatively sound popular control.

Yet the possibility puts the more difficult problems of the primary in their most acute form. Is it desirable to continue moving toward preconvention campaigns that will require a fund of at least a million dollars as the entrance fee? Is it desirable to force candidates into still more extensive campaigning at the grass-roots, with attendant strain and physical exhaustion? In the states that are developing a more competitive two-party system to good effect, is it desirable to risk splitting the state party organization by a focused contest?

These questions may explain why the present authors have only moderate enthusiasm for the Florida primary as it has operated in recent years, despite the fact that they had a good deal to do with designing its statute. They still believe, however, that it was a constructive development under the conditions prevailing in that state, as it might be in a considerable number of other states.

OTHER SOLUTIONS

Whatever is done about the presidential primary laws, the other factors that have recently stimulated more popular interest and desire for control will still exist. The mass media will continue to operate, public opinion polls will continue to provide readings on the candidates, candidates who are eager and willing to campaign openly will continue to appear, and factional interests will continue to exploit the situation in any way they can.

The expense and pressures of preconvention campaigning would be at least reduced if offsetting action were taken—for instance, moving the primaries closer in date to the conventions, simplifying the filing requirements, and holding open the filing opportunities for a longer time. More self-restraint on the part of the candidates would also be a desirable change. This may seem a hopeless counsel, but is not whenever the candidates in either party are closely bound together in a web of intra-party relationships and are clearly aware that continued friendly relations will be necessary for party success in the election. Such self-restraint would solve many of the problems of excessively bitter factional conflict in the campaigns. If it is ever achieved, however, it will be the combined result of many factors—among which the competitive situation between the parties tends most to control the behavior of the leading actors on both sides.

The conventions themselves will need improvement if popular control is to be maintained and extended. This subject is dealt with more fully in the next section, but here it may be noted that the abandonment of the two thirds rule in the Democratic party in 1936 was at least as important a step in the direction of popular control as anything that has been done to reform delegate selection. Majority rule is basic to the conception of popular control in any representative body; and not only is the principle of majority rule important, but also the mechanisms for making it effective. This is why the remaining vestiges of the unit rule should be removed from Democratic conventions as unwanted excrescences; and it is why also it is important to maintain rules under which a roll call vote can be obtained when necessary under conditions of sufficient decorum to permit an honest count. Attempts to manipulate convention action will always continue, and the conventions need more effective rules for their own protection than they have so far provided.

Under existing conditions, popular control may be indirect, but it appears to be highly effective, despite all the difficulties, whenever the national parties are closely competitive. The most compelling restraint that can be placed upon the behavior of a majority party is an increase in the votes of the other party. The history of state politics since the end of the 1930's displays case after case on the Democratic side, and some on the Republican, in which the party in the minority retrieved itself by effort and intelligence—and by holding out to the voters a set of specific political goals. If the Republican party could mount a vigorous effort during the next twenty years in states where it has typically been in the minority, many of the more acute problems of popular control in both parties would disappear.

Problems in Bringing the Conventions Up to Their Potentialities

If the conventions need reforming—and many people believe they do—there is also need for a more general recognition that the way to reform lies in improvement rather than in abolition. Some sixty years of propaganda on behalf of presidential primaries have tended to highlight the failings of the conventions, since the primary proposals have in general emphasized the desirability of replacing the convention system with another instrumentality rather than remedying its failings. Yet the continuing contributions made by the conventions to the survival and stability of the American political order are unique, indispensable, and, granted our form of Constitution, probably irreplaceable.

The durability of the two-party system is not something to be taken for granted. An effectively competitive two-party system is an artificial creation dependent for its maintenance upon suitable mechanisms, among which a regularly meeting national convention in each party would seem to be one of the most essential. The services of the convention as a general conclave for the selection and recognition of top leadership in each party, and for its replacement when necessary, could be abandoned only at serious national peril.

In the performance of the nominating function, the record of the conventions has been good and, especially in recent decades, has also been improving. Further improvement in nominating performance can reasonably be expected, on the basis of the record. For the three other functions of the convention, the performance record is ambiguous; the main problems in realizing convention potentialities lie here.

THE RALLY FUNCTION AS A PROBLEM

The convention's role as the rally that starts the national political campaign is clearly being given increasing recognition by the parties themselves and by the electorate and the public at large. The rally function is in a sense inherent in the fact that the conventions project an image of the parties in their collective, corporate identity and provide a setting within which the major leaders and the eventual candidates can be subjected to intense public scrutiny. Recent voting studies have demonstrated that many voters review their party preferences at the time of the conventions, with the coming election in mind. All of these aspects and effects have been amplified by television broadcasting; the conventions repeatedly attract television audiences larger than most of those that will later view the speeches and rallies in the election campaign.

A desire to abolish the rally function appears to be implicit in some of the proposals for drastically reducing the size of the conventions, restricting the time given to showmanship, and making the agenda more businesslike. A reform that would curtail the exaggerated tendency toward showmanship might improve the effectiveness of the conventions even as campaign rallies—evidences of gross incompetence in putting on a production inspire no public enthusiasm—but for the most part the problems of massive size must be accepted. A convention as big as the Democrats held in 1960 is not necessary, but something comparable to the recent Republican conventions and the conventions of each party in 1952 is probably a minimum in a country as big as the United States.

Granting this, a program for dealing with some of the problems might consist of several specific steps. The first five of these have been treated briefly in earlier chapters; the sixth was mentioned earlier and is here expanded; the seventh is presented here for the first time, but is related to a proposal made in 1955 by one of the authors.

1. *More effective scheduling and execution of preparatory work in advance of the convention.*

2. *Changing the structure of the national committee*

and convention committees to make them more representative, with each state given a number of votes proportionate to its importance in the party.

3. *Cutting back the Democratic convention to approximately 1,600 voting members by eliminating all fractional votes and bonus votes; holding the Republican convention at approximately its present size of 1,300.*

4. *Eliminating alternate delegates in both parties, using the seating space instead for state quotas of official visitors.*

5. *Authorizing each delegation to appoint a small group of official advisers to be seated with it at the convention.*

6. *Providing an executive committee of heads of delegations to secure a more effective control of convention time and operations.* A representative agency is needed that can take measures on behalf of the whole body, such as making a daily review of the agenda proposed for action, the motions that will be made from the floor, the division of time in any prospective debate, and the floor managers who will be responsible for the use of time on each side. The committee should be convened by the national chairman on the day before the convention opens, and it might either continue him as its chairman or elect a new one.

On the face of it, an executive committee to secure tighter control over what happens on the floor may seem undemocratic, but in a meeting so large some control is necessary to allow any business to be transacted. In present practice the control is mainly in the hands of one man—the permanent chairman, customarily the party leader in the House of Representatives. Since the viewpoints of the congressional and presidential wings of the party so often differ, the desires of the majority might often be more closely satisfied by a system of control that represented the whole presidential constituency than by the control exercised in recent years by the permanent chairman and the associates with whom he inevitably surrounds himself.

7. *More frequent meetings of the conventions, with biennial meetings as a first step.* These would provide a means for focusing national attention upon the parties and their current status at the beginning of each contest for control of Congress.

For the party in power, the meeting could be similar in form to the convention that renominates an incumbent President. In view of the President's vital interest in having a Congress controlled by his party, he would be received at the convention as the head of the party, responsible jointly with the congressional leaders for leading its mid-term campaign. A new platform would be adopted, expressing the party consensus in the Executive Branch, in Congress, and in the electorate. Most of all, the convention would be a central dramatic rally to mobilize the party for the kind of campaign that could prevent the weakening of congressional strength typically affecting the in-party in its off-year elections.

For the party out of power, the organization of a successful mid-term convention would be more difficult, because of the ambiguities surrounding its leadership. But leadership problems are not solved by refusing to take action, and it is the out-party that needs a mid-term convention most of all—to discover how to reach agreement in the name of the whole party on those problems involved in reversing the verdict of the previous election. Platform issues could reach their greatest importance, with a genuine clarification of the extent to which various leaders have been really speaking for the party. A new national committee could be elected, at the point in time when changes in national committee structure are usually most critical in an out-party.

The party, if it saw fit, could take special action to designate a campaign leader who would serve explicitly as the principal party spokesman for the period of the mid-term campaign. The Democratic party in 1954, for example, might have designated Adlai Stevenson, who would then have had the explicit backing of the whole party in the campaigning that he actually undertook. In 1958, the Democrats might have chosen Stevenson again, or they might have looked elsewhere—perhaps calling former President Truman back to a temporary task or tapping Senate leader Lyndon Johnson. All three men were active nationally in the 1958 campaign, but no one of them could lay claim effectively to the title of official spokesman. In 1962, the Republicans, having resumed the out-party role, had no generally recognized national spokesman who could meet the President on equal terms—except former President Eisenhower, and he did not campaign actively or extensively. Nixon, running for governor in California, was unable to campaign elsewhere and was seldom referred to as the titular leader of his national party. Yet, with the President and Vice President moving increasingly into leadership roles for the party in power in mid-term campaigning, the party out of power very much needs a voice correspondingly entitled to national attention.

In either party, of course, a mid-term convention would immediately place a claim on a large block of prime network time on television and radio—valuable free advertising that would help to offset the cost and trouble of the meeting.

THE AMBIGUITIES

OF THE PLATFORM FUNCTION

Only on a few rare occasions—all of them foreshadowing a basic reconstruction of the party system—has some great issue of public policy so dominated convention proceedings that the nominating act became secondary. But there is no doubt that the platform hearings at each successive convention involve a vast amount of work, time, and activity. Members of Congress are becoming increasingly involved—the result of a developing tradition that congressmen serving as delegates are especially eligible for service on the platform committee. With the growing importance of all public policies, there may be an increasing tendency to hold the parties actually responsible for the promises made in their platforms.

The platform function nonetheless remains ambiguous, because it is mainly a pronouncement of the presidential wing of the party. Platform adoption has only a loose connection with the conduct of the congressional election campaigns—and an even looser one with the future behavior of the candidates who by winning will represent the party in Congress. Platforms are written for use in *presidential* campaigns, yet they consist mainly of proposals for legislation that will be meaningless unless there is *congressional action.* The function seems likely to remain ambiguous until the parties find some means for giving greater coherence to the congressional campaigns that trade on the party name and are conducted under the party banner. Midterm conventions, with their inevitably greater emphasis on platform action for a purely congressional campaign, might be a substantial step in that direction.

THE GOVERNING OF THE PARTIES

The party-governing function of the conventions is the least understood and the most difficult to appraise. Originating as an activity incidental to the more central activities of the parties, in recent years it has begun to be recognized as capable of making its own contribution to party survival, stability, and adaptation to new conditions. It is the aspect that offers the greatest opportunity for further development, precisely because it has so far been least developed.

The work as a governing body includes all the decisions that are necessary to constitute the assembly; when a convention decides which delegates or delegations are entitled to seats, it is making the most elemental of all constituting decisions. Yet these decisions can have far-reaching consequences for the state parties concerned as well as for the total structure of the national party. Here are the national party's own instruments for developing greater consistency and cohesion within its own ranks—instruments of such potency that they can be used only infrequently and with the greatest caution.

Each convention most conspicuously governs the party when it acts to ensure the continuity and effectiveness of national party activity in non-convention years by regularly designating the members of the national committee for the term continuing until the next convention. The national committee is clearly subordinate to the convention by which it is created, and, in theory, may be limited to approved activities. In practice, between conventions it is largely on its own, since the convention adjournment is *sine die*. Essentially the committee tends to approve whatever is put before it by its chairman on most matters, but divided votes have become more common, and especially in the party out of power. The headquarters organizations of some strength that have grown up under the leadership of the national committee chairmen in recent decades are more and more a source of initiative in focusing the internal relationships of each party.

Both parties need to find a more rational and dependable base for the financial support of the national activities. Many state party organizations have always been casual about meeting their quotas for the support of the national party—the natural result of the fact that the financial relationships that are considered essential in any other national voluntary organization (farm, business, veterans, or whatever) have never been built into the structure of the parties.

What is needed is recognition of the principle of "no representation without taxation." When a state organization has failed or refused to meet its financial responsibilities to the national party, there is ample reason for withholding the voting rights of its delegation at the next convention, and voting rights should also be withheld in the national committee. The methods of determining state financial quotas have always been surrounded by obscurity in both parties. More vigorous action to enforce the quotas would inevitably involve putting them on some publicly defensible basis, and probably adopting them in the full national convention.

As currently organized, the conventions are more representative of the whole following than any other party body, but reforms are still needed in the basic apportionment system. The parties did not give fair representation or serve their own needs in 1956 when, in the eight mountain states, there was one Democratic convention vote for each 7,000 party voters and one Republican convention vote for each 12,000, but in

New York, Pennsylvania, Ohio, Illinois, and California, only one Democratic vote for each 29,000 party voters, and only one Republican vote for every 39,000 voters. In 1960 the situation was no better. Some plan of reapportionment should be adopted that would move closer to fair representation, not so much of the state populations as of the voters who constitute the parties.

The achievement of any of these party government reforms will require leaders who are convinced of the need to strengthen the national parties, and who are prepared to act firmly to that end. But any important innovating change also requires the approval of the convention, implied or express, if the change is to become a permanent feature of the party institutions.

Dilemmas in Out-Party Leadership

The structure of national party leadership—or, as some critics see it, the lack of structure—presents several dilemmas in connection with every problem of party effectiveness. In recent years the dilemmas have usually been most acute in the party out of power.

COORDINATE FACTIONALISM

First and most characteristic are the dilemmas of coordinate factionalism: the situation where several factions are struggling for control of the major posts of party leadership. The situation existed within both parties during most of the nineteenth century, whether ostensibly in power or not. Since no sectional leadership was beyond challenge the practice of coalition among sectional leaders was fostered. It was equally true that no machine-type of national party organization could become genuinely effective. The parties were free to choose the man of the hour, if he had become visible under the prevailing conditions of career advancement. It was possible to nominate and elect, though as a minority choice, a President who could win the Civil War, but only after twenty years of failure to find, install, and support the kind of President who might have prevented it.

Factionalism is still defended by those who prefer open conflict within the parties to any clarification of competitive roles that might produce greater cohesion in each party. But it is impossible to disregard the changes brought by the rising strength of the Presidency, by the disciplinary effects of responsibilities of government, and by the long-term tendencies toward more cohesion of leadership in the party in power. When the out-party displays all of the characteristics of factional disruption while attempting to compete with an incumbent party that has taken on some qualities of unity, the contest can become highly one-sided. Typically, under these conditions the out-party cannot win unless the in-party defeats itself—or is defeated by circumstances beyond its control.

CONGRESSIONAL LEADERSHIP

One frequently advocated solution for the dilemmas of out-party factionalism is to let the out-party leaders in Congress take control. They hold positions of recognized legitimacy within the government, even when their party is in the minority in Congress and out of power in the Executive Branch. At the convention, when they have mobilized behind a particular candidate for the nomination, they have almost invariably been able to assemble a substantial block of votes in his favor.

But other dilemmas result when the leaders in Congress dominate their party nationally while it is out of power in the Executive Branch. Typically, they are more responsive to their own special constituencies, even when they have regard for all the interests of the national party. In seeking a presidential nominee, they usually prefer a candidate who can be expected to defer to Congress on issues between the branches of government. There is nothing unethical about these attitudes. They are the natural product of the separation of powers, but they do tend to unfit the leaders of Congress for the leadership of their party's national electorate.

THE ROLE OF THE TITULAR LEADER

The review of experience suggests another alternative to the dilemmas of factionalism in the out-party— an active role for the party's titular leader, including renomination at the next convention, when this is appropriate, and influence on the choice of a successor, when a new choice must be made. But this course, too, has its dilemmas, some of them impossible to test by experience.

So far no renominated titular leader has yet won the Presidency—except Cleveland, who had previously been President. Were the titular leaders renominated only in losing situations? Are they useful in stabilizing the leadership in the presidential wing of the out-party *only* during long periods when victory is hopeless? Is it possible for a previously defeated candidate to win if given the chance when prospects are favorable? Various opinions could be and have been offered in response to these questions; the opinions of the authors of this book are as follows.

Bryan's renominations in 1900 and 1908 occurred in losing situations, but he probably did more to maintain the strength of the party vote in those years than any other available candidate could have done. Stevenson's renomination in 1956 also occurred in a losing situation. Dewey's renomination in 1948, however, was not in what was considered a losing situation. He ran well, and if the Republicans had not fallen prey to overconfidence he might have won. He also suffered from the reluctance of congressional and certain other party leaders to accept him as the titular leader of his party between 1944 and 1948.

All the titular leaders who were active as such did much to maintain party strength during periods when severe attrition could have been expected. Their usefulness continued, moreover, even after the tide had turned. Bryan's continued between 1908 and 1912, reaching its climax in Wilson's nomination. Smith was highly useful to his party between 1928 and 1932. Dewey's usefulness between 1948 and 1952 was limited by the circumstances of his defeat; yet he was largely responsible for the choice of the successor who brought victory to the party in 1952.

There is no doubt that previous defeat has consequences for future electoral success. A defeated candidate is the victim of an unfair psychological phenomenon: his inevitable human frailties will be fully appraised and probably magnified. A candidate who has reached the top through an unbroken series of resounding electoral successes takes on luminous qualities of charisma that make him seem larger than life.

In the political systems of other democratic countries, a party suffering defeat while in power is likely to re-examine its leadership and may then change it. But a party already out of power will usually share widely the responsibility for defeat, with little tendency to make its leader the scapegoat, and loyal service during subsequent years of defeat is his best claim to a commanding position when victory again becomes possible.

American attitudes toward defeated candidates for high office seem to be in part the product of the special circumstances of a political system where it is possible, in effect, to elect the man without electing the party and to defeat the man without defeating the party—as seems to have occurred in 1956, and came very near to happening again in 1960. The effect on the defeated candidate is redoubled when he holds no public office or holds one in which the term is expiring; with no appropriate public or official position, he may find it very difficult to maintain his prestige and his claim to public attention.

Until a titular leader is finally able to lead his party to victory, the ambiguity of the position will continue. Nevertheless, the evolution of a more mature attitude toward the potentialities of defeated candidates has recently been indicated. There seems to be increasing recognition that a nominee who has run well even in defeat has important assets—a name that is widely known, a popular following, and the reputation for leadership implied in his original selection by the party. In recent years defeated candidates for governor and senator who have kept on running have eventually marked up some impressive victories. The same phenomenon could have occurred at the presidential level forty years ago if Charles Evans Hughes had been willing to run in 1920.

COLLECTIVE LEADERSHIP OF THE PRESIDENTIAL OUT-PARTY

The recognition already achieved by the titular leaders suggests that it will not be easy in the future for the congressional leaders of either party to seize control when a party loses its hold on the White House. The experience of the Democratic Advisory Council between 1956 and 1960 further suggests that it is possible for the presidential wing of a party out of power, as represented in its national committee, to build and maintain its own continuing structure of leadership, not only without the consent of the party's congressional leaders, but also in the face of their opposition.

If the presidential wing and the congressional wing of a party each built a strong leadership structure to meet the demands of their overlapping but different constituencies, would the result be open warfare, carrying over into the next national convention? Or could conflict be held within bounds, with both groups joining to pass the torch to whatever candidate is finally nominated? In 1960, the Democratic experience was ambiguous. The conflict continued up to and into the convention, symbolized by Sam Rayburn's campaign to make Lyndon Johnson the presidential nominee. But when Johnson accepted the nomination for Vice President, the conflict was bridged in consolidating the ticket.

The dilemma could be avoided if the congressional and executive leadership of the out-party were merged in the same party council, but such a merger would risk doing violence to the inherent logic of the American scheme of government. It is not attempted even in the party in power. Although the President and his aides now customarily meet with the congressional leaders of his party and the national committee chairman at weekly intervals when Congress is in session, neither group is in a position to bind the other. Joint statements are never issued; nothing is settled by a vote. The relationship goes forward essentially as a negotiation between representatives of differing constituencies.

This seems a more appropriate model for the out-party than the composition originally proposed for the Democratic Advisory Council. The refusal of the congressional leaders to become members can be seen, in retrospect, as having permitted the emergence of the Council as the focus of the presidential wing of the party—an organization that might in time be able to achieve a fairly equal negotiating balance with the congressional leaders. Meanwhile, the experience of the Council is too recent and too brief to demonstrate how much weight similar groups might have in planning the internal structure of either party in the future.

What is important is the apparently increasing recognition of the need for some form of stability and continuity in the leadership of the out-party's presidential wing—which is inevitably out of office when it is out of power. The conventions, meeting only once in four years, have taken no responsibility for assuring leadership continuity in the presidential wing of their parties. Lacking such continuity, the out-party is never really ready to assume the tasks of government even if it does happen to win.

Goals for the Party System

Any attempt to formulate goals for the party system is hazardous, yet there is probably no other area of American life in which agreement on a set of workable goals is so greatly needed. The party system underlies the government and links it to the body politic; if the system is unhealthy, the nation itself may be endangered, along with the world-wide interests with which the nation is associated. A set of minimum goals might be stated thus:

1. A party system in which each of the major parties is sufficiently in accord with the underlying national consensus to be safely entrusted with power.
2. A party system in which each of the parties is

sufficiently strong and internally cohesive to develop
and carry out a governmental program of at least
minimum adequacy if it succeeds in gaining power.

3. A party system in which the two major parties are
sufficiently competitive to be able to replace each other
in power at intervals of reasonable frequency.

The third goal seems essential for the other two. Alternation in power—primarily in the holding of executive authority—seems to be the only means of demonstrating on a current basis that each of the parties can
be safely entrusted with power and can pull itself together sufficiently when in office to operate a government. When one party is too long in executive authority, the party out of power may become merely a dissident minority, so far out of accord with the national
consensus that it is not even a useful opposition party;
if it does again gain power, years of rebuilding will be
necessary before it can become adequately effective.
Or it may even die, as the Federalist party did in the
1820's, leaving the two-party system then dependent
for rebirth on a split of the dominant party.

However, party overturn can be an alternation of
weakness as well as strength. When both parties are
alternately voted out of office on every consecutive opportunity as occurred from 1840 to 1852 and again
from 1884 to 1896, it is obvious that neither party is
achieving much success in resolving either its own inner
conflicts or the problems of government.

All the concerns of this book are relevant in one
way or another to the attainment of the three goals
specified above, but the topics emphasized in this final
chapter seem especially relevant. To recapitulate, the
following changes are needed:

• • • wider acceptance of the principle that the
party organizations have a positive responsibility to

recruit able candidates into the channels of political career advancement at all levels of elective office;

• • • a wider distribution of opportunities through which the most able governors and senators may secure timely preparation for further political advancement;

• • • further development of the posts of party leadership in the Senate, of the Vice Presidency, and of the titular leadership of the out-party to give preparation for those who may later become President;

• • • adequate provision for popular influence in the nominating process, but with recognition also of the requirements for party cohesion and stable leadership;

• • • renewed efforts to protect and enhance the institutional integrity of the national conventions and to utilize their powers effectively;

• • • more effective organization of the leaders of the presidential wing of each national party, especially for the periods when it is out of power in the White House, as an essential means to the legitimate achievement of the previous objectives.

Each of the three goals to which these changes are related was deliberately stated in relative terms; each needs to be attained sufficiently for the requirements of the body politic under the circumstances prevailing. From one point of view, for example, the party system could be assessed as grossly out of accord with all three goals from 1896 to 1952, in view of the infrequency of party overturn, the difficult situation of whichever party was out of power at any given time, and the recurring crises of war and depression that could be attributed in considerable part to previous political ineptitude. Yet the nation fought two world wars successfully, had long periods of prosperity, and from almost any point of view enjoyed a rising level of well-being.

The present and the future, however, are already bringing greater demands than the past. No one knows what it will take to meet those demands in the future or whether they are being met sufficiently in the present. What we do know is that we live in a different world from that of 1896, one that will severely test all political and governmental institutions.

For the future, we shall need a party system that can do a better job in the achievement of all three goals than has been done so far. Before we can have it, we shall need much clarification of many aspects of the party system, including some changes in statute law, other changes in the organization of political bodies, and, most of all, changes in the customs and practices of the national political parties, with appropriate action by the national conventions to indicate consent or give active approval.

All of this implies a considerable development in the American political culture. Culture change seldom comes rapidly, but it does come in response to events, environmental pressures, and those qualities of vision without which the people perish. The events and the environmental pressures are here. It remains to be seen whether the necessary qualities of vision will be provided for sound institutional reforms, and soon enough, by some inspired national leadership.

Recent Changes in the Presidential Nominating Process

Of all the changes that have taken place in American political and governmental institutions in the past twenty years, perhaps the most far-reaching has been the change in the process by which the two major political parties' presidential candidates are chosen. Before the change, presidential aspirants in both parties were screened mainly by national, state, and local party organization leaders and chosen mainly by bargaining and "deals" among those leaders. Today the aspirants are screened mainly by the mass communications media, particularly the national networks' news programs, and chosen mainly by voters in presidential preference primaries.

Sources of the Change

Most of the change in the nominating process was initiated by a series of new rules adopted by the Democratic party between 1969 and 1971 to implement the recommendations of its McGovern-Fraser Commission on Party Structure and Delegate Selection. The new rules, which governed the selection of delegates to national party conventions, had three main thrusts: (1) to end the party leaders' traditional domination of the selection of delegates (and therefore the choosing of presidential candidates) by giving any enthusiast for a political cause or presidential aspirant an equal chance to become a delegate and by abolishing all guaranteed delegate slots for party leaders; (2) to make sure that certain groups in the population that had previously been discriminated against in the selection of delegates—notably women, blacks, and young people—would be chosen in rough proportion to their presence in the population (for example, a rule adopted in 1977 required that henceforth at

least half of the delegates must be women); and (3) to provide
for "fair reflection" of the voters' presidential preferences in
the composition of each state's delegation: today if candidate
X gets 30 percent of the popular vote in a state's primary, he
or she will also be guaranteed 30 percent of the votes cast by
the state's delegation at the national convention. The Republicans changed their delegate selection rules less drastically
than the Democrats, but to a degree they also weakened their
party leaders' powers, tried harder to represent formerly
disadvantaged groups, and widely installed proportional
representation of the voters' presidential preferences in the
composition of state delegations.

In response to changes initiated by the political parties, a
number of states also revised their laws governing the selection of delegates to the national conventions. By far the most
widespread change was the replacement of selection by state
conventions, state central committees, state caucuses, and
the like with selection by direct primaries. The figures are
dramatic: in 1968, the last of the "pre-reform" conventions,
only sixteen states and the District of Columbia held presidential primaries, and only about 36 percent of the delegates
at both parties' conventions were chosen by primaries. In
1980, the most recent of the "post-reform" conventions,
thirty-six states held presidential primaries, and about 75
percent of all convention delegates were chosen by primaries.

The principal change in the relevant federal laws came
with the 1974 amendments to the Federal Election Campaign
Act. They provided for public financing not only of the
general election contest between the Democratic and Republican nominees but also of the prenomination contests among
the aspirants for the nominations in both parties. The 1974
laws also put low limits on the amount of money persons and
groups could contribute to the presidential aspirants and on
the amounts that could be spent on campaigns for nomination
and election.

Taken together, these changes in party rules and state and
federal laws add up to a truly radical revision of the cir-

cumstances in which presidential nominations and elections take place, and, on the well-known principle that "changing the rules changes the game," it was inevitable that the process by which presidential candidates are chosen in the 1980s would be very different from the process that operated in the 1960s and before.

Characteristics of the New Selection Process

The main characteristics of the new process appear to be the following. First, the conventions now register choices that have already been made. As was noted above, about three-quarters of the delegates to both parties' conventions hold their positions not because of their own fame or service to the party or the patronage of party leaders but because they were chosen by presidential aspirants who received sufficient proportions of the popular vote in the states' presidential preference primaries. They are bound, by party rule, state law, or, most important, political custom to vote for the aspirant who got them there, and they are expected to remain faithful as long as their aspirant remains in the contest. The result is that the national conventions have become to the nominating process what the Electoral College is to the electing process.

Second, the mass communications media play a critical role in screening the choices. Over 30 million people now vote in the presidential primaries and thus choose the parties' nominees. Obviously, only a tiny handful of those people can ever know anything about the candidates except what they learn from the mass communications media, especially the television networks' newscasts. If the media make the news judgment that a particular aspirant (such as Philip Crane or Robert Dole in the 1980 Republican contest) has no realistic chance of being nominated, they will give him little or no coverage, his name recognition will remain low, and few people will vote for him because they simply have not heard of him. On the other hand, if the media determine that a particular candidate is doing "better than expected" (that is, better than expected by the media analysts, as was the case with McGovern in 1972, Carter in 1976, and Bush and Anderson in 1980), then that candidate will get considerable coverage, his name recognition will go up, and his ability to raise money will improve. In short, the more he is treated as a serious candidate, the more he actually becomes a serious candidate. Thus whom the media cover and whom they ignore is the main factor in deciding which aspirants drop out early and which stay in.

Third, primary scheduling and media interpretation "frontload" the process. Presidential primaries are not held on one day; they are strung out from early March to mid-June. A number of studies have shown that the media pay much more attention to the early primaries, when the true "front runners" and "apparent winners" are still being established, than to the late primaries, when a particular candidate is thought to have the nomination all locked up. Consequently, two clear winners usually have emerged by late March or early April, when less than one-third of the delegates have been selected. Clearly, then, the voters who vote in the New Hampshire primary in March have a great deal more impact on who wins the nominations than those who vote in California and Ohio in June.

Fourth, the process has become almost continuous. Prior to the 1970s, most presidential aspirants did not start intensive campaigning for their parties' nominations until a year or eighteen months before the time of the convention, but that is no longer the case. Jimmy Carter began full-time campaigning for the 1976 Democratic nomination in early 1974. Ronald Reagan began his campaign for the Republican nomination in the same year, and while he tailed (narrowly) in 1976, he won handsomely in 1980. Recognizing these facts of life, Walter Mondale openly started seeking the Democratic nomination for 1984 soon after he had left the vice presidency in early 1981. He has been actively campaigning ever since. Other Democratic candidates for 1984, such as John Glenn, Alan Cranston, and Gart Hart, did not start their campaigns until late 1982, but their late starts (twenty years ago they would have been regarded as very early starts) are widely believed to be serious handicaps in their contests with Mondale.

Fifth, campaigns are dominated by professional consultants. Presidential campaigns used to be dominated by "old pols," such as Jim Farley (for Franklin Roosevelt), John Hamilton (for Alfred Landon), Herbert Brownell (for Thomas Dewey), and Robert Kennedy (for John Kennedy and then for himself). More and more, however, modern presidential campaigns require direction by well-paid professional "campaign consultants" who have mastered such specialized operations as preparing television advertisements, getting the best free exposure on network newscasts, raising money from small donations by large numbers of people through the use of computerized direct mail, measuring the impact of the campaign by the use of privately commissioned public opinion polls, and so on. Among the best-known names in this new profession are John Deardourff, David Garth, Joseph Napolitan, Gerald Rafshoon, Matt Reese, and Richard Viguerie. Some will work only for candidates of a particular party of ideology, and some are available to any aspirant who will pay their fees. But they all come from backgrounds in advertising rather than party politics, and they have largely displaced party politicians in the planning and execution of campaign strategy.

Consequences of the New Process

There is now greater participation in the process than ever before. In 1968 and before, all the party and candidate activists and primary voters taken together added up to not much more than 5 million people. But more recently, an estimated 32 million people took part in choosing between Jimmy Carter and Ronald Reagan in 1980, and the number of participants will probably increase in 1984. It is also true that the proportion of the voting age population voting in the general elections for president has declined steadily since 1960 and in 1980 it was barely over half. But the proportion of the adult population participating in the selection of the party nominees has become thousands of times greater than it is in any other democratic country.

Labels aside, we have something very close to a no-party system in modern presidential politics. It is just as true in the 1980s as it has ever been that only a candidate labeled "Democrat" or "Republican" can have a serious chance of being elected to the presidency. But those labels are no longer bestowed by powerful groups of party leaders; rather they are won in a competition among personalities and organizations formed by and on behalf of particular aspirants. The national conventions, as we have seen, no longer "choose" the candidates; they merely register the choices already made by the primary voters. The national party chairmen and committees no longer play significant roles in raising campaign money or directing the campaigns. The money is provided by the federal government and by the nonparty PACs (political action committees) representing particular interests, and the campaigns are directed by professional campaign consultants.

Peer review has been eliminated. As was noted above, in the pre-reformed presidential selection process the candidates were effectively screened by their peers—that is, by other politicians who knew most of the aspirants personally, worked with them, observed them under conditions of stress, and had some first-hand knowledge of their weaknesses and strengths as candidates and as potential presidents. This kind of peer review did not, of course, guarantee that excellent candidates were always chosen by both parties: after all, Warren G. Harding and Barry Goldwater as well as Franklin Roosevelt and Dwight Eisenhower were nominated under the old system. It is also true, however, that public opinion studies of the 1972, 1976, and 1980 elections have shown substantially higher levels of public dissatisfaction with the candidates chosen by both parties than earlier studies showed about the candidates chosen in the 1950s and 1960s. Perhaps we are participating more but enjoying the results less.

In the past, nominating politics, electing politics, and governing politics were interwined and reinforcing. Since the pre-reformed nominating process required an aspirant to secure the approval of as many of his party's leaders as possible, he had to meet with them and try to work out accommodations with them. In the course of those meetings, the successful aspirants built the networks of acquaintance, accommodation, and communication that played important roles in their postnomination election campaigns and in their conduct of the presidency after they were elected. Thus no president assumed office as a stranger to most of the congressmen and other party leaders with whom he had to do business.

The two most recent successful candidates under the new presidential selection process, Jimmy Carter and Ronald Reagan, had never served in any federal office before assuming the presidency. Both of them directed much of their campaigns against the "mess in Washington," and made a good deal of the fact that, never having served in Washington, they were not responsible for the mess and were therefore especially qualified to clean it up. Carter went even further than Reagan: he often proclaimed that he was proud of the fact that he had won his party's nomination and the presidency without making any deals with his party's leaders and with the "Washington establishment." He was correct, and as a consequence during his entire tenure in office he remained more of an outsider than any other president in history. Many analysts believe that his unfamiliarity and unease with the leaders of Congress and the major interest groups was a significant factor in his inability to accomplish many of his legislative and administrative goals. Reagan campaigned against Washington almost as strenuously as Carter did, but, unlike Carter, he has tried hard to know and to work with the Capitol's leaders in Congress and elsewhere.

More Reforms?

Since the 1980 presidential nominations and election, a number of political scientists, politicians, journalists, and other citizens have formed various organizations to consider the new nominating process and to recommend further reforms. One group was headed by former governor Terry Sanford of North Carolina, another was sponsored by the Miller Center for the Study of the Presidency at the University of Virginia, and a third is now being conducted under the leadership of Alexander Heard, the former chancellor of Vanderbilt University. These groups generally agree that the post-1968 reforms have had a number of unforeseen and undesirable consequences that should be corrected as soon as possible. They recommend various reforms of the reforms, including such measures as giving *ex officio* delegate positions in the national conventions to each party's governors, senators, representatives, state chairs, and other party leaders; substantially raising the limits on the amounts individuals can contribute to presidential campaigns; requiring that all states within a particular region that choose to hold presidential primaries hold them on the same date; and trying in other ways to reintroduce some element of peer review into the process. On the other hand, public opinion polls show consistently that about 70 percent of the American people would like to see the national nominating conventions abolished altogether and both parties' nominees chosen by one-day national presidential primaries.

In 1982, the Democratic party, on the recommendation of yet another reform commission, this one chaired by Governor James Hunt of North Carolina, made some changes in delegate selection rules governing the 1984 convention and nomination. They include requiring that up to 14 percent of each state's delegation be set aside for governors, congressmen, and other party leaders; shortening the period in which the states may hold presidential primaries; and repealing the requirement (upheld in the 1980 convention) that a delegate must vote for the presidential aspirant who selected him or her. Whether or not these changes will make any significant difference in the presidential selection process for 1984 is hard to say, but it seems likely that the smoke-filled rooms and leader-controlled delegations of the past have permanently disappeared from the nominating conventions and that both parties' presidential nominating procedures will remain essentially what they have been since the early 1970s: wide-open contests among candidate-centered organizations led by professional political consultants in campaigns centered mainly on the mass media. Whether this process will eventually produce pairs of candidates with as much popular approval as those in the 1950s and 1960s remains to be seen.

By Austin Ranney. Reprinted with permission of The Key Reporter, Vol XLVIII, No. 4, The United Chapters of Phi Beta Kappa.

NATIONAL PARTY NOMINEES, 1832–1980

Democratic [a]

Year	Presidential Candidate	Vice-Presidential Candidate
1832	Andrew Jackson*	Martin Van Buren
1836	Martin Van Buren*	Richard M. Johnson
1840	Martin Van Buren	(no nominee)
1844	James K. Polk*	Silas Wright [b]
		George M. Dallas [c]
1848	Lewis Cass	William O. Butler
1852	Franklin Pierce*	William R. King
1856	James Buchanan*	John C. Breckinridge
1860	Stephen A. Douglas	Benjamin Fitzpatrick [b]
		Herschel V. Johnson [d]
1864	George B. McClellan	George H. Pendleton
1868	Horatio Seymour	Francis P. Blair, Jr.
1872	Horace Greeley	B. Gratz Brown
1876	Samuel J. Tilden	Thomas A. Hendricks
1880	Winfield Scott Hancock	William H. English
1884	Grover Cleveland*	Thomas A. Hendricks
1888	Grover Cleveland	Allen G. Thurman
1892	Grover Cleveland*	Adlai E. Stevenson
1896	William Jennings Bryan	Arthur Sewall
1900	William Jennings Bryan	Adlai E. Stevenson
1904	Alton B. Parker	Henry G. Davis
1908	William Jennings Bryan	John W. Kern
1912	Woodrow Wilson*	Thomas R. Marshall
1916	Woodrow Wilson*	Thomas R. Marshall
1920	James M. Cox	Franklin D. Roosevelt
1924	John W. Davis	Charles W. Bryan
1928	Alfred E. Smith	Joseph T. Robinson
1932	Franklin D. Roosevelt*	John N. Garner
1936	Franklin D. Roosevelt*	John N. Garner
1940	Franklin D. Roosevelt*	Henry A. Wallace
1944	Franklin D. Roosevelt*	Harry S Truman
1948	Harry S Truman*	Alben W. Barkley
1952	Adlai E. Stevenson	John J. Sparkman
1956	Adlai E. Stevenson	Estes Kefauver
1960	John F. Kennedy*	Lyndon B. Johnson
1964	Lyndon B. Johnson*	Hubert H. Humphrey
1968	Hubert H. Humphrey	Edmund S. Muskie
1972	George McGovern	Thomas F. Eagleton [e]
		Sargent Shriver [d]
1976	Jimmy Carter*	Walter F. Mondale
1980	Jimmy Carter	Walter F. Mondale

[a]Winning party candidate is indicated by asterisk (*). [b]Nominated but refused. [c]Named by convention. [d]Named by Democratic national committee. [e]Nominated but resigned during campaign.

NATIONAL PARTY NOMINEES, 1832–1980

Republican [a]

Year	Presidential Candidate	Vice-Presidential Candidate
1832	Henry Clay	John Sergeant
1836	(no convention)	
1840	William Henry Harrison*	John Tyler
1844	Henry Clay	Theodore Frelinghuysen
1848	Zachary Taylor*	Millard Fillmore
1852	Winfield Scott	William A. Graham
1856	John C. Frémont	William L. Dayton
1860	Abraham Lincoln*	Hannibal Hamlin
1864	Abraham Lincoln*	Andrew Johnson
1868	Ulysses S. Grant*	Schuyler Colfax
1872	Ulysses S. Grant*	Henry Wilson
1876	Rutherford B. Hayes*	William A. Wheeler
1880	James A. Garfield*	Chester A. Arthur
1884	James G. Blaine	John A. Logan
1888	Benjamin Harrison*	Levi P. Morton
1892	Benjamin Harrison	Whitelaw Reid
1896	William McKinley*	Garret A. Hobart
1900	William McKinley*	Theodore Roosevelt
1904	Theodore Roosevelt*	Charles W. Fairbanks
1908	William Howard Taft*	James S. Sherman
1912	William Howard Taft	James S. Sherman [b]
		Nicholas Murray Butler [c]
1916	Charles Evans Hughes	Charles W. Fairbanks
1920	Warren G. Harding*	Calvin Coolidge
1924	Calvin Coolidge*	Frank O. Lowden [d]
		Charles G. Dawes [e]
1928	Herbert Hoover*	Charles Curtis
1932	Herbert Hoover	Charles Curtis
1936	Alfred M. Landon	Frank Knox
1940	Wendell L. Willkie	Charles L. McNary
1944	Thomas E. Dewey	John W. Bricker
1948	Thomas E. Dewey	Earl Warren
1952	Dwight D. Eisenhower*	Richard M. Nixon
1956	Dwight D. Eisenhower*	Richard M. Nixon
1960	Richard M. Nixon	Henry Cabot Lodge
1964	Barry Goldwater	William E. Miller
1968	Richard M. Nixon*	Spiro T. Agnew

NATIONAL PARTY NOMINEES, 1832–1980

Republican [a]

Year	Presidential Candidate	Vice-Presidential Candidate
1972	Richard M. Nixon*	Spiro T. Agnew[f] Gerald R. Ford[g]
1976	Gerald R. Ford	Nelson Rockefeller[h]
1980	Ronald Reagan*	George Bush

[a]Includes National Republican and Whig. Winning party candidate is indicated by asterisk (*). Willim Henry Harrison and Zachary Taylor were Whig winners; the first nominee of the new Republican party was John C. Frémont. [b]Died October 30, 1912. [c]Named by Republican national committee. [d]Nominated but refused. [e]Named by convention. [f]Resigned from office October 10, 1973. [g]Appointed October 12, 1973, under provisions of Twenty-fifth Amendment. Succeeded to presidency on August 9, 1974, upon resignation of President Nixon. [h]Appointed under provisions of Twenty-fifth Amendment on December 19, 1974, by President Ford and Congress.

Index of Names
People, Parties, and States

Adams, John, 45, 47, 48, 164
Adams, John Quincy, 51, 52, 53, 164
Alabama, 81, 173, 175, 195, 197, 214, 215
Alaska, 81, 171, 173, 192
Allred, James V., 187
American party. *See* Know-Nothing party
Antifederalist party, 45
Antimason party, 54, 55, 63, 186
Arizona, 81, 173, 175, 179, 214
Arkansas, 81, 173, 175, 214, 215, 236, 251, 258, 302, 304
Arthur, Chester A., 128, 130, 148 n., 164

Barkley, Alben W., 87, 90, 148, 255, 259, 260, 263
Baruch, Bernard, 101
Bell, John, 59
Blaine, James G., 129, 133, 136, 158, 313
Borah, William E., 90
Brancher, Charles L., 230, 234
Breckinridge, John C., 59
Brice, Calvin S., 121
Bricker, John W., 108
Brown, Clarence J., 116
Brown, Edmund (Pat), 13
Brown, George, 63 n.
Browning, Gordon, 261
Bryan, William Jennings, 71, 72, 73, 104, 105, 129, 131, 133, 136, 156, 157, 158, 161, 271, 283, 286, 293, 294, 303, 313, 349, 350
Bryce, James, 331-32
Buchanan, James, 59, 104, 128, 133, 136, 164, 187, 313
Bull Moose party. *See* Progressive party
Burr, Aaron, 45, 46, 47-48
Butler, Paul M., 111, 123, 170
Butler, R. A., 63 n.
Byrd, Harry F., 188
Byrnes, James F., 90

Calhoun, John C., 51, 52, 53, 55, 215
California, 5, 81, 109, 123, 146, 147, 171, 173, 175, 178, 196, 200, 201, 202, 206, 211, 249, 254 n., 257, 259, 260, 269, 272, 273, 276, 277, 303, 304, 343, 347
Callaghan, James, 63 n.
Cameron, Simon, 121
Canal Zone, 81, 173
Cass, Lewis, 129, 131, 133, 134, 158, 187, 313
Childs, Marquis, 120
Clark, Bennett Champ. 188, 283
Clay, Henry, 51, 52, 54, 64, 129, 131, 132, 133, 134, 137. 148 n., 155, 158, 313
Cleveland, Grover, 64, 70, 71, 83, 104, 105, 117, 128, 129, 131, 133, 134, 164, 183, 310, 313, 349
Clinton, De Witt, 48, 50
Clinton, George, 45, 48, 49, 50
Collins, LeRoy, 96
Colorado, 81, 173, 175, 214
Commager, H. S., 121
Conkling, Roscoe, 121
Connecticut, 81, 172, 174, 214, 215
Conservative party (British), 63 n.
Constitutional Union party, 59
Coolidge, Calvin, 74, 83, 86, 90, 128, 130, 148 n., 164, 205, 313, 318
Cox, Eugene E., 187
Cox, James M., 105-06, 117, 129, 133, 136, 157, 161, 286, 302, 313
Crawford, William H., 50, 51, 52
Curtis, Charles, 88, 90, 91

Daugherty, Harry, 121
David, Paul T., 76 n., 82, 214, 230, 250, 254 n., 334 n.
Davis, John W., 106, 129, 133,

135, 141, 156, 158, 161, 272, 286, 300, 302, 303, 313, 318
Dawes, Charles G., 90
Dawson, William L., 233
de Grazia, Alfred, 176
Delaware, 81, 172, 174, 178, 179, 214, 302
Democratic party, 5, 6, 56, 58, 59, 61, 64, 66, 67, 68, 69, 70, 71, 72, 73, 74, 75, 76, 77, 78, 79, 87, 114, 118, 119, 123-24, 128, 129, 130, 133, 138, 140, 145, 148, 162, 169-70, 180, 183, 186, 194, 216, 231, 248, 250, 264, 269, 284, 288, 294, 295, 296, 300, 302, 311, 317, 318, 337-38, 343
Democratic Republican party, 48, 51, 52, 55, 56, 61
Dewey, Thomas E., 3, 6, 8, 10, 20, 21, 22, 32, 36, 104, 107-08, 114, 117, 129, 131, 133, 137, 158, 162, 206, 207-08, 258, 271, 284, 286, 294, 313, 316, 318, 334, 349-50
Dirksen, Everett M., 125
District of Columbia, 81, 173, 175, 195, 197, 208, 264
Dixiecrats, 317
Douglas, Stephen A., 59, 133, 136, 158, 162, 220, 313
Douglas, William O., 90

Eisenhower, Dwight D., 4, 6, 11, 12, 15, 17, 20, 21, 32, 37, 78, 83, 85, 88, 92, 94, 96, 97, 100, 108, 114, 115, 116, 121, 128, 133, 137, 149, 154, 158, 162, 171, 181, 188, 203, 207, 216, 222, 233, 237, 256-57, 262, 263, 264, 271, 272, 279, 283, 289, 293, 306, 307-08, 313, 317, 318, 343

Fairbanks, Charles W., 90
Farley, James A., 187, 218
Farmer-Labor party, 73
Federalist party, 43, 44, 45, 47, 48, 49, 354
Fillmore, Millard, 57, 58, 128, 130, 148 n., 164
Fine, John S., 217
Florida, 75, 81, 109, 116, 123, 172, 175, 194, 196, 199, 206, 207, 210, 212, 231, 264, 302, 336

Foraker, Joseph Benson, 121
Ford, Henry, II, 120
Franklin, Benjamin, 90
Freeman, Orville L., 262
Frémont, John Charles, 59, 129, 133, 134, 313

Gallup, George, 76 n.
Garfield, James A., 133, 135, 313
Garner, John Nance, 88, 89, 91
Georgia, 52, 81, 172, 174, 214, 215, 222, 258, 276
Goldberg, Arthur F., 94
Goldman, Ralph, 76 n., 82, 214, 230, 250
Grant, Ulysses S., 104, 127, 128, 133, 134, 154, 158, 164, 313
Greeley, Horace, 101, 133, 134, 313
Greenback party, 71

Hailsham, Viscount, 63 n.
Halleck, Charles A., 98, 125
Hallett, Benjamin, 58
Hamilton, Alexander, 44, 46, 47, 48
Hancock, Winfield Scott, 129, 133, 134, 154, 158, 313
Hanna, Mark, 121, 221, 273
Harbord, James, 154
Harding, Warren G., 5, 121, 133, 135, 136, 141, 158, 162, 163, 164, 273, 285, 289, 305, 306, 313
Harriman, Averell, 15, 35, 87, 115, 254-56, 263, 264
Harris, Louis, 118
Harrison, Benjamin, 127, 128, 129, 133, 137, 158, 164, 286, 313
Harrison, William Henry, 57, 91, 133, 137, 149, 158, 313
Hawaii, 81, 171, 173, 192, 238
Hayes, Rutherford B., 83, 128, 133, 135, 164, 313
Heard, Alexander E., 14, 18
Herter, Christian A., 88
Hill, David B., 121
Home, Lord, 63 n.
Hoover, Herbert C., 86, 88, 94, 99, 106-07, 128, 129, 132, 133, 149, 157, 162, 163, 164, 205, 271, 288, 292, 301, 313

Howe, Louis McHenry, 121
Hughes, Charles Evans, 105, 129, 133, 134, 154, 162, 273, 306, 313, 351
Hull, Cordell, 89
Humphrey, Hubert H., 4, 13, 15, 18, 21, 116, 195 n., 203, 210
Hyman, Sidney, 135, 160

Idaho, 70, 81, 173, 175, 214
Illinois, 73, 81, 146, 147, 171, 172, 174, 178, 186, 195, 196, 202, 214, 220, 249, 254 n., 276, 277, 347
Indiana, 73, 81, 146, 172, 174, 203, 214, 217
Iowa, 81, 172, 174, 214, 276

Jackson, Andrew, 39, 51, 52, 53, 55, 72, 127, 128, 148 n., 160, 164, 313, 321
Jay, John, 48
Jefferson, Thomas, 44, 45-46, 47, 48, 49, 50, 70, 164
Johnson, Andrew, 128, 130, 134, 139, 148 n., 164
Johnson, Hiram, 4, 273, 288
Johnson, Lyndon B., 4, 13, 15, 35, 37, 93, 114, 115, 123, 130, 207, 303, 343, 352

Kansas, 81, 172, 174, 184, 214
Kefauver, Estes, 7, 9-10, 15, 38, 109, 115, 199, 201, 204, 207, 237, 254-56, 259, 263, 264, 272
Kennedy, John F., 4, 7, 11, 13, 15, 20, 21, 35, 37, 93, 94, 96, 109, 110, 115, 123, 133, 137, 148, 153, 158, 162, 164, 200, 201, 203, 207, 210, 271, 286, 287, 302-03, 313, 318
Kennedy, Robert, 94
Kentucky, 81, 146, 172, 175, 214, 223, 236, 260, 302
Kerr, Robert, 237, 264
Khrushchev, N., 18
King, Rufus, 49, 50
Knowland, William F., 97
Know-Nothing party, 58
Knox, Frank, 146

Labour party (British), 63 n.
La Follette, Robert M., 73, 194
Landon, Alfred M., 7, 30, 106-07, 117, 129, 133, 134, 158, 162, 313

Lewis, William B., 55
Lincoln, Abraham, 59, 60, 127, 128, 133, 137, 158, 164, 188, 286, 313
Lodge, Henry Cabot, 116
Long, Huey, 187
Louisiana, 81, 173, 175, 214, 221, 222, 236
Lowden, Frank O., 4, 90, 288

MacArthur, Douglas, 334
Madison, James, 44, 45, 46, 50, 104, 164
Maine, 40, 81, 146, 172, 174, 214
Marshall, Thomas R., 88, 91, 148
Martin, Joseph W., Jr., 97, 98
Maryland, 81, 171, 172, 174, 203, 214, 257
Massachusetts, 5, 49, 53, 81, 146, 172, 174, 196, 197, 198, 202, 203, 276, 301
Maudling, Reginald, 63 n.
McClellan, George B., 129, 133, 134, 154, 158, 313
McKeldin, Theodore Roosevelt, 256, 257
McKinley, William, 71, 72-73, 117, 121, 127, 128, 133, 137, 149, 158, 162, 163, 164, 221, 271, 273, 286, 293, 313
Meyner, Robert R., 13
Michigan, 73, 81, 146, 147, 172, 174, 214, 238, 257, 276, 277, 301, 303
Minnesota, 11, 81, 109, 116, 171, 172, 174, 200, 204, 205, 206, 214, 257, 276, 301
Mississippi, 81, 173, 175, 214
Missouri, 81, 172, 174, 214, 276
Mitchell, Stephen A., 108, 222
Monroe, James, 50, 51, 104, 164
Montana, 70, 81, 173, 175, 179, 214
Moody, Dan, 281
Moos, Malcolm, 76 n., 82, 214, 230, 250
Morison, S. E., 121
Morse, Wayne, 195 n., 207

National Republican party, 45, 46, 47, 49, 50, 52, 54-55, 57, 59 n., 67, 77, 128, 129, 133
Nebraska, 81, 146, 172, 174,

195, 197, 202, 206, 264, 302

Nevada, 81, 173, 175, 177, 178, 179, 214

New Hampshire, 4, 11, 81, 146, 172, 174, 196, 199, 202, 206, 207, 208, 210, 212, 264, 302

New Jersey, 72, 81, 146, 172, 174, 196, 197, 198, 199, 202, 217, 236, 243, 276, 301, 303

New Mexico, 81, 173, 175, 179, 214, 302

New York, 45, 49, 51, 57, 68, 70, 72, 81, 146, 162, 171, 172, 174, 178, 180, 183, 186, 195, 196, 198, 208, 211, 214, 220, 225, 249, 270, 275, 276, 277, 301, 330, 347

Nixon, Richard M., 14, 18, 88, 91, 92-93, 109, 110, 125, 132, 133, 148, 163, 200, 213, 318, 343

North Carolina, 81, 172, 174, 214, 215, 223

North Dakota, 70, 81, 172, 174, 214, 237, 301

Ohio, 4, 73, 81, 146, 147, 171, 172, 174, 196, 200, 249, 260, 276, 302, 347

Oklahoma, 81, 173, 175, 214, 236

Oregon, 6, 11, 81, 109, 173, 175, 194, 195, 203, 206, 207, 210

Parker, Alton B., 133, 134, 161, 271, 313

Pennsylvania, 45, 51, 72, 81, 146, 147, 171, 172, 174, 184, 186, 194, 195, 196, 202, 214, 215, 217, 219, 249, 254 n., 257, 276, 277, 301, 303, 347

People's party. See Populist party

Philippine Islands, 81

Pierce, Franklin, 58, 128, 133, 135, 158, 164, 187, 313

Pinckney, Charles C., 47, 48, 49, 50

Pinckney, Thomas, 47

Platt, Tom, 121, 245

Polk, James K., 63, 64, 128, 133, 135, 155, 158, 164, 186, 216, 313

Populist party, 71, 72

Powell, Adam Clayton, Jr., 233

Progressive party, 73, 98-99, 168, 194, 301, 306

Puerto Rico, 81, 173, 175, 238

Quay, Matthew Stanley, 121

Randall, Samuel J., 121

Raskob, John J., 106

Rayburn, Sam, 95-96, 98, 114, 187, 262, 352

Reece, Carroll, 116

Republican party, 4, 5, 6, 22, 58-59, 61, 66, 67, 68, 69, 71, 72, 73, 74, 75, 76, 77, 78, 79, 99, 105, 107, 109, 113, 114, 118, 120, 123, 124-25, 128, 129, 131, 133, 134, 138, 139, 141, 145, 147, 162, 167-69, 180, 181, 183, 188, 216, 221, 222, 223, 231, 233, 237, 250, 262, 269, 271, 273, 274, 284, 288, 294, 295, 296, 306, 317, 319, 338, 343

Rhode Island, 81, 172, 174, 179, 214, 260

Robinson, Edgar F., 294 n.

Rockefeller, Nelson, 13-14

Roosevelt, Franklin D., 5, 7, 8, 30, 32, 83, 88, 89, 92, 96, 100, 106, 107, 117, 120, 121, 128, 133, 137, 148, 158, 161, 162, 163, 164, 187, 205, 272, 286, 313, 317, 318

Roosevelt, Theodore, 73, 83, 86, 88, 90, 91, 128, 130, 148 n., 164, 168, 194, 304, 313

Russell, Richard B., 99, 233, 254-55, 259, 263, 264

Schlesinger, Arthur M., 163, 164 n.

Scott, Winfield, 58, 129, 133, 136, 154, 158, 286, 313

Sergeant, John, 54

Seward, William H., 59

Seymour, Horatio, 70, 129, 133, 136, 313

Sherman, James S., 91

Shivers, Allan, 241

Sikes, Robert L., F., 116

Smathers, George, 200

Smith, Alfred E., 104, 106,

117, 129, 132, 133, 158, 161, 187, 271, 272, 288, 300, 301-02, 303, 313, 350
Socialist party, 73
South Carolina, 81, 172, 174, 214
South Dakota, 11, 70, 81, 172, 174, 196, 197, 198
Stassen, Harold E., 3, 4, 6, 9-10, 88, 108, 201, 206, 207, 256, 257, 334
Stephens, Thomas E., 85
Stevenson, Adlai E., 4, 7, 10, 12, 15, 17, 20, 21, 22, 35, 37, 86-87, 104, 108-09, 110, 114, 115, 116, 117, 123, 129, 131, 133, 136, 157, 161, 199, 204-05, 206, 217, 254-56, 263, 264, 270, 271, 293, 294, 303, 304-05, 307-08, 313, 316, 318, 343, 349
Symington, Stuart, 4, 13, 15, 37, 123

Taft, Robert A., 3, 4, 6, 15, 22, 28, 32, 37, 107, 108, 114, 116, 118, 171, 181, 203, 204, 216, 222, 226, 233, 237, 256-57, 259, 262, 263, 266, 279, 283, 289, 307
Taft, William Howard, 73, 86, 88, 94, 105, 128, 129, 130, 132, 133, 154, 157, 162, 163, 164, 168, 194, 205, 271, 293, 304, 305, 313
Taylor, Zachery, 133, 137, 154, 158, 164, 313
Tennessee, 40, 53, 81, 146, 173, 175, 214, 215, 223, 261
Texas, 63, 75, 81, 147, 167, 171, 173, 175, 214, 221, 222, 236, 266, 276, 277, 303
Tilden, Samuel J., 70, 129, 133, 137, 286, 313
Tillett, Paul, 254 n.
Truman, Harry S., 5, 7, 35, 83, 86-87, 89-90, 96, 99, 100, 108, 109, 114, 123, 128, 130, 136, 148, 149, 205, 218, 254, 255, 264, 271, 281, 303, 313, 318, 343
Tumulty, Joseph P., 86
Tuttle, Daniel W., 230, 234, 235, 239
Tyler, John, 57, 91, 128, 130, 164

Utah, 81, 173, 175, 214

Van Buren, Martin, 53, 55, 56, 63, 127, 128, 129, 131, 132, 133, 164, 186, 215, 219, 313
Vandenberg, Arthur, 32
Vermont, 81, 172, 174, 178, 179, 214, 215
Vinson, Frederick M., 86
Virginia, 43, 51, 75, 81, 146, 167, 172, 174, 214, 223, 262-63, 276
Virgin Islands, 81, 173, 175

Wallace, Henry A., 89, 90, 92, 99
Warren, Earl, 3, 4, 204, 256, 257, 259, 260
Washington, 70, 81, 173, 175, 214
Washington, George, 39, 43, 44, 45, 46, 164
Weed, Thurlow, 54, 57, 58, 59, 67-68, 101
West Virginia, 11, 81, 146, 161, 172, 174, 195, 197, 202, 203, 209-10, 302
Wheeler, Burton K., 73
Whig party, 54, 56, 57, 58, 61, 66, 67, 68, 77, 128, 129, 133, 139, 148 n., 286, 288, 323
White, T. H., 254 n.
Williams, G. Mennen, 13
Willkie, Wendell, 5, 8, 20, 22, 104, 107, 129, 131, 133, 135, 137, 152, 156, 158, 206, 271, 286, 294, 307-08, 313, 318
Wilmot, David, 220
Wilson, Charles E., 120
Wilson, Harold, 63 n.
Wilson, Woodrow, 73, 86, 100, 105, 117, 128, 133, 137, 148, 151, 158, 161, 162, 163, 164, 188, 271, 283, 286, 293, 304, 306, 313, 350
Wirt, William, 54
Wisconsin, 4, 11, 73, 74, 81, 172, 174, 183, 194, 196, 199, 200, 202, 204, 206, 208, 238, 260, 276, 301, 334
Wood, Leonard, 4, 154, 288
Wyoming, 70, 81, 173, 175, 177, 178, 179, 214

(373)

A Note on the Authors

The senior author, PAUL T. DAVID, is professor of political science at the University of Virginia. Previously he had been a Brookings Institution staff member from 1950 to 1960. He was on leave from Brookings for the academic year 1959-60 as a Fellow at the Center for Advanced Study in the Behavioral Sciences, Stanford, California. Trained originally as an economist, he was mainly employed in the federal government from 1932 to 1950. In 1946, he helped develop the plan for the Committee on Political Parties of the American Political Science Association, and he later contributed one chapter of the Committee's report, *Toward a More Responsible Two-Party System* (published 1950). With Malcolm Moos and Ralph M. Goldman, he edited the five-volume report *Presidential Nominating Politics in 1952*. He attended both party conventions in 1952 and 1960, and the Democratic convention in 1956. In 1961 he edited *The Presidential Election and Transition 1960-1961: Brookings Lectures and Additional Papers,* and he is author and editor of several other books.

RALPH M. GOLDMAN, who was a research associate at Brookings from 1953-56, is professor of political science at San Francisco State College. Previously he had taught at Michigan State University and the University of Chicago. In 1952 he was a consultant to the research division of the Democratic National Committee and subsequently was a research associate with the American Political Science Association. A co-editor of *Presidential Nominating Politics in 1952,* he has also written numerous articles on parties and elections for *Encyclopaedia Britannica, Midwest Journal of Political*

Science, Western Political Quarterly, Public Opinion Quarterly, and other journals.

RICHARD C. BAIN, who joined the Brookings staff in 1953, resigned early in 1960 to become Legislative Research Assistant to Congressman Joel T. Broyhill (R, Va.). He attended Republican and Democratic national party conventions in 1956 and was chairman of the Platform Committee for the past three successive Virginia State Republican conventions. He formerly headed statistical and accounting offices at Columbia University and later at Louisiana State University, and was Director of the Educational Statistical Service Bureau, sponsored by the Carnegie Foundation. He was a naval officer during World War II and the Korean conflict. He is the author of the Brookings book, *Convention Decisions and Voting Records* (1960). Since 1962 he has been doing free-lance writing.

KATHLEEN SPROUL, an editorial associate at Brookings since 1959, prepared the condensation and worked with the authors on editing the original edition. She has been a newspaper reporter, college teacher, and an editor on the staffs of *Survey Graphic* and *Saturday Review* magazines. She is the author of several novels and short stories. Her book editing background includes free-lance work for many New York publishers, among them Permabooks, for whom she prepared the condensation of *Bartlett's Familiar Quotations* (1953). Before coming to Washington as a technical editor for the National Institute of Mental Health in 1955, she had been a senior editor for the University of Texas Press. From 1956 to 1958 she was chief editor for the Washington branch of Human Relations Area Files.